HEAD
IN THE
CLOUD

Also by William Poundstone

William Poundstone

HEAD
IN THE
CLOUD

Dispatches from a
Post-Fact World

ONEWORLD

A Oneworld Book

First published in Great Britain and Australia
by Oneworld Publications, 2016

This mass market edition published 2017

A CIP record for this title is available from the British Library

ISBN 978-1-78607-115-6
eISBN 978-1-78607-285-6

Typeset by Tetragon, London
Printed and bound in Great Britain by Clays Ltd, St Ives plc

Oneworld Publications
10 Bloomsbury Street
London WC1B 3SR
England

Stay up to date with the latest books,
special offers, and exclusive content from
Oneworld with our monthly newsletter

Sign up on our website
www.oneworld-publications.com

To Kathy, for all the good times

The only thing I ever learned in school that did me any good in after life was that if you spit on a pencil eraser, it will erase ink.

—*Dorothy Parker*

If you repeat a lie often enough, people will believe it.

—*A quotation so often incorrectly attributed to Nazi propaganda minister Joseph Goebbels that fourteen percent of the public believe Goebbels said it*

Contents

HEAD IN THE CLOUD

Introduction

Facts Are Obsolete

On December 3, 2016, Edgar M. Welch put an AR-15 rifle in his car and drove the six hours from his North Carolina home to Washington, D.C. The twenty-eight-year-old father of two was on a mission to save the children. He'd read on the Internet that a pizza restaurant called Comet Ping Pong was imprisoning child sex slaves for a paedophile ring with shadowy links to Hillary Clinton.

Some might have found this claim—about a former first lady, senator, secretary of state, and presidential candidate—prima facie unbelievable. Welch was not one of those people. However, when he entered the restaurant brandishing two guns, he found nothing more suspicious than customers eating pizza and playing ping-pong. Welch pointed his AR-15 at a restaurant employee, demanding information. He fired the rifle at the floor. Welch went into the kitchen looking for secret tunnels and dungeons as customers and employees fled the restaurant. Police quickly arrested Welch and charged him with felony assault with a deadly weapon and carrying a gun without a license.

Welch had been conned by a fake news story. He wasn't alone. The tale may have been created for political gain, to damage Clinton's presidential bid. A perhaps more disturbing possibility is that it was created by an apolitical opportunist looking to make easy money. Disinformation has become a cottage industry of the global village. "News" stories that go viral on social networks can earn handsome advertising revenues for those who create them.

Welch was not the end of the story, only its prologue. The mainstream news media reported on the incident, carefully debunking the claim of a child-sex ring linked to an intensely vetted leader and candidate. Soon afterward Representative Steven Smith of Georgia's 15th district told his Twitter followers that the only "fake news" was the media's debunkings.

Georgia does not have a 15th Congressional district, and there is no Congressperson Steven Smith. It's a fake Twitter account with 24,000 followers.

Another wave of fake stories said that Welch was a hired actor. He was supposed to search for captives and fail, making the child-sex claims look baseless. He would thereby provide cover for the "real" and ongoing conspiracy.

As Welch demonstrates, the information age has devolved into a post-fact world. Some politicians and media pundits take that as a cynical new normal. Others are fighting back, or trying to do so. Facebook CEO Mark Zuckerberg has vowed to crack down on the spread of fake news, but the problem is not so much in the lies as in ourselves. People are gullible. Zuckerberg can rewrite the algorithms but not human nature.

"Gullible" is not an immutable personality trait. It is really a matter of prior probabilities, of having a built-in sense of what is possible, what is probable, and what is so improbable that only extraordinary evidence could ever render it credible. To someone lacking this epistemic compass, the Internet's fire hose of information is bewildering and dangerous.

Welch said he did a lot of online research before heading for Washington. One article on the Comet Ping Pong conspiracy led to another, and another. Each article linked to other articles to "document" its claims. The profusion of interlocking articles ultimately convinced Welch that there had to be something to the story. That's the problem with the Internet: you can look up anything, but you can't look up everything.

What didn't Welch know? Well he apparently didn't know that child-sex rings linked to innocuous businesses and celebrities are a standard motif of urban legends going back decades. Perhaps he didn't know that Hillary and Bill Clinton's combined net worth was a reported $111 million, presumably diminishing the incentive to invest in high-risk criminal enterprises. He apparently didn't know that presidential candidates like Clinton are the object of opposition research. That Clinton's political opponents ignored a potential scandal of this magnitude, leaving it to a few fringe websites, ought to have raised a red flag. Welch could have learned all this from the Internet, had he looked for it. The Internet is a powerful oracle only to those who know enough to ask the right questions.

This book explores the roots, and the consequences, of that fact. The part that's easy to understand is that we've offloaded much of our factual knowledge to the cloud. In many cases, that's okay. We know fewer facts but we also know where and how to look things up. The less-appreciated part is that the Internet has made broad-based contextual knowledge more important than ever. It is this that allows us to put news (and "news") in perspective. It is this that helps us decide what to believe in a post-fact world.

To those who know little, nothing is incredible. That is the scariest news of all.

Part One

The Dunning–Kruger Effect

One

"I Wore the Juice"

At five foot six and nineteen stone, the bank robber was impossible to miss. On April 19, 1995, he hit two Pittsburgh banks in broad daylight. Security cameras picked up good images of his face—he wore no mask—and showed him holding a gun to the teller. Police made sure the footage was broadcast on the local eleven o'clock news. A tip came in within minutes, and just after midnight, the police were knocking on the suspect's door in McKeesport. Identified as McArthur Wheeler, he was incredulous. "But I wore the juice," he said.

Wheeler told police he rubbed lemon juice on his face to make it invisible to security cameras. Detectives concluded he was not delusional, not on drugs—just incredibly mistaken.

Wheeler knew that lemon juice is used as an invisible ink. Logically, then, lemon juice would make his face invisible to cameras. He tested this out before the heists, putting juice on his face and snapping a selfie with a Polaroid camera. There was no face in the photo! (Police never figured that out. Most likely Wheeler was no more competent as a photographer than he was as a bank robber.)

Wheeler reported one problem with his scheme. The lemon juice stung his eyes so badly that he could barely see.

Wheeler went to jail and into the annals of the world's dumbest criminals. It was such a feature, in the 1996 *World Almanac*, that brought Wheeler's story to the attention of David Dunning, a Cornell psychology professor. He saw in this tale of dim-witted woe something universal. Those most lacking in knowledge and skills are least able to appreciate that lack. This observation would eventually become known as the Dunning–Kruger effect.

Dunning and a graduate student, Justin Kruger, embarked on a series of experiments testing this premise. They quizzed undergraduate psychology students on grammar, logic, and jokes, then asked the students to estimate their scores and also estimate how well they did relative to others (on a percentile basis). The students who scored lowest had greatly exaggerated notions of how well they did. Dunning had expected that, but not the magnitude of the effect. His first reaction to the results was, "*Wow*". Those who scored near the bottom estimated that their skills were superior to two-thirds of the other students.

Those who scored higher had, as might be expected, more accurate perceptions of their abilities. But (are you ready for this?) the group that scored highest slightly *underestimated* their performance relative to others.

As the researchers observed, the only way to know how well you did on a grammar quiz is to know grammar. Those lacking that knowledge were also least able to gauge their knowledge. They were oblivious to their own ignorance.

Everyone thinks he or she knows what's funny. The joke test included these two examples:

1. Question: What is as big as a man but weighs nothing?
   Answer: His shadow.

2. If a kid asks where rain comes from, I think a cute thing to tell him is, "God is crying." And if he asks why God is crying, another cute thing to tell him is, "Probably because of something you did."

The goal was to rate the funniness of each joke. Dunning and Kruger had a panel of professional comedians rate the jokes, and their averaged opinions were then considered "correct." The comedians judged the first joke as not funny at all, while the second (written by *Saturday Night Live* writer Jack Handey) was rated very funny. Some quiz takers struggled to make that kind of distinction—yet were confident of their ability to determine what's funny.

Later research went far beyond the university. For one experiment Dunning and Kruger recruited gun hobbyists at a trap-shooting and skeet-shooting competition. Volunteers took a ten-question gun safety and knowledge quiz adapted from one published by the National Rifle Association. Again, the gun owners who knew the least about firearm safety wildly overestimated their knowledge.

Like most rules, this one has exceptions. "One need not look far," Dunning and Kruger wrote, "to find individuals with an impressive understanding of the strategies and techniques of basketball, for instance, yet who could not 'dunk' to save their lives. (These people are called coaches.)" But of course coaches understand their own *physical* limitations. Similarly, "most people have no trouble identifying their inability to translate Slovenian proverbs, reconstruct a V-8 engine, or diagnose acute disseminated encephalomyelitis."

The Dunning–Kruger effect requires a minimal degree of knowledge and experience in the area about which you are ignorant (and ignorant of your ignorance). Drivers, as a group, are subject to the effect—bad drivers usually think they're good drivers—but those who have never learned how to drive are exempt.

Since Dunning and Kruger first published their results in the 1999 paper, "Unskilled and Unaware of It: How Difficulties in Recognizing One's Own Incompetence Lead to Inflated Self-Assessments," the effect named for them has become a meme. It strikes a universal chord: as Dunning put it, the overconfident airhead "is someone we've all met." The Ig Nobel Prize committee awarded the duo one of its satirical prizes in 2000. Actor John Cleese concisely explains the Dunning–Kruger effect in a much-shared YouTube video: "If you're very, very stupid, how can you possibly realize that you're very, very stupid? You'd have to be relatively intelligent to realize how stupid you are...And this explains not just Hollywood but almost the entirety of Fox News." The Dunning–Kruger effect is now part of the vocabulary of Internet snark (and some who think they know what it means don't quite get it). But the 1999 paper makes clear the authors' opinion that the first place to look for a Dunning–Kruger ignoramus is in the mirror.

The Knowledge

The first successful search engine took its name from a synonym for "noisy simpleton." In the mid-1990s, Yahoo introduced a world in which facts are accessible to all. A few keystrokes or spoken words summon a genie that lays almost any recorded fact at our feet. There was a time when bartenders were arbiters of debates over trivia relating to sports, sex, celebrities, and politics. Now customers whip out their phones or watches. Those alluring mobile devices have brought the cloud to the dining table, the gym, the backseat—and of course to the boardroom, the classroom, and the bedroom.

So why should we bother filling our heads with facts?

A case in point is the Knowledge, the notoriously difficult test required of London taxi drivers. As the guidebook for applicants explains:

To achieve the required standard to be licensed as an "All London" taxi driver you will need a thorough knowledge, primarily, of the area within a six-mile radius of Charing Cross. You will need to know: all the streets; housing estates; parks and open spaces; government offices and departments; financial and commercial centres; diplomatic premises; town halls; registry offices; hospitals; places of worship; sports stadiums and leisure centres; airline offices; stations; hotels; clubs; theatres; cinemas; museums; art galleries; schools; colleges and universities; police stations and headquarters buildings; civil, criminal, and coroner's courts; prisons; and places of interest to tourists. In fact, anywhere a taxi passenger might ask to be taken.

There are twenty-five thousand streets to be learned within this six-mile radius. Not only that, the London taxi driver is also expected to be a living GPS, capable of promptly describing an efficient route between any two named points.

But change is in the air. In London, as in other big cities, the ride-sharing service Uber has disrupted the taxi business. It is safe to assume that your Uber driver will not have anything like the London taxi driver's vaunted Knowledge. It is equally safe to assume that the Uber driver will have Google Maps.

Is there any advantage to having a knowledgeable driver rather than one who simply defers to an app's turn-by-turn directions? That debate is currently raging. Taxi drivers and their supporters speak of the limitations and glitches of GPS navigation (as if human drivers never make a mistake). The subtext is that the Knowledge is another uniquely British tradition in danger of extinction.

It's not hard to guess how the story will end. Whether London bans ride-sharing apps or embraces them, whether change happens quickly or is drawn out for decades, at some point the digital juggernaut will prevail. Drivers for hire will cease memorizing city maps.

The outsourcing of knowledge to the digital commons is one of the grand narratives of the twenty-first century. Whatever your own professional knowledge is, the cloud already knows it or soon will. The network's knowledge will be more up to date than yours, and the network will be faster at retrieving it and better at drawing connections. What then?

The great twentieth-century fear was the fear of being replaced by a machine. The great twenty-first-century fear is the fear of being replaced by a lower-paid, less knowledgeable human augmented by a machine. In place of Knowledge, the low-paid human has McKnowledge—such as knowing how to use a GPS app. Tech enthusiasts say this kind of creative destruction is inevitable and ultimately good for all. They're right about the inevitable part. Sadly, there is no guarantee that inevitable changes produce the best of all possible worlds.

The Knowledge exam is a pure meritocracy, something still hard to come by in class-bound Britain. Class, race, religion, sex, and age don't matter. All that matters is knowing the streets. Though applicants may spend years studying for the exam, the outlay of time and money is usually much less than one would spend for a university education. A London taxi driver earns more than many graduates do and has the ability to set his or her own hours.

Uber's barriers to entry are a lot less stringent than that. "A lot less" also describes the earnings of Uber drivers. Driving for Uber is neither a career nor a vehicle of upward mobility. That is likely to remain true up until the inevitable day when Uber drivers find themselves replaced by self-driving cars.

Are You Smarter Than a Year One Student?

It's said that changing curricula is like moving a cemetery. Yet change does happen. In 2013 US schools dropped cursive writing from the list of skills required of schoolchildren. Idaho state representative Linden Bateman was outraged. "Modern research indicates that more areas of the brain are engaged when children use cursive handwriting than when they keyboard," he said. "It's beyond belief to me that states have allowed cursive to slip from the standards." Bateman added that he wrote 125 cursive letters a year.

At seventy-two, Bateman was a bit older than the nation's schoolchildren. But he wasn't alone in his views. The curriculum change drew quick rebuke from…the nostalgia lobby? The objectors had enough pull in seven states, including California and Massachusetts, to get cursive written back into the state curricula.

The question is not whether cursive writing has some value. It's whether it's got *more* value than what could be taught in its place. Every hour spent teaching cursive writing is an hour not spent teaching something else.

An eternal dilemma of education is whether to teach facts or skills. At one extreme is rote memorization of multiplication tables, dates, and canons. At the other is an emphasis on critical thinking and skills (such as how to look up facts on the Internet, should you ever need a fact). When the issue is presented in this simplistic way, most of us lean towards the skills approach. Better to teach someone to fish than to supply a fish dinner.

"Should schoolchildren be taught the capital of Colombia?" In 2009 Kingston University journalism professor Brian Cathcart posed that question to David Fann, chair of the primary schools committee of Britain's National Association of Head Teachers. Fann's answer was a resounding no. "They just don't need to learn the capital cities of the world," he said. "The capital of France, yes, but not the capital of Colombia. They will be much better off learning to use atlases as a skill."

Fann's sentiment is an old one. Charles Dickens caricatured the Victorian method of teaching by rote in the character of Thomas Gradgrind, the flint-hearted headmaster of *Hard Times* (1854).

"Now, what I want is, Facts," Gradgrind says. "Teach these boys and girls nothing but Facts." In due course Gradgrind has an Ebenezer Scrooge-esque epiphany. He realizes that every fact is just another brick in the wall of education we don't need.

Dickens's novel (and Pink Floyd's rock opera) is half right. You can't justify the cost of one fact or brick to a Scrooge-ish auditor. Remove the brick, and the wall stands. Remove many bricks—not too many, not too close together—and still the wall stands.

The error is in projecting this too far—in thinking that you can dispense with *most* of the bricks. That would leave bricks hanging in mid-air. The wall collapses. The learner must acquire a critical mass of facts, permitting her a rough map of her knowledge and its gaps. Only then can she avoid the Dunning–Kruger fate of not knowing her own ignorance, and only then can she use Google to fill in the gaps.

Consider what it means to "look up" the capital of Colombia. That requires not just atlas-reading or Web-searching skills but also knowledge of a couple of facts:

1. There is a country called Colombia.
2. Almost every country has a capital.

Fact 1 is taught in school. Fact 2 is rarely stated explicitly, in school or anywhere else. It is a surmise that students make on their own, after learning of many countries and many capitals. Unless you know both 1 and 2, you're not going to know that there is a capital of Colombia to be looked up. In practice, facts and skills are not so readily disentangled. An educational programme that privileges either one too strongly risks running afoul of the way the learning mind operates.

The Common Core curriculum is a US initiative specifying standards for English and mathematics education. Its godfather was

E. D. Hirsch Jr, an English professor at the University of Virginia who felt that the anti-fact movement had overreached. He noticed that his students arrived lacking the basic cultural background that former generations of students had. Hirsch recalled his father, a Memphis cotton trader who dropped Shakespearean allusions into his business letters—allusions that were meaningful to fellow Memphis cotton traders.

Hirsch blamed an educational system that emphasized skills and "critical thinking" while slighting the teaching of facts. In many cases, children were being taught facts only as "for instances." Hirsch argued that facts *do* matter. He and his collaborators compiled a list of about five thousand persons, events, and ideas that they believed every educated person should know about. The list includes terms such as *gamma rays*, *rococo*, *absolute zero*, *faux pas*, and *penis envy*. These were, as Hirsch wrote, part of "the network of information that all competent readers possess...the background information, stored in their minds, that enables them to take up a newspaper and read it with an adequate level of comprehension, getting the point, grasping the implications, relating what they read to the unstated context which alone gives meaning to what they read."

Hirsch's list became the basis of his bestselling 1987 book, *Cultural Literacy: What Every American Needs to Know*. In it Hirsch cited an experiment: Harvard undergraduate Douglas Kingsbury asked Harvard Square passers-by, "How do you get to Central Square?" Most gave quick directions, like "First stop on the subway."

Kingsbury then assumed the guise of a tourist and said, "I'm from out of town. Can you tell me how to get to Central Square?" This time the answers were much longer.

> Yes, well, you go down on the subway. You can see the
> entrance over there, and when you get downstairs you buy

a token, put it in the slot, and you go over to the side that
says Quincy. You take the train headed for Quincy, but
you get off very soon, just the first stop is Central Square,
and be sure you get off there. You'll know it because there's
a big sign on the wall. It says Central Square.

Without even thinking about it, everyone realized that a tourist
would need more detailed directions. He would lack the shared
points of reference; things that might be obvious to Bostonians
would have to be spelled out. Kingsbury found that slipping into a
Missouri accent could trigger the more detailed directions. Hirsch
took that as evidence that shared points of cultural reference
improve the ease and richness of communication, to everyone's
benefit.

It's easy to buy Hirsch's basic argument; less clear is how far
to take it. Hirsch's list is heavy on terms from ancient Greece and
Rome, a civilization that lives on in figures of speech such as *mentor*,
platonic, and *lesbian* (though an ancient Greek would be hard put
to guess precisely how these terms are being used today). Still, you
don't have to read Sophocles to know what these words mean.

Today few fret that the rising generation will miss classical
allusions in Trollope or Thackeray. We're more likely to be puzzled
by op-ed pieces referring to TV series that most have never seen;
by Facebook posts alluding to micro-subcultures of food, music,
politics, movies, and fashion. Is this a problem to worry about or
just one of life's little anomalies?

In any case, Hirsch's ideas remain influential (and controversial). They were the motivation behind the Common Core
curriculum, now used by forty-two US states and the District of
Columbia. To many American parents and politicians, *Common
Core* are fighting words. Some have concluded that Common Core
is an attempt to foist progressive curricula—including Darwin and
the contributions of women and minorities—on the nation's less

progressive school districts. As South Carolina governor Nikki Haley put it, "We don't ever want to educate South Carolina children like they educate California children."

In reality Common Core is a rather innocuous set of guidelines prescribing the topics that should be taught at each grade level. For instance, Common Core's English Language Arts domains for first graders say that children should leave the first grade with the ability to:

- identify Mesopotamia as the "Cradle of Civilization";
- locate Egypt on a world map or globe and identify it as part of Africa;
- identify hieroglyphics as the system of writing used in ancient Egypt;
- explain that Christianity developed after Judaism;
- classify the sun as a star;
- explain that other parts of the world experience nighttime while we have daytime;
- classify Pluto as a dwarf planet;
- define the heart as a muscle that never stops working;
- identify "one if by land, two if by sea";
- explain that the first Africans in the English colonies came to Jamestown as indentured servants, not slaves; and
- explain the significance of the Fourth of July.

You may be saying, "Hold on, *that's* not Common Core. I saw this crazy homework assignment on Facebook…" Indeed, the words *Common Core* have morphed into an Internet meme. It is now the all-purpose hashtag for any bizarre homework assignment that turns up in the states that are using the guidelines. Of course, individual teachers create the homework, and inevitably a handful of them are loopy or just having a bad day. (No one ever posts *sensible*

Are You Smarter Than a Common Core First-Grader?

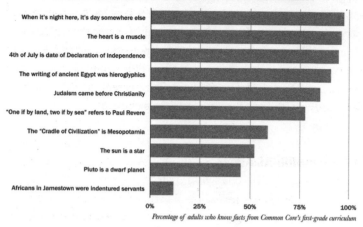

Percentage of adults who know facts from Common Core's first-grade curriculum

homework assignments originating in the Common Core states.) The perception that Common Core is crazy is attributable to the selective reporting of our social networks. It is an object lesson in how information technologies can misinform.

One criticism of Common Core holds water, though: it is ambitious, perhaps unrealistically so, for many students. I conducted a survey testing American adults' knowledge of the first-grade items I just listed. The average adult could answer only seven of the ten questions.

To put the most optimistic spin on these results, American grown-ups have the night-here, day-there concept nailed. Perhaps we can forgive the fact that fewer than half of them got the memo about Pluto's demotion to a dwarf planet in 2006, an essentially semantic change that inspired a glut of media attention. It's harder to understand how half the public goes around not knowing that the sun is a star. That's not exactly breaking news.

Demonstrations of public ignorance are by now familiar; in fact, they're a staple of late-night comedy. For several years the Pew

Research Center has been polling the public with some general knowledge questions. A September 2010 Pew survey found that forty-one percent of adult Americans couldn't name the nation's vice president. Twenty percent said that lasers work by focusing sound waves—this was a true-false question. Fifty-eight percent didn't know the author of *Moby-Dick*, and four percent identified him as Stephen King (the question was multiple choice).

What Millennials Know

The Millennial generation is a bellwether for new ways of knowing—and not having to know. Loosely defined as people born from the early 1980s to the early 2000s, Millennials were the first generation to do homework by copying from Wikipedia instead of *World Book*; to get their news from *The Daily Show* or the Internet rather than the network news. If contemporary media have fried our collective brains, the damage ought to be most evident in Millennials.

Psychologists John Dunlosky and Katherine A. Rawson tested the general knowledge of 671 Kent State and Colorado State university students using a set of three hundred questions. Here are five of the questions they asked:

> What is the last name of the author of *The Brothers Karamazov*?
> What is the name of the mountain range that separates Europe from Asia?
> What was the last name of the captain of the British ship *Bounty* when the mutiny occurred?
> What is John Kenneth Galbraith's profession?
> What is the last name of the leader whom Fidel Castro overthrew?

These are questions you might find in a trivia game promising fun for the whole family. Would you care to guess how many under-graduates could answer them?

Nobody. Not one single student, out of 671, could answer *any* of these five questions.

It should be emphasized that Millennials are the nation's most educated generation. But more education doesn't always mean more knowledge. That's the takeaway from a 2015 report prepared by the Educational Testing Service, the organization that creates the SATs. It compared the verbal, mathematical, and digital media skills and knowledge of Millennials in twenty-three nations. The British, Irish, and US scores were among the lowest in all categories. Canadian scores were somewhat better but below average.

The ETS broke out its findings into three figures: a national median, a tenth-percentile score (attained by those who scored just better than the worst ten percent of Millennials in each nation), and a ninetieth-percentile score (of those who just topped ninety percent of Millennials in each nation). This tripled the number of data points, but not one offered a salve to the English-speaking world's self-esteem.

America's least-informed ten percent were unparalleled in their ignorance, scoring lower than their peers in any other nation tested. The news was almost as grim for the ninetieth-percentile group. America's best and brightest outscored Spain's and were in a statistical dead heat with a few other nations. The highest-scoring US Millennials were still significantly behind those of the Slovak Republic, Norway, Japan, and Germany.

The ETS report concluded that:

> despite having the highest levels of educational attain-ment of any previous American generation, these young adults on average demonstrate relatively weak skills in lit-eracy, numeracy, and problem solving in technology-rich

environments compared to their international peers.... Equally troubling is that these findings represent a decrease in literacy and numeracy skills for US adults when compared with results from previous adult surveys.

No one really knows why American Millennials are falling behind. One hypothesis—though it's unproved—is that mobile devices are a factor. American Millennials are more likely to own smartphones than Millennials elsewhere. In 2014, eighty-six percent of Americans under thirty had a smartphone versus sixty-nine percent for China, forty-six percent for Russia, and twenty-five percent for Brazil. A smartphone puts the Internet's answers at your fingertips; for those growing up with such instant access, a re-evaluation of the importance of memorizing facts seems inevitable. In that sense, American Millennials could be the global future: less informed because there is less need to be informed.

My surveys confirm what others have found. Millennials don't know many facts that might be considered fundamental to cultural literacy. To give you some idea…

Most—more than fifty percent of—Millennials can't name anyone who shot a US president or discovered a planet; they don't know Socrates's most famous pupil (or the poison that killed Socrates); they can't say who wrote *The Canterbury Tales*, *A Streetcar Named Desire*, or *1984*; they can't name the palace built by Louis XIV or the Virginia estate of Thomas Jefferson; they are unable to supply the word for "deer meat" or "people who explore caves" or "the three-leaf clover that is the emblem of Ireland"; they can't identify the pop star who recorded "Heartbreak Hotel" and "All Shook Up" or the male or female leads of *Gone with the Wind* or *Casablanca*; they don't know the artists who painted *Guernica*, *The Persistence of Memory*, or *American Gothic*, or the escape artist who died of a ruptured appendix; they don't know who invented the telegraph, steamboat, radio, or phonograph; who proposed that the earth moves around the sun, demonstrated that lightning is electricity, or formulated the theory of relativity; they can't name the brightest or second-brightest stars in the sky (that's the sun and Sirius, by the way); they can't name the largest ocean on earth, the longest river in South America, the city whose airport is Heathrow, or the mountain range that contains Mount Everest; they can't name the woman who discovered radium, the one who (in popular myth) designed and sewed the first American flag, or the Egyptian queen who allied with Mark Antony against Rome; they are unable to recognize Karl Marx, Queen Victoria, or Charles Dickens from a photograph; they can't identify the group of extinct creatures whose name means "terrible lizards," the big hairy spiders that are sometimes found in banana bunches, the deadly snake used by Indian snake charmers, or the furry animal that attacks this kind of snake; they draw a blank when asked for the capital of New York or the metal that is liquid at room temperature; they don't know what Frank Lloyd Wright did for a living; they can't name the captain of the *Pequod* in *Moby-Dick*, the ship of Charles Darwin's scientific voyage, the secret project that built the first atomic bomb, or the first artificial satellite; they don't know the ancient city celebrated for its hanging gardens, the one destroyed by Mount Vesuvius, or the emperor said to have fiddled while Rome burned; and most Millennials can't name the single word uttered by the raven in Edgar Allan Poe's poem.

Rational Ignorance

The conventional reaction to such reports is a blend of shock and amusement. It's terrible how little young people/ordinary citizens know—right? It's worth asking how we *know* it's so terrible and whether it's terrible at all.

Ignorance can be rational. Economist Anthony Downs made that claim in the 1950s. He meant that there are many situations in which the effort needed to acquire knowledge outweighs the advantage of having it. One example is a voter who follows politics. Why bother? A voter has no power beyond a single vote, which has never swung an election and never will.

Or maybe you got your diploma and a high-paying job without ever learning about that poem with the raven in it. Why learn it now?

The contemporary world regards knowledge with ambivalence. We admire learning and retain the view that it is a desirable end in itself. But our more entitled side sees learning as a means to an end—to social advancement, wealth, power, *something*. We are suspicious of education that lacks an ulterior motive; we click on listicles entitled "8 Degrees with the Worst Return on Investment."

Ours is the golden age of rational—and rationalized— ignorance. Information is being produced, devalued, and made obsolete at a prodigious rate. Every day the culture changes beneath our feet. It is harder than ever to keep up or even to be sure that keeping up matters any more. We are left speculating about how important it is to stay current on the Middle East, contemporary novels, local politics, wearable technology, and basketball. A friend recently wondered aloud whether it was okay to not know anything about *Game of Thrones*. The observation that you can look up any needed bit of information dodges the issue. You can't Google a point of view.

The poorly informed don't necessarily know less. They just know different things. A gamer who spends all his free time play-ing video games will have an encyclopedic understanding of those games. He is ill informed only by arbitrary standards of what's important. Not everyone agrees with Hirsch that there is a fixed set of facts that all should know. But absent such a set, the concept of being well informed becomes a hopelessly relative one.

Today's mediascape does not provide much guidance. It encourages us to create personal, solipsistic filters over informa-tion, making it unprecedentedly easy to gorge on news of favourite celebrities, TV shows, teams, political ideologies, and tech toys. This leaves less time and attention for everything else. The great risk isn't that the Internet is making us less informed or even misinformed. It's that it may be making us *meta-ignorant*—less cognizant of what we don't know.

The Google Effect

There is now an active field of research into how the Internet is changing what we learn and remember. Start with the "Google effect." In a 2011 experiment helmed by Daniel Wegner of Harvard, volunteers were presented with a list of forty trivia facts—short, pithy statements such as "An ostrich's eye is bigger than its brain." Each person was instructed to type all forty statements into a computer. Half the volunteers were told to remember the facts. The other half weren't. Also, half were informed that their work would be stored on the computer. The other half were told that it would be erased immediately after the task's completion.

The volunteers were later given a quiz on the facts they'd typed. Those instructed to remember the information scored no better than those who hadn't been told to do so. But those who believed that their work would be erased scored much better compared to those who believed it would be saved. This was true whether they were trying to remember the facts or not.

Proust was not the first to propose that memory is a great mystery. We remember the madeleine dipped in tea and forget many experiences and facts of greater consequence. The conscious mind exercises little choice in remembering and forgetting. Nobody decides to forget a client's name or to remember for ever the lyrics of a detested pop tune. It just happens.

The Harvard experiment's results are consistent with a pragmatic system of memory. It is impossible to remember everything.

The brain must constantly be doing triage on memories, without conscious intervention. And apparently it recognizes that there is less need to stock our minds with information that can be readily retrieved. (It may be a very long time before you need to know how big an ostrich's eyeball is.) So facts are more often forgotten when people believe the facts will be archived. This phenomenon has earned a name—the Google effect—describing the automatic forgetting of information that can be found online.

The Google effect raises some interesting and even disturbing possibilities. One is that messages sent in apps like Snapchat and Confide—in which a photo or message disappears immediately after viewing—may be better remembered than texts and e-mails are. If true, that would defeat Snapchat's purpose as a drunk-sexting medium.

If you take the Google effect to the point of absurdity, selfies would cause amnesia. But a 2013 study conducted by Linda Henkel of Fairfield University pointed in that direction. Henkel noticed that visitors to art museums are obsessed with taking cell-phone shots of artworks and often are less interested in looking at the art itself. So she performed an experiment at Fairfield University's Bellarmine Museum of Art. Undergraduates took a guided tour in which they were directed to view specific artworks. Some were instructed to photograph the art, and others were simply told to take note of it. The next day both groups were quizzed on their knowledge of the artworks. The visitors who snapped pictures were less able to identify works and to recall visual details.

Our unconscious curators of memory must be aware of how quickly and easily any needed fact can be called up. This implies that our broadband networks have created a new regime of learning and memory, one in which facts are less likely to be retained and are more quickly forgotten. In a few years, we'll probably all be wearing devices that shoot a 24-7 video stream of our lives. Will social media make amnesiacs of us all?

What Google Knows

Source memory is the recall of when or where a fact was learned. It is often fallible and has been implicated in false memories. "Yeah, chameleons are water creatures. I forget where I heard that…"

One Harvard experiment showed how much we are coming to depend on source memory. Subjects in this study were presented with a list of trivia facts and told that they would be stored in a specific folder with a name such as *Facts*, *Data*, or *Info*. It turned out that the volunteers were more likely to remember which folder stored the trivia facts than the facts themselves, despite their being quirky and memorable ("An ostrich's eyeball…") and despite the folder names being boringly generic.

Could we function if we knew almost nothing except where to look up what we need? There are already people who work that way. Some of them are called attorneys. "Ignorance is no excuse," is a sardonic dictum of American jurisprudence. Congress alone adds about twenty million words of new law each year, an amount that would take something like ten months to read, were anyone to try. That's just the words that are added to new federal laws. Combine that with a couple centuries of old law—federal, state, and local—and all the judgments ever passed on those laws, and you've got yourself a physically impossible task of reading. Attorneys can know only a bare outline of the law, but they need to be expert at looking up relevant cases.

One of the most impressive memory experiments of recent years demonstrated that relying on source memory is becoming automatic. The study, conducted by Daniel Wegner and Adrian F. Ward, used a twist on the classic Stroop task, that amusing Psychology 101 demonstration in which you are presented with names of colours in the "wrong" colour ink or pixels. Picture RED printed in blue ink. The challenge is to call out the colour (not read the word aloud). It's harder than you might think.

For instance, call out the colours of these words:

GREY
WHITE
BLACK

Frustrated laughter is a common reaction. It takes about twice as long to name the colours as it does when the words and colours agree.

This finding was described in the 1935 dissertation of John Ridley Stroop, who must possess one of the highest name-recognition-to-achievement ratios of any psychologist. Stroop took a PhD in psychology, and then decided that he was less interested in the colours of words than in the Word. He left psychology for a career as a country preacher in Tennessee.

Meanwhile Stroop's discovery went on to achieve fame, inspiring thousands of other psychological studies. The Stroop task can be useful for gauging attention and unarticulated thoughts. There have been experiments in which subjects went without food, then did a Stroop task with a list of seemingly arbitrary words. The hungry subjects slowed down when they encountered a word like *hamburger* or *dinner*. Because thoughts of food were foremost in their minds, the meanings of food-related words were hard to tune out.

Back to Wegner and Ward. They used this principle in an experiment in which volunteers answered tough questions such as, "Do all countries have at least two colours in their flags?" Immediately afterwards, they were given a Stroop task with a series of familiar brand names printed in various colours. The goal was to name the colour of each brand name as quickly and accurately as possible.

NIKE
GOOGLE
TARGET
YAHOO

The subjects slowed down when reading off the colours of words like *Google* and *Yahoo*—but not words like *Nike* and *Target*. Evidently the difficult trivia quiz had directed attention to searching for answers on the Web.

To confirm this, the researchers did another version of the study with a ridiculously easy trivia quiz, in which everyone could be assumed to know the right answers. When those subjects did the brand-name test, they did not slow down over *Google* and *Yahoo*. It was only the hard questions that evoked thoughts of searching on the Web.

Wegner connects the Google effect to the general phenomenon of distributed memory. Uploaded keystrokes are just one of many ways we have of storing information outside our brains. Long before our virtual social networks, we shared memory, knowledge, and expertise among our real social networks. I'm not a foodie, but I have friends who can recommend interesting new restaurants. I don't know doctors, but I have a general practitioner who can recommend a specialist. We get by in the world not by knowing everything but by knowing people.

Distributed memory can counteract misinformation—to a degree, anyway. Surveys have shown that most people think antibiotics will fight viruses. *Wrong.* But, as Dan M. Kahan of Yale points out, it hardly matters. "Most people" are not going to self-prescribe azithromycin. The important thing is to know that it's a good idea to go to a doctor when we're sick and to follow that doctor's instructions.

The Google effect is another adaptation to distributed memory. The cloud is a friend who happens to know everything. It's always available, provides the answer in seconds, and never gets upset with dumb questions. It's little wonder we depend on it to the point of absurdity. Economist Seth Stephens-Davidowitz noted that the third-most-common Google search containing the phrase "my penis" is "How big is my penis?" You'd think a ruler would have a better answer.

When Senators Plagiarize

Our reliance on the cloud recalls a job title that was familiar to ancient Greeks and Romans: *mnemon*. A *mnemon* was a professional memorizer. He stood by during senatorial speeches and debates, supplying needed facts. Apparently no one thought this reflected poorly on the speaker's expertise. Today the Internet is the common *mnemon*, and politicians of our own time struggle with it.

US Senator Rand Paul has been accused of lifting material from Wikipedia and other online sources. Here's part of a 154-word passage from a *Forbes* article (by Bill Singer) that appeared verbatim and without credit in Senator Paul's 2012 book, *Government Bullies*.

As part of a plea agreement, both Kinder Caviar and Black Star Caviar Company have each agreed to pay a $5,000 fine and serve a three-year term of probation, during which time those companies will be prohibited from applying for or receiving a CITES Export Permit.

The marvel is that this court-reporter prose was deemed worthy of swiping—by anyone for anything. And this is just one of many reports of politicians, journalists, and celebrities cribbing from online sources. Though most of the high-profile plagiarists are well into middle age, a younger staffer is often blamed. The rising generation is growing up thinking that cutting and pasting are as natural, and as ethically neutral, as streaming music.

Hofstra University journalism professor Susan Drucker sees a generational divide even among her students. "The graduate students still see literary theft as stealing, but the 17- and 18-year-old undergraduates don't see this as wrong. 'It's so easy to copy material on the Internet,' they say. 'How can it be wrong?'"

Besides encouraging breach of copyright, the mnemonic Internet may also be coaxing us into groundless intellectual arrogance. In another trivia-quiz experiment by Daniel Wegner and Adrian F. Ward, half the participants were allowed to look up answers on the Web, and the other half weren't. Afterwards, all filled out questionnaires rating their memory, knowledge, and intelligence.

As expected, there was a connection between performance on the quiz and self-ratings. The eye-opener was that the ratings were higher for those who had just looked up everything. Copying answers from Google or Wikipedia made people feel, "I am smart" (one of the agree-or-disagree statements).

Naturally, looking up answers also tends to result in a high score. Wegner and Ward did another version of the experiment in which all participants were told they had got a near-perfect score. Even then, the people who had looked up the answers online reported feeling smarter.

You may counter by saying that "feeling smart" has nothing to do with the ethics of taking other people's words without credit. That's true enough, but subjective feelings underpin actions, rationalizations—and ultimately our sense of ethics. This experiment demonstrates that we have come to "own" the Internet as collective memory.

The cloud is easy to access now, and the process can only get more seamless in the near future. A bit in the movie *Annie Hall* (1977) already seems dated—or is it prophetic? Woody Allen finds himself standing in line in front of a man pontificating to his date about Marshall McLuhan. Allen interrupts to tell him he's got McLuhan's philosophy all wrong. The man says he teaches a class in media studies at Columbia. Allen does not whip out his smartphone, because they didn't exist at the time. Instead he pulls Marshall McLuhan from off-screen to denounce the poseur in person.

We're getting closer to something like that. Carnegie Mellon computer scientist Chris Harrison envisions "active listening," whereby a smartwatch could monitor a user's conversation and perform searches in the background. Whenever you speak (or a nearby loudmouth speaks) of Marshall McLuhan, the watch could display information about McLuhan—just in case you needed it. A discreet glance at the watch might prompt you with a better, more relevant talking point. Maybe a video of a McLuhan lecture would pop up, queued to the point where he refutes what your debating partner just said.

This hardly counts as science fiction. Voice recognition as a gateway to Web searching is already impressive. It's only battery life and the cost of cellular data that make active listening presently unfeasible. Solve that, and most of Harrison's vision will fall into place.

It's not too early to ponder the value of knowledge in a world like that. Of course, humans must know enough about Marshall McLuhan in the first place to have clashing opinions about him—otherwise there's no value in channelling McLuhan from the cloud.

The Value of Knowing

Is there value in knowing facts in a world where facts are so easy to look up? This book is an attempt to answer that simple question. I address it primarily through analysing original surveys of the public's knowledge.

The surveys reported in this book have been conducted by means of a new type of polling technology that may not be familiar to many. It's worth saying a little about it. An *Internet panel survey* is one conducted by an organization that has recruited a large group of people (a panel) who agree to participate in future surveys. Once a new survey begins, software selects a random sample of the panel to contact. E-mails containing links to the survey are sent to the selected participants, typically in several waves to achieve a demographic balance closely approximating the general population's. The sample can be balanced for sex, age, ethnicity, education, income, and other demographic markers that concern pollsters and marketers.

Internet panels have two substantial advantages over traditional phone polling. One is that there are few refusals. Traditional pollsters call phone numbers at random. Since in most people's eyes a call from a pollster is hardly more welcome than one from a telemarketer, many don't take the call or hang up when they find out what the call is about, which compromises the randomness of the sample. If it turns out, say, that fifty-year-old married white women are more likely to stay on the line, the survey sample becomes skewed. In an Internet panel survey, everyone has already stated a willingness to participate (and well over ninety percent do). So the invitation algorithm to any particular study is more readily able to achieve demographic balance.

One obvious caveat: everyone in an Internet panel has an Internet connection. Those who do have Internet are a bit more affluent, educated, and digitally savvy than the total population. This should be kept in mind. Still, almost everyone who has a phone has Internet access (if only via a smartphone's cellular data). The limitation of the field to Internet users isn't much of a disadvantage relative to the disadvantages of phone polling.

Internet panel surveys are conducted by non-profit organizations (such as RAND American Life Panel) and a number of tech firms and start-ups (GfK KnowledgePanel, SurveyMonkey, Amazon's Mechanical Turk). Typically the poll organization rewards volunteers by making a small donation to a charity of the volunteer's choosing. This provides a modest incentive while discouraging participation for money. No one can volunteer for a specific poll, and the polling algorithm limits any individual's participation to no more than a few surveys a year.

The instructions to my surveys explained that I was interested in measuring the state of public knowledge and requested that participants not look up answers. It's possible that a few cheated, even though there was nothing to be gained by getting a high score. But most of the surveys were filled out quickly, scarcely allowing time to research answers. The overall results—which often show a shockingly low state of public knowledge—argue against cheating being much of a factor.

In recent years Internet panels have been embraced by the academic and business worlds. For social scientists they promise a considerable improvement over the old method of putting up flyers on campus and polling undergraduates. Marketers now use online panels for testing new products, ads, and designs. Media such as *The Wall Street Journal*, the *Los Angeles Times*, and Bloomberg News use Internet panels for political polling.

Another of the technique's virtues is that it is fast and cheap compared to traditional surveys, making it possible to map public knowledge in ways that would have been impractical just a few years ago. You'll see a number of examples in this book.

The surveys document what the public knows and doesn't know in scores of key areas, from quantum physics to contemporary art to pop culture. They also reveal connections between factual knowledge and wealth, health, happiness, politics, and behaviour. Most of the chapters supply a few of the survey questions (shown in a box) so you can get a sense of where you stand relative to everyone else.

The book is divided into three parts. They focus (with some overlap) on three themes:

- *The Dunning–Kruger Effect.* The Internet isn't making us stupid, but it can make us less aware of what we don't know. Incomplete knowledge creates distorted mental maps of the world. These misperceptions affect choices, behaviour, and opinions in both the personal and public realms.
- *The Knowledge Premium.* The ability to answer so-called trivia questions correlates with higher income and other indexes of a successful life. This knowledge premium often remains even when you factor out formal education and age. There is a real-world value to knowing things, above and beyond a diploma or social connections made in university.
- *Strategies for a Culturally Illiterate World.* I will explore the ways individuals can best use today's media to stay informed, how companies and organizations can adapt to a society with limited cultural literacy, and how democracies can make wise choices despite low-information voters.

Age Test

How many US senators are there?

What is the capital of Brazil?

Where does a shortstop play?

If you answered one hundred, Brasilia, and between second and third base, you're right. And statistically speaking, you're probably older than those who can't answer these questions.

Though the above facts might seem timeless and generation-neutral, these are things that young people are less likely to know. Those who answered the senators question correctly were nine years older, on average, than those who got it wrong. For the Brazil and shortstop questions, the age differences were six and seven years.

Two

A Map of Ignorance

Susan Sherman, a Kentucky Catholic schoolteacher and nurse, returned home from a mission to Kenya to discover that she was no longer welcome in her Louisville school. It was late 2014, and an Ebola virus outbreak was ravaging Guinea, Liberia, and Sierra Leone. Parents at Sherman's school feared she might have the Ebola virus and transmit it to their children.

There had been no outbreak in Kenya. The school nonetheless barred Sherman from teaching for twenty-one days and requested that she submit a note from her doctor declaring her Ebola-free. Instead Sherman chose to submit her resignation.

This is one demonstration of the way that geographic knowledge and ignorance affects us all. To many Westerners, Africa is a compact and homogenous locale, like Las Vegas. In reality Kenya is 3,500 miles from the nations that experienced the 2014 Ebola outbreak. That's a couple hundred miles more than the distance separating Louisville, Kentucky and Manaus, Brazil. By the logic of Sherman's school, visitors returning from Louisville ought to be checked for piranhas in their luggage.

The classic demonstration of public narcissism and idiocy is the map test. How many Britons can find Austria on a map? Only forty-six percent, I found, in a survey asking people to locate ten nations. Less than a third could locate Myanmar, Nicaragua, or Gabon.

Nation	How Many Britons Can Find It on a Map?
Ireland	98%
Austria	46%
Estonia	41%
Kazakhstan	31%
Myanmar	26%
Nicaragua	21%
Suriname	18%
Burkina Faso	17%
Gabon	13%

Polling organizations have been asking questions like that for years, with predictable hand-wringing over the state of education. I took advantage of the speed and flexibility of Internet panel polling to do a more ambitious map test. Instead of asking about a few countries in the news, I asked Americans about all fifty US states, 170 of the globe's sovereign nations, and a few miscellaneous territories and regions. Each participant was asked to find ten to fifteen states or countries chosen from the total set, using an outline map of the United States, a continent, or the world with boundaries indicated but not labelled.

I then used the survey results to create cartograms. These are the distorted maps in which each region's area is scaled to population, electoral votes, or another variable of interest. In this case, the states or countries were digitally scaled to the percentage of the survey

A Map of Ignorance: The United States

The area of each state is scaled to the percentage of Americans who can't find that state on a map

sample that *wasn't* able to locate those regions on a map. These are maps of ignorance.

Virtually every adult American can locate Florida, Texas, and California on a US map. "Corner" states like Maine and Washington are easy, too. So in the cartogram, they shrink to almost nothing. Alaska and Hawaii aren't shown, but they would be mere dots, as nearly everyone could find them.

The bloated states are those that Americans have trouble finding. The most difficult state to find was Delaware: fifty-eight percent of the public couldn't locate it. More than a third were unable to find Nebraska, Missouri, or Alabama.

Why are so many Americans bad at finding states? Similar shapes and similar spellings threw some off. Illinois was regularly confused with Indiana and other "vowel-belt" states. Missouri and Mississippi were commingled.

Mistakes were rampant in the northern plains and Rocky Mountain states, with uncertainty about which more-or-less rectangular state was which. Also confused were not-so-identical twins such as New Hampshire and Vermont and Alabama and Mississippi.

For the world map, I tested every nation with a land area of more than three hundred square miles. The omitted countries were

A Map of Ignorance: The World

Each nation's area is scaled to the percentage of Americans who can't find it on a map

mostly island nations (Grenada, Tuvalu, the Maldives) and a few tiny European countries (Lichtenstein, Monaco, Vatican City, San Marino). They would be dots on the map in any case.

Just about everyone in my sample could find the United States, Canada, Mexico, and Australia. These readily located nations collapse to a small fraction of their usual size in the cartogram. Americans also do well with Russia, China, Japan, and the tourist-friendly zone of western Europe. The survey's participants were as able to find Italy as they were to find the United States. That must mean something—maybe that Americans eat a lot of pizza. Pizza boxes often reproduce Italy's boot as a de facto trademark.

Africa is the largest continent of all in a map projection based on American cluelessness. The Balkans and the Middle East have taken over much of Eurasia, diminishing more readily identifiable Russia and China. Easy-to-find Brazil no longer dominates the South American continent.

Reasonably enough, the survey sample was best at locating big nations and territories. The exaggerated size of Greenland and Antarctica in familiar map projections may have boosted their recognition rates (shrinking them in the cartogram).

Nation	How Many Americans Can Find It on a Map?
United States	98%
Australia	98%
Italy	98%
Mexico	97%
Russia	92%
China	91%
Japan	90%
Brazil	88%
India	84%
United Kingdom	82%
France	80%
North Korea	73%
Iran	53%
Israel	45%
Kazakhstan	42%
Venezuela	40%
Nigeria	27%
Costa Rica	10%
Republic of the Congo	5%

Kazakhstan, the ninth-largest country on the face of the earth, is almost four times the size of Texas, yet less than half the sample could find it on a map. In general Westerners fumble with almost any nation ending in *stan*. Many of us are still not up to speed on the post-Soviet Union and post-Yugoslavia political map.

Admittedly, some of these nations rarely make international news. But most couldn't find nations constantly in the news, such as Israel. Barely half could locate Iraq and Afghanistan, where Britain and the United States fought recent wars.

There are some truly confusing pairs of nations. The Republic of the Congo (the capital of which is Brazzaville) is distinct from its much larger neighbour to the east, the Democratic Republic of the Congo (the former Zaire, the capital of which is Kinshasa). The smaller Congo was the *least* locatable nation of all on my survey, with only five percent of the sample getting it right.

The map test aside, there is abundant evidence of how shaky our geographic knowledge is. A 2006 National Geographic–Roper Public Affairs and Media poll found that eighteen percent of young Americans, aged eighteen to twenty-four, thought the Amazon is in Africa. Twenty percent had Sudan in Asia, and ten percent put it in Europe. Three-quarters thought English was the most commonly spoken language in the world (it's Mandarin Chinese, with 2.6 times as many native speakers as English). The National Geographic folks concluded, with no little exasperation: "Americans are far from alone in the world, but from the perspective of many young Americans, we might as well be."

In 2013 the *Harvard Crimson* made a video in which a reporter asked students to name the capital of Canada. Answers included "I don't know—probably Vancouver or something," "Alberta? I have no idea," and "Is it Toronto?"

Such ignorance has spawned a new video genre, now familiar on talk shows and YouTube. It's easy: just point a camera at people, ask a simple question, and string together the most brain-dead responses for laughs. But don't show the people who gave correct answers, because that wouldn't be funny. For all the viewer knows, the producers had to interview hundreds of people to get a few wrong answers. I used to think these segments were patronizing and instances of selective reporting. I now know better. The videos *are* patronizing, but the ignorance is not invented in the editing bay.

In my own survey, using an American sample of all ages and educational levels, forty-seven percent knew that the capital of Canada is Ottawa. This was a multiple-choice question with five answers (an easier format than "fill in the blank"). "What is the capital of Canada?" has also been asked in two serious peer-reviewed surveys on the knowledge of US university students. The most recent survey, from 2012, found that just 1.9 percent answered correctly.

I have found that about nine percent of adult Americans don't know what country New Mexico is in. "Mexico" is the most popular wrong answer. New Mexico has been a state for the whole lifetime of virtually everyone drawing breath; its votes have counted in every presidential election since its admission; *Breaking Bad* was shot there. But almost one in ten people just weren't paying attention.

One bright spot in the 2006 National Geographic–Roper poll is that Millennials scored well on a test of abstract map-reading skills. They were shown a map of a fictitious no-man's-land and asked questions like "Which of the cities is most likely to be a port?" Most knew to pick a city on the water with multiple highways converging on it. Our educational system is turning out a generation that understands the map but not the territory.

So maybe geography is going the way of cursive writing. Is that so bad?

There is some alarming evidence that it is. In 2014 Russian troops entered Ukraine's Crimean peninsula. Americans were debating what, if anything, to do about it. Three political scientists—Kyle Dropp, Joshua D. Kertzer, and Thomas Zeitzoff—ran a survey asking Americans to locate Ukraine on a world map.

The survey used an unlabelled world map with national borders indicated. Participants were asked to click on the point best representing the Ukraine's location. Only one in six clicked within Ukraine's borders.

Other guesses were, literally, all over the map. There were clicks in every populated continent, with a cluster in Greenland and a few within the continental United States. There were a few clicks in the world's oceans. They weren't on an island. Either the clickers imagined Ukraine to be some lost Atlantis or they couldn't tell which part of a world map was water and which was land.

Here's the upshot. The researchers found that the further a person's guess was from the actual location of Ukraine, the more likely it was that that person supported a US military intervention in Ukraine.

There's a reason why war rooms have maps. Geography helps determine whether a military operation is essential to national security or immaterial to it; feasible or ruinously costly. A decision about sending troops to war in Ukraine ought to be informed by fine details such as whether Ukraine is in the United States or is a foreign country and whether Ukraine is on land or under water.

The correlation between factual knowledge and political opinion doesn't stop there. I ran a survey of sixteen assorted general-knowledge questions, including two about maps (asking the location of North Carolina and Ukraine), with American subjects. The survey also asked an issue then prominent in US media: "There has been talk of building a border fence to prevent illegal immigration. On a scale of 0–10, how do you feel about this idea?"

The more factual questions a person answered correctly, the *less* likely that person was to favour a border fence. The correlation was impressively strong, even when holding educational level and age constant. It's not just that the fence supporters were less educated. They knew less than others of the same educational level and age.

Those who aced the factual part of the survey, getting all sixteen questions right, put their support for a border fence at an average of 2.25 out of 10—that is, very low. Those who flunked the survey, failing to answer any question right, rated their support of the border fence at 7.22 out of 10. They were in favour of it.

Those who couldn't find Ukraine on a map were also more likely to want a border fence. And here's another question that was strongly connected to border-fence support:

> Scientists believe that early humans hunted dinosaurs such as Stegosaurus and Tyrannosaurus. True or false?

Those who said *true* wanted the border fence; those who said *false* didn't.

A border fence is a matter of practicality as well as ideology. At least some immigration hawks are signing on to the idea of a magic immigrant-deterring fence that can be constructed quickly, at minimal cost. More thoughtful people have to ask tough questions. How much would it cost the taxpayers? How effective would it be? A knowledge of geography is helpful in estimating the cost, and history provides a basis for judging how successful it would be. (Dynastic China's border fence, the Great Wall, spectacularly failed to keep out the Mongols.)

Democracies do not depend on every single citizen being well informed. There are always going to be voters who are less knowledgeable than others. That's okay, as long as the politics of the ignorant don't diverge too much from those of the better informed. But when the ignorant have different policy views and outnumber the better informed, there is cause to worry. Call this the border-fence principle: that certain political ideas can best be understood as examples of the Dunning–Kruger effect.

The National Deficit, Debt, Whatever

Ignorance of geography distorts our mental maps and sometimes shapes opinions. In the same way, other kinds of ignorance can distort our world views. This is often true of topics involving very large numbers.

How much is the UK's debt? I posed this question to British residents in late 2015, when the correct answer was about £1.6 trillion. I made the question as easy as possible. It was multiple choice,

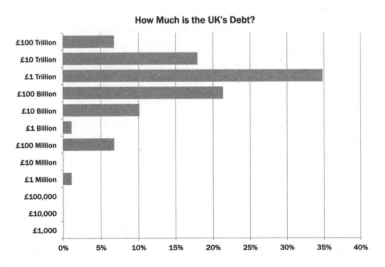

How Much is the UK's Debt?

asking only for an order of magnitude estimate. The most accurate response (£1 trillion) was indeed the most popular one. However, it was chosen by only about thirty-five percent of respondents. The rest chose answers that were wildly incorrect.

Then there's the issue of debt versus deficit. In 2013 David Cameron apparently confused the two, earning a rebuke from the UK Statistics Authority. This type of confusion is widespread. Later the same year *Business Insider* asked five hundred Americans to estimate the size of the US deficit. The most common answer, chosen by twenty-three percent of responders, was the range $1 billion to just under $10 billion. The actual 2013 deficit was $642 billion. That's about a hundred times bigger than the typical respondent thought it was.

Others underestimated the deficit even more drastically. More than ten percent put it at a few million dollars or less. That segment of the public inhabits an alternative universe in which a retired optician in Florida could write a cheque covering this year's federal deficit.

The survey also asked what had happened to the US deficit in the previous year. Was it bigger, smaller, or about the same?

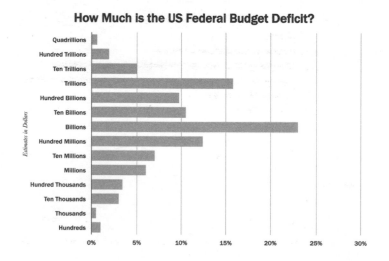

How Much is the US Federal Budget Deficit?

Well-informed Americans would have known that the slowly recovering economy, spending cuts, and tax increases had combined to cut the deficit from $1.09 trillion in 2012 to $642 billion in 2013. But sixty-eight percent believed that the deficit was larger in 2013.

I followed up that survey with a similar one using the same Internet panel firm that *Business Insider* used. A new randomized national sample of Americans was asked the same two questions, except I replaced the word *deficit* with the word *debt*.

Just so everyone's on the same page here: they're different! The debt is what the nation owes (like a credit-card balance). The deficit is how much the debt *grows* in a fiscal year (like how much a credit-card balance has increased over a year's time).

Under tax-and-spend George Washington, the United States ran up a huge Revolutionary War debt that wasn't paid off until 1830. For about a decade after that, the United States had no debt at all, but ever since 1840 the United States has always had debt. At the time of my survey, US debt stood at more than $17 trillion. Here are the answers to the survey asking about debt, overlaid onto the results of the survey asking about deficit.

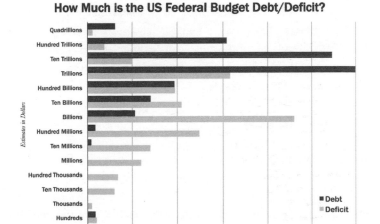

How Much is the US Federal Budget Debt/Deficit?

There's a fair amount of overlap in the guesses. That's despite the fact that the debt is about twenty-six times larger than the deficit. Compared to the deficit guesses, the debt answers skew larger—towards the top of the chart—as they should. But only twenty-seven percent of responders picked the correct range ($10–100 trillion), and it was not the most popular answer.

About two-thirds of my survey sample believed the debt had got larger in the past year. Just as a broken clock is right twice a day, that is correct.

It's no great mystery what's going on. People relate to words more than numbers and to emotions more than words. Every politician and journalist knows this. The deficit hawks have convinced voters that the deficit/debt/*whatever* is a threat to the nation's existence. They have achieved this without imparting many actual facts and by suggesting some "facts" that are not facts at all. Most people don't know the numbers: they just understand that there's a problem that's always getting worse (even when it's not).

One can question whether the size of the debt/deficit matters all that much to the average citizen. In any case, a number that would supply needed context is population. It's debt per capita that really matters. To figure that out, you need to know the population. A National Geographic survey asked participants to pick the current US population from four multiple-choice ranges. Sixty-nine percent picked outrageously wrong answers or said they didn't know.

Facts and Inequality

In 2011 psychologist Dan Ariely and business professor Michael I. Norton ran an Internet panel survey asking 5,522 Americans to estimate the nation's distribution of wealth. The participants were instructed to divide the nation into quintiles (fifths of the population) by wealth. There would be the wealthiest twenty percent, the

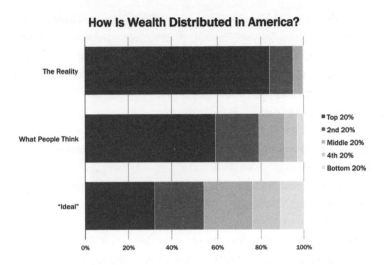

How Is Wealth Distributed in America?

second-wealthiest twenty percent, and so on, down to the poorest twenty percent. They were then asked to estimate what percentage of the nation's total wealth each quintile owned.

Note that the survey asked for wealth, not income. The survey spelled out the fact that it was asking for "net worth...defined as the total value of everything someone owns minus any debt" and gave examples ("property, stocks, bonds, art, collections, etc., minus the value of things like loans and mortgages"). Participants were also asked to describe an "ideal" distribution of wealth.

Start with the reality (the top bar of the chart). In actual fact, the top twenty percent of Americans possess about eighty-four percent of the wealth. The second and middle quintiles split between them almost everything else. The two poorest quintiles are barely visible in the chart's top bar, as they account for only 0.2 and 0.1 percent of the total.

Now, remember, we're talking about assets. The bottom forty percent live mostly month to month. They are more likely to rent their homes or have an underwater mortgage; to have student debt and little or no savings.

The public understands that there is a lopsided distribution of wealth. But as the middle bar shows, they underestimate how lopsided it is. The survey subjects guesstimated that the top quintile holds about fifty-eight percent of the total wealth and that each succeeding quintile has progressively less, down to about three percent for the poorest group.

To put it another way, the public estimated the top quintile to be twenty times richer than the bottom quintile. In reality, the top quintile is 840 times wealthier.

When asked to describe the ideal wealth distribution, the survey answers produced another unequal distribution—but far less unequal than the others (bottom bar). In this people's-choice distribution of wealth, the top fifth would hold thirty-two percent of the nation's wealth, and the bottom fifth would have ten percent. The top-to-bottom quintile difference shrinks to barely threefold.

One especially provocative finding of the Norton–Ariely survey is that there wasn't much variation among the estimates (actual or ideal) made by different political and demographic groups. Sure, they did find that conservatives and men favoured a bit more wealth inequality than liberals and women did, but not by much. The wealthy had a better handle on how much the top quintile owned, and they envisioned a utopia with greater wealth disparity than the poor did. But again, the difference was only a few percentage points.

There was even consensus about what is not so ideal about the status quo. Most respondents felt that the richest quintile would, ideally, have less, while the three poorest ones would have more. The second quintile (roughly, the upper middle class) already has its optimal share or close to it—according to the survey's estimates.

These findings, coming in the year of Occupy Wall Street, were spun by pundits across the political spectrum. Discussions of minimum wage, income taxes, and Social Security inevitably invoke the presumptive opinions of a silent ninety-nine percent majority. But unless the public knows the status quo, how well can it know what it wants?

The media have inundated us with statistics along the lines of "x percent of the population controls y percent of the wealth." We retain the *idea* of inequality, and our emotional reactions to it, better than the actual numbers. In effect the Norton–Ariely survey asked participants to confabulate a wealth distribution consistent with the general tenor of the news reports. That's a tall order. An economy is a complicated machine with many moving parts.

Imagine that an airline requested that its passengers sketch designs for an "ideal" airliner. The sketches would doubtless emphasize spacious seats and extra room for carry-on bags. They would leave off mechanical and navigation systems that the public knows nothing about. An airline that implemented the ideas would find that the plane wouldn't fly and that the cost of the roomy seating would be so high that almost no one would buy a ticket.

The American public's "ideal" wealth distribution is not wildly unrealistic. It is marginally more egalitarian than that of Sweden, a country that seems to work well enough (and where taxes come to forty-eight percent of gross domestic product). But Americans, unlike Swedes, are expected to save for retirement rather than relying on private or public pensions.

In the United States the average senior citizen has eighteen times the wealth of the average young adult. That makes baby boomers (a quintile unto themselves) much wealthier than the youngest adult quintile. The disparity has nothing to do with one-percenters or socio-economic inequality. The lifetime savings cycle of regular working people can itself produce a wealth disparity much larger than what the public envisions as ideal.

Given that people confuse words such as *debt* and *deficit*, I wondered whether they might be failing to distinguish between *wealth*

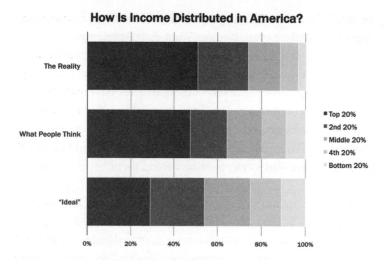

How Is Income Distributed in America?

The Reality

What People Think

"Ideal"

■ Top 20%
■ 2nd 20%
▦ Middle 20%
▦ 4th 20%
▦ Bottom 20%

0%   20%   40%   60%   80%   100%

and *income*. To check this, I conducted a survey patterned on the Norton–Ariely study, but asking about distribution of income rather than wealth.

America's income distribution is also top-heavy—but less so than its wealth distribution. The top twenty percent of earners account for just over half the total household income (versus the top quintile's eighty-four percent of wealth). At the other end of the spectrum, the bottom forty percent have some income, even if they have next to zero net worth.

There is, then, a big difference between income and wealth distributions in reality. But there was less difference in the public's estimates concerning the two. That's because the crowd thought that both income and wealth were more equally distributed than they are.

The most striking thing is that the "ideal" distributions of income and wealth were almost identical. Both samples felt that the top quintile ought to have about thirty percent (of income or wealth) and the bottom quintile should have eleven percent.

Related terms can be commingled in memory. Should you read an article on income equality and then, a couple of days later, be asked about the distribution of wealth, the income article may shape your answer even though it's not directly relevant.

The biggest issue, however, is that it's difficult to translate emotion and ideology into numbers that add up. Most are not used to thinking in terms of population quintiles. They start with the idea that the top quintile's slice should be "several times" the size of the bottom quintile's, then they fill in the middle quintile's proportions. They make a few nips and tucks to get the numbers to add up to 100 percent and are glad to put the task behind them.

Another study eliminated the quintile confusion. Michael Norton and Sorapop Kiatpongsan asked a huge sample of 55,000 respondents in forty industrialized nations to estimate the actual and ideal incomes of unskilled workers in their respective nations. They also asked for the actual and ideal incomes of the CEO of a large corporation.

The answers allowed the researchers to compute CEO-to-worker pay ratios, based on the estimates, and compare them to the reality. In the United Kingdom, for instance, the true ratio is about 183:1. But the British estimated it to be only 14:1. The ideal pay ratio was even closer—6:1.

This pattern was repeated around the globe. In every case citizens greatly underestimated their own nation's income inequality and said that an ideal distribution of pay would be much more egalitarian, with the average ideal ratio at 4.6:1. Once again, political beliefs didn't have much effect on the answers.

These studies show convincingly that conservatives and liberals alike *say* they consider an income distribution comparable to a Scandinavian welfare state ideal, leading Norton and Ariely to ask,

> Given the consensus among disparate groups on the gap between an ideal distribution of wealth and the actual level of wealth inequality, why are more Americans,

especially those with low income, not advocating for greater redistribution of wealth?

They came up with a few potential reasons:

> First, our results demonstrate that Americans appear to drastically underestimate the current level of wealth inequality, suggesting they may simply be unaware of the gap. Second, just as people have erroneous beliefs about the actual level of wealth inequality, they may also hold overly optimistic beliefs about opportunities for social mobility in the United States... Third, despite the fact that conservatives and liberals in our sample agree that the current level of inequality is far from ideal, public disagreements about the causes of that inequality may drown out this consensus.

You don't need a survey to conclude that the public's "ideal" number of gunshot deaths is zero. Some say the solution is to ban handguns, and others say the solution is for everyone to carry a loaded gun at all times. So what do we do?

Guns and Crime

Speaking of guns, a 2015 Pew Research Center poll showed a surge in support for gun ownership among Americans. More than half the US public says it's more important to protect the rights of gun owners than to impose further controls on gun buyers. That's an opinion. Some surveys have also asked about a fact: Has the US violent crime rate recently gone up, down, or stayed about the same?

A recent Gallup poll found that those who thought crime was up were less supportive of gun control. Specifically, among those who believed that the crime rate had risen in the previous year, forty-five percent supported stricter firearms laws. Among those who believed that the crime rate had stayed the same or decreased, fifty-two percent favoured stricter gun laws.

Now for some important context: From 1993 to 2010, the US violent crime rate has dropped precipitously. The firearms homicide rate was cut almost in half (from 7.0 to 3.6 per 100,000 people) while the rate of non-fatal violent crimes plunged to a little more than a quarter of what it had been. It's hard to think of another major social problem that has shown such a dramatic improvement.

This qualifies, however, as a little-known fact. A 2013 Pew Research Center poll asked whether gun crimes had gone up, down, or stayed the same over the previous twenty years. Fifty-six percent thought the crime rate had gone up (wrong), and twenty-six percent thought it had stayed the same (equally wrong). Just twelve percent knew it had gone down.

What's ironic is that both sides of the gun issue believe they have the better remedy for a surging crime rate that doesn't actually exist. Neither law-abiding gun owners nor gun-control laws likely had much to do with the plunge in firearms homicide. Some experts credit demographics. Violent crime is a young man's game, and the baby boomer generation moved out of that age cohort in the 1990s.

Big Macs and Democracy

The great challenge of a free society is making good choices when practically everyone is misinformed. Sometimes the crowd does better than you might expect.

I asked people, "How many calories are in a McDonald's Big Mac?"

The correct answer, according to the McDonald's website, is 550 calories. The most popular survey response was indeed the right one (a multiple-choice range of 400–799 calories). Forty-one

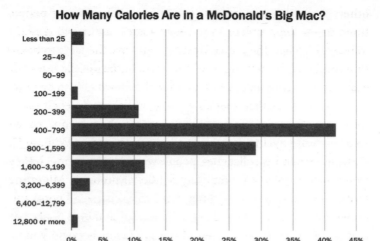

How Many Calories Are in a McDonald's Big Mac?

percent gave that correct answer, and the guesses clustered around it. About eighty percent gave an answer that at least wasn't completely ridiculous.

This may demonstrate the wisdom of crowds. When the public tries to estimate a numerical quantity, the average of the guesses is often surprisingly accurate.

The classic example is a contest to guess the number of jelly beans in a jar. Some guesses will be way too low, others will be way too high, and others may be just about right (though nobody has a way of knowing who's right). The mean guess (or, for that matter, the median or the mode) is often closer to the correct value than the vast majority of guesses.

The wisdom of crowds is not an immutable law. There was a time when everyone believed that the earth was flat. Everyone was wrong. The crowd's opinion of string theory would not be very enlightening to physicists. For the wisdom of crowds to work, the crowd must have some basis for reasoned opinions. In a jelly-bean-guessing contest, everyone can see how big the jar is and how small the beans are. Some resort to counting, others to maths, and others to intuition. When many people think about the problem from many angles, the crowd is likely to be wise. When the crowd doesn't even have the facts to begin thinking about something (the "flat" earth in the Middle Ages, for example, or string theory today), then the crowd fails to be wise.

You'll notice that guesses at national debt and deficit levels were way off base. One possible factor is a phenomenon called *scope insensitivity*. In a famous experiment devised by William H. Desvousges and his colleagues, people were asked how much they would pay to solve a (completely fictitious) problem. Migrating birds, it was said, were becoming mired in industrial oil pools and drowning. The birds could be saved by covering the oil pools, but that would be costly. The question was, how much would you be willing to pay to save the birds?

This question was put to three randomized groups. All were given identical descriptions, except that one group was told that the lives of 2,000 birds were at stake. Another heard there were 20,000 birds to be saved, and still another was told there were 200,000 birds whose lives were on the line.

The average amount that the members of the three groups were willing to pay was $80, $78, and $88 respectively. The number of birds didn't make much difference.

Desvousges's dilemma conjures, as the authors put it, the mental image of "a single exhausted bird, its feathers soaked in black oil, unable to escape." Either you care about that picture or you don't. Those who care find a single bird's death almost as tragic as the death of thousands. Logical or not, that's the way the human mind and "heart" work.

The scope-insensitivity experiment, which has been replicated many times with issues as different as chlorinated drinking water and the Rwanda genocide, is proof that emotions and not numbers rule. Scope insensitivity also affects the facts we retain. The emotional punch of a big number does not depend on its exact magnitude as much as on the fact that it's *big*. We know the national debt is big, just not how big. This mental imprecision, on the part of millions of voters, can thwart good decision-making. Democracy is predicated on the wisdom of crowds.

Marketers would do well to be aware of scope insensitivity. Apple has shown itself savvy on this point. Tech bloggers have slammed Apple for not releasing random-access-memory figures and other specs for its iPhones and iPads. But such numbers don't mean much to the vast majority of buyers.

I did a survey asking for an estimate of "the average amount of memory for a new tablet computer." I didn't specify what type of memory (the results make it all too clear that this wouldn't have mattered much).

Many consumers still don't get the distinction between kilobytes, megabytes, and gigabytes. But once again, the wisdom of crowds seems to have applied. The most common answer, 10–99 gigabytes, was also the most reasonable one at the time of the survey. It got forty percent of responses. But an equal portion of respondents

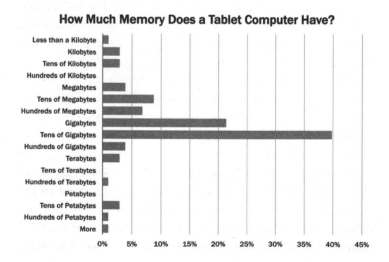

How Much Memory Does a Tablet Computer Have?

gave answers that were way off. These would be consumers who aren't likely to be impressed with talk of specs.

Apple's products generally don't have the *most* of anything (unless you count the highest prices and profit margins). Instead they offer an intelligent set of compromises. The firm's marketing moves the conversation away from numbers and on to intangibles such as ease of use and high-end design. That leaves the other tablet makers to play the war of specs. But talk of specs goes in one ear and out the other for about half the public. A specs-based pitch must educate before it can persuade, and it's not so easy to fold a Gigabytes 101 lesson into an ad.

The War on Christmas

I asked a national sample of Americans to estimate the percentage of Asians in the US population. The question didn't specify what nationalities count as "Asian" or how to classify those of mixed ancestry. The US Census Bureau *does* have a legalistically precise definition of "Asian American." It reports that, in the 2010 census, Asian Americans constituted 5.6 percent of the nation's population. In my survey, the public's average estimate was thirteen percent, more than twice the census figure.

These results fit into a pattern (see overleaf).

As you can see, the public has a tendency to overestimate the size of minority groups—and the smaller the minority, the more its size is overstated. On average, Americans think that 25 percent of people in the US are Hispanic or Latino (versus 17 percent, according to the census bureau), that 23 percent are African-American (versus 12.6 percent, according to the census), and that 11 percent are gay or lesbian. While there are no census numbers for gay people, a widely cited figure from a 2011 UCLA School of Law study is 1.7 percent for male and female homosexuals combined. The public

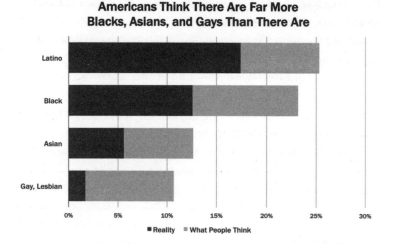

Americans Think There Are Far More Blacks, Asians, and Gays Than There Are

■ Reality　■ What People Think

overshot that by a factor of six. Overall the public believes Asians and gays to be comparably sized minorities, despite the fact that there are about three Asian Americans for every gay or lesbian American.

It's conceivable that some took "gay or lesbian" to mean "LGBT," a term often in the news. I also surveyed estimates of the LGBT population (spelling out that it means "lesbian, gay, bisexual, and transgender"), which logically has to be equal to or greater than the LG population. But the LGBT guesstimates tracked the gay and lesbian numbers rather closely. The crowd's LGBT estimate was fifteen percent, versus eleven percent for gays and lesbians. Like *debt* and *deficit*, *gay* and *LGBT* can be essentially synonymous in the public mind.

Millennials overestimate even more than others do. Those under the age of thirty put the proportion of Asians in the United States at twenty-one percent and gay people at fifteen percent. Thus younger people think there are twice as many Asians, and half again as many who are gay, than older people do. Age did not make much of a difference in estimates of the Latino and black populations.

There are at least three puzzles here. Why does the public overestimate the size of minorities? Why do young people overestimate even more? Why are small minorities overestimated to an even greater degree?

An extreme example of the latter phenomenon can be seen in the results of an Ipsos MORI survey that asked Americans for the percentage of Muslims in the US population. It's actually about one percent. The average estimate was fifteen percent.

Think about that. In the American mind, Latinos, blacks, Asians, gays, and Muslims constitute something like 25, 23, 13, 11, and 15 percent of the US population respectively. Add up these figures and you get 87 percent. Even when you allow for overlap, these high-profile minorities account for about two-thirds of the US population—*or so the average American estimates.*

This is a global phenomenon. The British, Ipsos MORI reported, believe that twenty-one percent of the UK population is Muslim (versus five percent in reality). In Hungary, Muslims are rare indeed, constituting one-tenth of a percent of the population. Hungarians estimated that seven percent of their fellow Hungarians were Muslim. That's about seventy times too high.

But not all the public's guesses are overestimates. Ipsos MORI asked Americans to estimate the percentage of the US population that is Christian. The average answer was fifty-six percent. In fact, seventy-eight percent of Americans are Christian. On this question America's perception gap was the greatest, but most Christian-majority nations considerably underestimated their Christian percentage as well. (A notable exception was Germany, where the average guess was right on the nose—fifty-eight percent of Germans are Christian.) By contrast, in Japan and South Korea, where Christians are a minority, the public *over*estimated the percentage of Christians. The rule seems to be that people underestimate the size of majorities and overestimate the size of minorities.

Our delusional demographics might be funny if it weren't for the fact that they influence attitudes and policy in reality. The misperception that minority groups are much larger than they are might feed into a narrative that straight, white, native-born Christians are an endangered species—and hence that every "Season's Greetings" card constitutes a war on Christmas.

Similar surveys have shown that people also greatly overestimate the percentage of teenage mothers, immigrants, senior citizens, and the unemployed. Britons guessed that a stupendous twenty-four percent of their compatriots were unemployed, when in fact only seven percent were at the time of the survey (2014). Thus the British public overestimated its unemployment rate by more than a factor of three. South Koreans overstated their unemployment rate eightfold. This kind of error is particularly alarming because, as politicians and journalists routinely remind us, voters often judge administrations by employment numbers—that is, their *perceptions* of employment numbers.

Errors can be hard to dislodge, as Ipsos MORI discovered when it debriefed some of its survey subjects. The company contacted those Britons who had overestimated the percentage of immigrants by a factor of two or more, informed them that the official figure was thirteen percent, and asked them to account for having guessed twenty-six percent or more. The subjects were allowed to pick as many explanations as applied. Most agreed with the statement, "People come into the country illegally so [they] aren't counted." Half said, "I still think the proportion is much higher." They cited "what I see in my local area," "information seen on TV," and "the experiences of friends and family."

While it would be unwise to place much faith in the precision of official figures on immigration, it would be *insane* to think that the non-expert can, just by recalling a few "experiences," come up with an accurate figure. Yet that was the logic used by much of the sample. Only a third admitted, "I was just guessing," which ought to have applied to almost everyone.

The wisdom of crowds does not require that everyone know the right answer. And in many ways, democracy ought to meet the conditions for wise crowds. Voters choose from among candidates and policies that campaigns strive to make understandable. The voters have many sources of news and plenty of time to deliberate.

But crowds are less wise when too many share the same distorted mental maps. In order to make reasoned decisions on most policy issues, it is imperative that voters know some demographic statistics and understand the difference between a million, a billion, and a trillion. As journalist Andrew Romano put it,

> [P]oll after poll shows that voters have no clue what the budget actually looks like. A 2010 World Public Opinion survey found that Americans want to tackle deficits by cutting foreign aid from what they believe is the current level (27 percent of the budget) to a more prudent 13 percent. The real number is under 1 percent. A Jan. 25 [2011] CNN poll, meanwhile, discovered that even though 71 percent of voters want smaller government, vast majorities oppose cuts to Medicare (81 percent), Social Security (78 percent), and Medicaid (70 percent). Instead, they prefer to slash waste—a category that, in their fantasy world, seems to include 50 percent of spending, according to a 2009 Gallup poll. Needless to say, it's impossible to balance the budget by listening to these people. But politicians pander to them anyway, and even encourage their misapprehensions.

As Romano's account makes painfully clear, one problem with the premise that people don't need to know facts because they can always look them up is that we *don't* look them up. Most people will never Google facts such as the location of Ukraine, the percentage of Muslims in the population, or the size of the nation's budget. We just don't care enough; we don't feel we need to know. Yet we walk around with misperceptions that shape attitudes, votes, and policy.

Distorted Mental Maps

Find Colombia on a world map.

How many Britons are immigrants?

What percentage of the British population is over sixty-five?

If you know where Colombia is, your map knowledge is better than about half the public's.

Immigrants comprise about thirteen percent of the British population. But the average estimate, according to an Ipsos MORI survey of the British population, is twenty-four percent.

Those over sixty-five make up 17 percent of the UK population. Ipsos MORI found that the British public guessed thirty-seven percent—a misperception that presumably skews discussions of pensions.

The percentage of both senior citizens and immigrants was wildly overstated in all surveyed nations, often by a factor of two or more.

Three

Dumb History

Those wishing to become British citizens are required to take the "Life in the UK" test, a set of questions about British history and culture. Here are some sample questions:

- In the UK, April 1 is a day when people play jokes on each other (true or false).
- What flower is traditionally worn by people on Remembrance Day? (lily, daffodil, iris, or poppy).
- Which landmark is a prehistoric monument which still stands in the English county of Wiltshire? (Stonehenge, Hadrian's Wall, Offa's Dyke, or Fountains Abbey).

By design, the questions are easy (the correct answers are true, poppy, and Stonehenge). The grading is easy too. A score of seventy-five percent correct is enough to pass. I surveyed British residents on a sample of the "Life in the UK" questions. About fourteen percent would have failed the test, scoring less than seventy-five percent correct.

Is the glass half empty or half full? Those scores were actually better than those in a 2011 *Newsweek* survey of one thousand Americans asked questions on the US citizenship exam. Thirty-eight percent of Americans flunked. Most couldn't say who was president during World War I (Woodrow Wilson) or identify Susan B. Anthony as an activist for women's rights. About forty percent didn't know the countries the United States fought in World War II (Japan, Germany, Italy). A third couldn't name the date the Declaration of Independence was adopted (July 4, 1776). Six percent were unable to circle Independence Day on a calendar.

Such findings have mobilized public opinion. In 2014 Arizona governor Doug Ducey signed a law requiring that high school students be able to pass the citizenship test in order to graduate. An organization known as the Civics Education Initiative hopes to enact similar laws in all fifty US states.

Here's the thing: it's easier to rally support for well-meaning mandates than it is to figure out how to teach more effectively than we already do. Civics has always been a bulwark of education. Should teachers place less emphasis on reading, maths, and computer skills in order to focus on how a bill becomes a law? The vast reserve of ignorance is not reduced so much as shifted around.

Half of Subjective History Happened Since 1948

I did a survey in which US participants were asked to name "important news or historical events" that took place within specific time frames. These frames ran from 3000 BC to the present and covered single years, decades, centuries, and millennia. The time frames were each presented to a different randomized group so that no one was overwhelmed.

The survey took place in May of 2014. Eighteen percent of participants were unable to name *any* news or historic event that had happened in the previous calendar year, 2013. Another eleven percent gave a wrong answer.

Survey subjects did about as poorly in naming an event from 2012, and the recall rate for 2011 plummeted to thirty-six percent. That's right—most people couldn't remember anything of general importance that had happened three years prior to the survey's calendar year. There was a similar result for 2010.

A sizable proportion of responses did not concern news so much as sports, weather, crime, and celebrity fluff. Some mentioned sports victories; hurricanes and floods; high-profile murders; celebrity deaths and scandals. These were counted correct as long as the date was right.

There were two ways an answer could be wrong. A few gave events that never happened, such as "President Nixon impeached." (Nixon resigned to avoid that ignominy.) The more common type of wrong answer was assigning a real event to an incorrect time frame. There were those who put the death of Osama bin Laden in 2012 or 2010 instead of 2011. That's understandable. The general consensus is that there's less need to memorize dates now that we've

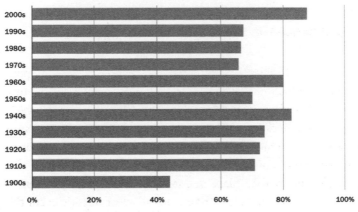

How Many People Can Name at Least One Important Event of Recent Decades?

got Google and that it's sufficient to have a general sense of what came after what. But many in my survey didn't. Some said that Columbus sailed to America in the 1600s and that the Ice Age was in the first millennium CE.

Eighty-eight percent of my sample could name an event that happened in the decade 2000–2009. The most popular answer was the 2001 terrorist attacks on the World Trade Center and the Pentagon. Recall rates dropped to about two-thirds for the 1990s, 1980s, and 1970s.

Memories perked up for the trippy 1960s (eighty percent), sagged back for the boring 1950s (seventy percent), and rebounded (eighty-four percent) for the 1940s. Most could recollect something about Hitler, Pearl Harbor, the Holocaust, or Hiroshima.

Then recall trended downwards. More than half of respondents were unable to name a single important historical event of the first decade of the twentieth century (1900–1909).

On to centuries.

Seventy-eight percent could name something that happened in the 1800s (the Civil War and the end of slavery were the most

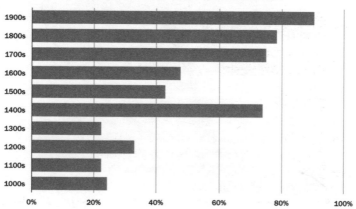

popular responses). Recall was almost as good for the 1700s (the US Revolutionary War and Declaration of Independence). But most could not name a single event of the 1600s.

A lot happened in that century. The Pilgrims landed at Plymouth Rock. There was the English Civil War and the Salem witch trials; the death of Shakespeare and the birth of Bach; the invention of the telescope and the beginnings of modern science in the persons of Galileo, Kepler, and Newton. None of these occurred to more than half the sample.

A few dates are burned into schoolroom memory, one being 1492. That was enough to produce a spike in recall for its century. Four out of five who were able to supply an event for the 1400s named Columbus's voyage. But most drew a complete blank for the centuries of the later Middle Ages.

From AD 1000 and back, I merely asked for events that happened in a given millennium. I didn't count on volunteers understanding admittedly confusing terms such as "first millennium AD." The survey asked for "an important historical event that happened in the years AD 1 to AD 999."

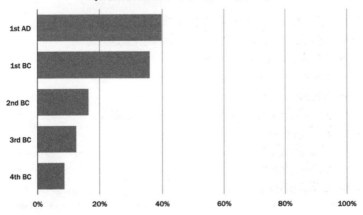

How Many Can People Name at Least One Important Event of Recent Millennia?

You might think it would be all but impossible for a person who understood the question to *not* be able to name something that happened in the first millennium AD (such as the life and death of Jesus and the decline and fall of Rome) or BC (classical Greece, Cleopatra). Most could not.

Historians infer that Jesus was born in either 6 or 4 BC. Thus the birth of Jesus fell in the first millennium BC. This threw a few people and accounted for some wrong answers, but not enough to change the results much.

Most of the earth's surface was literally prehistoric before 1000 BC, so it's not surprising that few were able to name any historic events for the earliest millennia surveyed. The correct answers mainly had to do with Egypt (building the Pyramids), the Old Testament (the Exodus of the Jews, King David rules Israel), and Stonehenge.

Some participants were able to name multiple events for each time frame. I collated all the remembered events (including those that were assigned to a wrong time frame) and used this data to create a timeline of subjective history. The midpoint of remembered history—splitting the timeline in half—is 1948. In very rough terms, it seems that people recall as much that happened after 1948 as before it—going back to the beginnings of civilization. This is another distorted mental map. Here the timeline's scale is weighted by the number of recalled events.

In making personal and collective decisions, we place too much weight on what has happened in the very recent past. You see this in the reactions to the world's catastrophes: mass shootings, wars, earthquakes, stock market crashes, terrorist attacks, economic depressions, and epidemics. After each dire event there are calls to be better prepared the next time—prepared, that is, for the thing that just happened. We fail to prepare for predictable challenges and catastrophes that have happened many times before—just not lately.

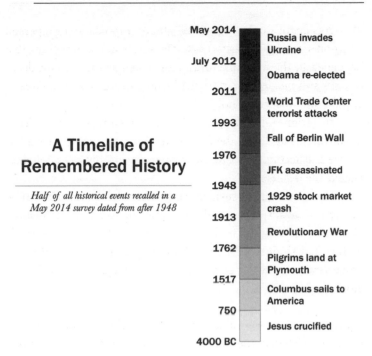

A Timeline of Remembered History

Half of all historical events recalled in a May 2014 survey dated from after 1948

May 2014	Russia invades Ukraine
July 2012	Obama re-elected
2011	World Trade Center terrorist attacks
1993	Fall of Berlin Wall
1976	JFK assassinated
1948	1929 stock market crash
1913	Revolutionary War
1762	Pilgrims land at Plymouth
1517	Columbus sails to America
750	Jesus crucified
4000 BC	

Forgetting the Presidents

For much of his career, Henry Roediger III has been studying how Americans forget their presidents. He came to this topic by accident. In some psychological experiments, it is useful to interpose a filler task in between the tasks of interest to the researchers. During one experiment, as a filler task, he tried asking undergraduates to write down all the US presidents they could remember in five minutes. The average Purdue or Yale student, he found, could recall only seventeen presidents out of the thirty-six or thirty-seven who had held office up to that point. This research, published in 1976, spanned the Richard Nixon and Gerald Ford administrations.

Roediger, now at Washington University in Saint Louis, Missouri, was not trying to make another case for the cultural illiteracy of students. His interest was human memory, and he found that there was huge variation in recall rates for individual presidents. Nearly everyone named Washington, Lincoln, and the few most recent presidents. Very few, less than twenty percent, remembered obscure presidents such as John Tyler and Chester A. Arthur.

Of course, you might argue that some presidents *are* more important, more worthy of being remembered. But Roediger made a chart that challenged this notion. He put the presidents in chronological order (on the x axis) and charted their recall rate (0–100 percent, on the y axis). This produced, very roughly, a U-shaped curve. The students best remembered the first few presidents and the few most recent ones. In between those two poles stretched a great slump of the forgotten, with the major exception of Lincoln, who had a very high recall rate (the U curve was actually a kind of W, rounded on the bottom).

Roediger and Robert G. Crowder identified this as a *serial position effect*. When memorizing a list, people best remember the first few items and the last few items. They are least likely to remember items a little more than halfway from the start of the list. In 2015, Rutherford B. Hayes, James A. Garfield, and Chester A. Arthur occupy that blind spot of memory.

Of course, with any list there are going to be items that are more memorable for reasons having nothing to do with their position in the list. Lincoln won a war that split and reunited the nation; he abolished slavery, an action that still fascinates and resonates; his dramatic assassination (in a theatre) is part of a tale taught to every American schoolchild. It's easy to see why Lincoln is an exception to the serial position effect. More surprising is that the few presidents before and after him were also better remembered than average, a Lincoln halo effect that especially benefited his successors Andrew Johnson and Ulysses S. Grant.

Roediger has been repeating the presidents experiment over the course of four decades with similar results—aside from the progressive slump of recent presidents into obscurity. In a 2014 experiment Roediger and K. A. DeSoto enlisted the participation of adults of all ages and found that age makes a big difference: people are far more likely to name presidents whose administrations they have lived through. Less than a quarter of Generation X participants—those born from the early 1960s to the early 1980s—named Eisenhower. This isn't to say that they'd never heard of Eisenhower but that he didn't come to mind when they were trying hard to think of US presidents. This tells us something about how future generations will think of Eisenhower—or rather, *not* think of him.

The gradual forgetting of presidents appears to be predictable. By 2040, Roediger forecasts, less than a quarter of the population will be able to remember Lyndon Johnson, Richard Nixon, and Jimmy Carter. One may imagine that certain presidents are exceptions, as Lincoln is—but usually they're not. Roediger began his experiments around the time of Watergate. It then seemed to him that Gerald Ford's status as the first president who was never elected to that office had earned him a permanent place in history and memory. The distinction counts for little now, and Ford has slid predictably into obscurity. After Roediger mentioned this fact in interviews, a spokesperson for the Gerald R. Ford Presidential Library and Museum contacted him, saying attendance at the institution was declining—did Roediger have any suggestions?

Reminiscence Bump

Beloit College's Mindset List, published annually since 1998, gently warns professors of dated cultural references that will be meaningless to the incoming class. The class of 2016 has "never seen an airplane 'ticket'…Robert De Niro is thought of as Greg Focker's long-suffering father-in-law, not as Vito Corleone or Jimmy Conway."

Even the teaching of history must, to some degree, accommodate the short memories of youth. Historians wrestle with what is relevant and what can be dropped from the syllabus. There are, however, no sharp lines between nostalgia and cultural history. Should young people know who Billie Holiday was? Groucho Marx? The Kray twins?

A disproportionate share of the memories that we have of our own lives are from adolescence and early adulthood, between the ages of ten and thirty or so, a tendency termed a *reminiscence bump*. These memories include the joys and pains of puberty, school and university, first love, first job, and first apartment. In contrast we remember nothing of infancy and little of early childhood. The middle-aged remember relatively little of what happened in the great valley of memory yawning between about age thirty and the very recent past. We thus have a biased perception of our own lives, one dominated by the two decades spent in an advertiser-prized demographic.

Danish psychologists Jonathan Koppel and Dorthe Berntsen have found that the reminiscence bump applies to world events as well. People are more likely to remember news events that occurred when they were between around ten and thirty years old. It may not be true that those who remember Woodstock weren't there, but it's a safe bet that they were between ten and thirty years old when it happened.

The participants in my history survey were adults, between twenty and seventy years old. Twenty-year-olds are in the middle of their golden memory zone right now. For seventy-year-olds, that zone is forty to sixty years in the past. You would therefore expect the surveyed public to have relatively good memories of events stretching back as far as sixty years. In fact, "living memory" commands about half the subjective timeline, compressing everything else into the other half.

The goal of history class—to provide a broad perspective, to introduce us to the great world that existed before we were born—entails an uphill battle against the realities of memory and attention spans.

The Thirty-Two Faces of History

History is not just about names and dates. Shakespeare, Queen Victoria, and Einstein live for us today a little more vividly because we can call to mind their faces, preserved in portraits that have become part of collective memory. I wondered how many historic faces are generally known to the public. Nearly everyone can identify Napoleon, Washington, and Lincoln, but there are surprisingly few people who have achieved that level of fame. They are far outnumbered by important personages whom most have heard of but can't recognize from a headshot. Furthermore, almost everyone can recognize contemporary entertainers and athletes better than they recognize historical figures. Consequently any estimate of the number of widely recognized faces from "history" depends on exactly where you draw the line between historical figures and contemporary celebrities.

I tested facial recognition of nearly all the top one hundred historical figures on a list published by Steven Skiena and Charles B. Ward in 2013. Skiena and Ward claimed to rank historical figures "just as Google ranks web pages, by integrating a diverse set of measurements about their reputation into a single consensus value." Their method drew heavily on Wikipedia entries: how long the entries are; how often they are viewed; how many links point to them. You may debate how valid this method is. For my purpose the important thing is that it casts a wide net. The top ten on the list are Jesus, Napoleon, Muhammad, Shakespeare, Lincoln, Washington, Hitler, Aristotle, Alexander the Great, and Jefferson. (All are male, as are most Wikipedia editors.)

I asked American survey participants to identify a tightly cropped headshot, 160 pixels square, of each figure. I made the survey as easy as possible, using the most iconic and recognizable portraits I could find. Of course, the features of some of history's most influential people have gone unrecorded, but a portrait does not have to be authentic to be recognizable. Pictures of Jesus are pure fantasy. Despite that, people have a pretty clear idea of what Jesus is "supposed" to look like. The most iconic image of Christ is one painted by the otherwise obscure twentieth-century religious illustrator Warner Sallman. His *Head of Christ* was mass-produced as prints and greeting cards, starting in 1941. The Jesuses you see in films and *South Park* are ultimately modelled on Sallman's image.

One hundred percent of my sample recognized Jesus from a small, cropped version of Sallman's *Head of Christ*.

I was able to find usable likenesses for all Skiena and Ward's one hundred names with the exception of Muhammad (it being seen as blasphemous to represent him), King David, and several early Christian saints. These weren't tested. The survey was multiple choice, so the correct answer was in the list to jog verbal memory. Each question had five options plus "don't know."

Excluding recent US presidents, there are five historic figures that effectively everyone in the United States recognizes: Jesus, Hitler, Abraham Lincoln, Albert Einstein, and George Washington. The group of widely recognized figures was dominated by heads of state and included three authors (Shakespeare, Mark Twain, and Edgar Allan Poe), two scientists (Einstein and Newton), and scientist-statesman-polymath Benjamin Franklin.

Recognizability is not just a matter of historical importance. Unusual faces help. Henry VIII looks well fed, Abe Lincoln is gaunt, and Hitler has that creepy moustache. In contrast, Thomas Jefferson gets lost in a bewigged crowd of America's founders. Barely fifty percent could identify Jefferson from a picture, despite the fact that his face has been on the American nickel since 1938.

Of the hundred people on Skiena and Ward's list, only thirty-one were recognized by more than fifty percent of participants (though the error bars of a dozen or so straddled that threshold). I believe that understates the total number of widely recognizable historical figures, though not by very much.

Here's why. The Skiena–Ward one hundred is a ranked list. The last ten of the hundred are:

91. Pope John Paul II
92. René Descartes
93. Nikola Tesla
94. Harry S. Truman
95. Joan of Arc
96. Dante Alighieri
97. Otto von Bismarck
98. Grover Cleveland
99. John Calvin
100. John Locke

You don't need me to tell you that the only person here whom most average Americans might recognize from a picture is Harry S. Truman (and only fifty-eight percent of my sample did).

The first half of Skiena and Ward's hundred included twenty-three people whom more than half my sample could recognize. The second half (numbers 51–100) included only eight. If we assume that the above rate of decrease is typical, then you'd expect the third fifty (numbers 101–150) of a hypothetical extended list to have around three recognizable faces and the fifty after that (numbers 151–200) to have maybe one. Model this as a converging series, and the total number of all historical figures recognized by more than half the public would be about thirty-five.

The Skiena–Ward list includes recent presidents. As Roediger's research shows, their fame is likely to be fleeting. It is surely a temporary anomaly, in the grand scheme of things, that Gerald Ford's face is about as recognized as Shakespeare's or Napoleon's.

I adopted this admittedly arbitrary definition: a historical figure is someone whose main achievement occurred at least fifty years earlier than the time of the survey. That means we drop Nixon, Reagan, and George W. Bush as being too recent. I was able to find just four additional faces not on the Skiena–Ward list that most people recognized: those of Walt Disney, Dwight Eisenhower, Andy Warhol, and Lyndon Johnson (who barely makes the fifty-year cut-off). That comes to about thirty-two figures. There are fewer widely recognized faces from ancient and modern world history than there are US presidents.

The US public's visual history is undeniably a distorted map. Fifty-eight percent of the recognized faces are those of white

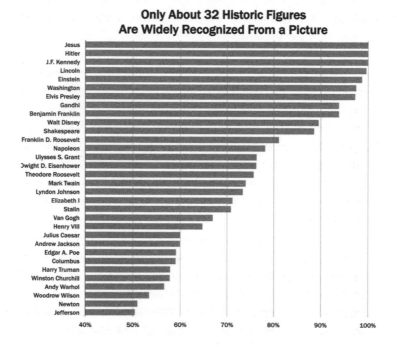

Only About 32 Historic Figures Are Widely Recognized From a Picture

American men. There is only one woman on the list (Elizabeth I) and one who is non-white (Gandhi). No one ever said history was politically correct.

Misquoting Einstein

Surveys gauge historical knowledge narrowly—how many people can recognize a face, know a fact, think of an event. Connections between facts are as important—maybe more so. This book began with the tale of an educated woman who knew of Shakespeare and of *Hamlet*, just not the connection between them. That kind of fragmented knowledge is universal.

One survey of undergraduates found that only thirty percent could name the man who proposed the theory of relativity. The students surely knew the name Albert Einstein and the face. But the question didn't ask about Einstein. It asked about the theory of relativity.

Like every other figure of history, Albert Einstein exists as a free-floating cloud of ideas, associations, and catchphrases not always tethered to a name or face. Not only are great people and events progressively forgotten, they are also progressively simplified. In life Einstein was a complex and multidimensional figure. He was a failure who couldn't get an academic job and worked in the Swiss patent office, a Jew who escaped the Third Reich, an American celebrity, a civil-rights activist who called racism "a disease of white people." Gradually Einstein's narrative has been simplified and oversimplified. Ambiguity gets left on history's cutting-room floor.

In one memory experiment, Roediger and his colleagues asked people of various ages to list events that occurred during the Civil War, World War II, and the Iraq War. There was much more agreement about what happened during the Civil War than during the Iraq War. Those who lived through a war had personal and idiosyncratic memories of it. Those who learned about a war purely from school and the ambient culture had more consistent interpretations.

Thus the past devolves from complicated reality to "history for dummies." Along the way, the story gets garbled. I asked survey participants to identify the author of the following statement:

> The definition of insanity is doing the same thing over and over and expecting different results.

The epigram is widely attributed to Einstein on Internet quote mills, and politicians love to cite it. (Mis)quoting Einstein remains one of the cheapest brands of instant gravitas. But the insanity quote isn't in any of Einstein's published writings or interviews. It appears to have originated decades after the physicist's death. With slight variations the quote surfaces in two rather different books published in 1983, the basic text of *Narcotics Anonymous* (*not* attributed to Einstein, who was never in rehab) and Rita Mae Brown's *Sudden Death*, a *roman-à-clef* about the women's tennis circuit (where it's credited to a fictional character who is female and not a physicist). This is an example of "Churchillian drift," whereby apt quotations by the marginally famous get attributed to someone more famous (such as Winston Churchill). The phenomenon is older than the Internet, but the profusion of poorly vetted quote sites has enabled it.

Another popular error is confusion about $E=mc^2$ and the atomic bomb. The July 1, 1946 cover of *Time* magazine depicted Einstein with a mushroom cloud in the background. Inscribed on the cloud was $E=mc^2$. Ever since then Americans have assumed that the iconic equation was somehow central to the bomb. It's true that $E=mc^2$ was Einstein's equation and that Einstein co-authored the 1939 letter to President Franklin D. Roosevelt warning him that Germany might build an atomic bomb. But the bomb had nothing to do with relativity and could have been made without Einstein's

Who Is Albert Einstein?

Almost everyone can identify the older, white-haired Einstein from photos, but only 68% recognize him in this 1921 photo (at age 42)

Physicist

48% can say what Einstein did for a living ("scientist" was also counted correct)

German

42% can name the country where Einstein was born

$$E=mc^2$$

66% know who formulated this equation

Relativity

30% know who devised the theory of relativity

Intelligence

98% understand that "Einstein" has become synonymous with intelligence

Atomic Bomb

42% say Einstein created the atomic bomb (which is incorrect)

"The definition of insanity is doing the same thing over and over and expecting different results."

41% believe that Einstein said this, though it doesn't appear in any of his published writings or interviews

theory. It was certainly made without Einstein, a pacifist who didn't have security clearance.

I asked a survey sample to identify "the father of the atomic bomb." That vague phrase is applied to several physicists—though never, by the well informed, to Einstein. Einstein was nevertheless the most common response (forty-two percent), beating out J. Robert Oppenheimer (eight percent) and Edward Teller (three percent).

Frida Kahlo ranks high in popularity among twentieth-century artists. On closer inspection, public understanding of Kahlo's life and

Who Is Frida Kahlo?

8% recognize Kahlo from a portrait

Artist — 53% know what Frida Kahlo did for a living

Dead — 44% don't know whether Frida Kahlo is living or dead, and 4% believe she's still alive

Mexican — 48% know Kahlo's nationality

Surrealist — 18% can identify the art movement associated with Kahlo

Diego Rivera — 9% can name the famous person who was married to Kahlo

Not Georgia O'Keeffe — 15% incorrectly identify Kahlo as "the woman artist who lived in New Mexico and created colourful paintings of flowers, cattle skulls, and desert landscapes"

Not Grant Wood — 5% identify Kahlo as the painter of *American Gothic*

achievement is incredibly threadbare. Scarcely half of Americans know that she was an artist or that she was Mexican. Few can connect her to surrealism, a famous self-portrait, or Diego Rivera. What is left of Kahlo if you don't know anything important about her? It's like the joke about Santa Claus being real—only he's skinny, lives in Miami, and hates children.

Textbook Wars

In the summer of 2014, the College Board announced a new framework for Advanced Placement US history courses. Within days this normally boring development was in the news. The Republican National Committee called the framework a "radically revisionist view of American history that emphasizes negative aspects of our nation's history while omitting or minimizing positive aspects." The Texas Education Agency drew up plans to shun College Board materials in favour of Texas-sanctioned ones. Ken Mercer, who was behind the Texas proposal, explained: "I've had kids tell me when they get to college, their US History 101 is really I Hate America 101."

By September of 2014, one Colorado school board had drawn up a policy limiting instruction to subjects promoting patriotism, the free-market system, and respect for authority. In 2015 an Oklahoma legislative committee formally banned the College Board's US history framework, finding it lacking in the above values.

Why did a history syllabus hit a nerve? Stanley Kurtz, in the *National Review*, complained that the College Board was in thrall to historians who want "early American history to be less about the Pilgrims, Plymouth Colony, and John Winthrop's 'City on a Hill' speech, and more about the role of the plantation economy and the slave trade in the rise of an intrinsically exploitative international capitalism."

Kurtz (his surname is the same as that of the colonializing anti-hero of Joseph Conrad's *Heart of Darkness*) identified a disconnect between parents and historians. Whereas most parents would be happy to have their children learn the same history they did, professional historians tend to be revisionists. They see their role as "revising" the existing understanding in the field. Textbooks gradually incorporate new scholarship, with the result that they change from generation to generation.

It all depends on perspective. A thirty-nation study of historical knowledge organized by James H. Liu, a psychologist at Victoria University of Wellington, New Zealand, illustrates this problem perfectly. The study asked volunteers around the globe to identify the individuals who had most influenced world history, for good or for ill. For one nation, the ten most important figures in *world* history were:

1. Gandhi
2. Hitler
3. Osama bin Laden
4. Mother Teresa
5. Bhagat Singh
6. Shivaji Bhonsle
7. Einstein
8. Subhas C. Bose
9. Lincoln
10. George W. Bush

You can probably guess what nation was responsible for this list. If you're not from that nation, you may have trouble guessing who numbers 5, 6, and 8 are.

The point is not that Indians have an exaggerated notion of their nation's global importance. Every nation does. Another question in Liu's survey asked participants to rate the relative importance of their nation in world history as a percentage, somewhere between 0 and 100 percent. Henry Roediger, who helped collect the US data, told me he "cringed" when he saw the estimates. Americans estimated that America was responsible for something like thirty percent of world history!

Roediger felt a little better when he learned that Canadian estimates of Canada's importance were in the same range. In fact, around thirty percent turned out to be a typical answer in the nations surveyed (mostly large industrialized nations where Liu had colleagues). Add up all the averaged estimates, and they came to about 900 percent. Logically the figure shouldn't exceed 100 percent, and realistically it should be less, for Liu surveyed only about thirty of the world's 196 sovereign states.

Historians who choose to write textbooks understand that they have to sell to an assortment of finicky parents and school boards. For better or worse, history textbooks aim for a politically neutral and inoffensive style. The subtler issue is that historians make thousands of judgement calls about what to include, what to leave out, how much emphasis to give certain events, and what connections to draw. The cumulative effect of all these choices is to reflect the authors' world views. Kurtz, and his liberal counterparts, aren't being paranoid when they perceive cultural and political agendas in history curricula. The question is, what viewpoints are acceptable?

It would be possible to write a textbook presenting a positive (and factual) view of Adolf Hitler—they had them in Nazi Germany. It would be possible to write a Marxist, or libertarian, history that was scrupulously accurate and free of heavy-handed rhetoric. Most of us can agree that such histories would not be suitable as primary textbooks for teaching history in elementary and high schools. All we can rationally expect of our textbooks is that they embody the political and cultural values of the median citizen—and subtly, at that.

But this rational expectation is increasingly embattled. We live in an age of immersive narrowcasting. Partisan 24-7 TV networks react to news in real time and spill out onto social networks, becoming all-encompassing in ways that the yellow journals of old were not. Accustomed to such news sources, parents and politicians want history textbooks to narrowcast, too. The Fox News motto—"Fair and balanced"—captures this new sense of epistemological entitlement. We feel we are entitled not only to a history tailored to our politics but also to the belief that *our* history is uniquely objective and neutral—while all others are biased.

Dead White Males

Americans are not that good at identifying the European males who fill the nation's history textbooks. The two faces above are recognized by only about half the US public.

A multiple-choice survey gave these options for the bearded man at left: Charles Darwin; Alfred, Lord Tennyson; Karl Marx; Charles Dickens; and Henry Wadsworth Longfellow.

Options for the gent at right were: Samuel Johnson, Marquis de Sade, Johann Sebastian Bach, Peter the Great, and Molière.

The correct answers are Darwin and Bach. It is of course true that their achievements have nothing to do with how they looked. Nevertheless we live in a visual society that is only getting more so. Textbooks, biographies, documentaries, and museum displays have pictures. That half the public doesn't recognize Darwin or Bach implies that it hasn't been much exposed to these figures.

Four

The One-in-Five Rule

You don't have to explore the world of ignorance long to encounter the one-in-five rule. It's claimed that about twenty percent of the public believes...well, just about any nutty idea a survey taker dares to ask about. A 2010 *Huffington Post* article sampled recent surveys to report that the under-informed twenty-percenters

- believe witches are real,
- believe the sun revolves around the earth,
- believe in alien abductions,
- believe Barack Obama is a Muslim, and
- believe the lottery is a good investment.

Is the one-in-five rule something to take seriously? Ask a stupid question, and you'll get a stupid answer. It is up to the survey maker to design questions whose answers are meaningful.

In 2014, Malaysia Airlines flight 370 vanished mysteriously, leading to extensive news coverage in a near-complete vacuum of facts. A CNN poll asked people to evaluate possible explanations for the missing airliner: terrorists, a rogue pilot, and so on. The survey's last option was "space aliens, time travellers or beings from another dimension." Three percent rated this explanation as "very likely," and six percent said it was "somewhat likely." That's nine percent giving it credence.

To ask about aliens or time travellers is to pose a leading question. Most will not take the bait, but a few will. It is far from clear that those who rated these outlandish ideas "likely" had given them any thought at all prior to the survey. Certain survey questions create their own lunatic fringes.

Had the survey simply asked, "What happened to Malaysia Airlines flight 370?" fewer would have volunteered an absurd answer. The moral is that it can be wrong to identify a survey response as "what people think." They may not have thought about it before they said they believed it, and afterwards they may go back to not believing it and not thinking about it.

With a suitably wacky question, and a little ingenuity, it's not hard to manufacture a one-in-five statistic.

Survey takers are told to make questions as neutral as possible. It's not always clear how to follow that prescription. A 2014 poll by the Anti-Defamation League that asked an extraordinarily large global sample (53,100 people in 100 nations) to describe their views on the Holocaust yielded a memorable one-in-five factoid: about one in five citizens of Western Europe and the US did not accept the standard, history-book account of the Holocaust.

The details of the survey tell a more complicated story. The interviewers first asked participants whether they had heard of the Holocaust. Those who said they had were then asked to characterize their views on it. The three options were:

- The Holocaust is a myth and did not happen.
- The Holocaust happened, but the number of Jews who died in it has been greatly exaggerated by history.

- The Holocaust happened, and the number of Jews who died in it has been fairly described by history.

"Don't know" was not explicitly offered as an option, but those who volunteered that answer were so tabulated. Here are a few results by nation.

Nation	Never Heard of the Holocaust	Holocaust Is a Myth	Holocaust Has Been Greatly Exaggerated	Holocaust Was Fairly Described	Don't Know
United Kingdom	1%	0%	6%	83%	10%
Germany	8%	0%	10%	79%	4%
United States	10%	1%	5%	79%	4%
China	31%	2%	22%	42%	3%
Egypt	71%	3%	15%	6%	6%
West Bank and Gaza	51%	5%	35%	4%	5%

Though it's shocking that there are any Holocaust deniers, they are a small minority everywhere. The proportion ranges from zero percent (in Britain and in Germany, where denial would require mental gymnastics) to five percent (in the West Bank and Gaza).

More surprising is the number of respondents who picked the middle option, saying that the Holocaust happened but that the number of Jews killed was "greatly exaggerated." In the United States, that's the talking point of white supremacists trying to sound "reasonable" for a TV interview. Ten percent of Germans and twenty-two percent of Chinese endorsed this view.

The number killed in Nazi death camps cannot be known exactly, so saying that estimates of the death toll might be "exaggerated" is not demonstrably wrong. For some, choosing this option may be a way of expressing cultural identity or politics. It may be attractive to supporters of a Palestinian state or those who disapprove of Israeli settlements in the West Bank. In fact, the ADL pollsters found that Holocaust minimization (as well as outright denial) tracked consistently with negative attitudes towards Jews.

Most unexpected is the number who say they've never heard of the Holocaust. In the United Kingdom, only one percent claimed ignorance, but the figure was seventy-one percent in Egypt and ninety percent in Indonesia. Throughout the Middle East, a majority said they'd never heard of the genocide that motivated the founding of Israel, an event with ongoing political and military relevance to the region.

But a claim of ignorance can also mask an unpopular or controversial opinion. Given that the ADL survey questionnaire asked fifteen questions about attitudes towards Jews before it got to the Holocaust, it would have been abundantly clear that the pollsters had a particular interest in the Jewish people, and those unsympathetic to them might have felt that it was easier to claim ignorance than to give an answer the pollster might disapprove of. The distinction between knowledge and opinions is not always absolute in a survey.

Ten Percent of Your Brain

Surveys demonstrating belief in Holocaust denial and jetliner-abducting aliens attest to a gullible public. What's needed, we're told, is more scepticism, more critical thinking, better baloney detectors. These are talking points of the sceptic movement. Yet our relationship to nonsense is more complex than it might at first appear.

"If you don't press the Clear button after buying gas, the next customer can charge gas to your credit card." This is a claim that has been posted widely on the Internet. It's not true. When I included it in a true-false survey, a resounding 80 percent said it was false, and a mere two percent said it was true. The rest said they didn't know. Apparently, it's the two percent who do a lot of posting on Facebook.

In general the public understands that there are false yet compelling claims that get repeated and taken for true. They just don't always connect that to what they heard the other day. We know *how* to be sceptical but not *when*. And blanket scepticism can lead one as far astray as blanket credibility can.

True or false: At the time of the 9/11 attacks, the World Trade Center contained a stockpile of gold in the basement.

True. Gold and silver bars worth about $230 million were retrieved from a precious-metals depository underneath the site in the weeks after the attack. I tested this statement because it sounds like an urban legend. Sure enough, seventy percent said it was false, and only nine percent called it true. The public seems to appreciate that 9/11 is the stuff of conspiracy theories. Adding a secret cache of gold raises another red flag. The survey answers were driven by a facile, intuitive scepticism rather than knowledge of the facts.

True or false: You only use about ten percent of your brain.

False. This ever-popular "statistic" drives neuroscientists up the wall. Debunkings of it are legion—yet somehow they never reach the crowd that most needs to see them. In my survey, sixty-six percent of the sample called the statement true.

Why is this claim so popular? The ten percent mythos tends to resonate with intuitive, creative, and unconventionally spiritual personalities. Some use it to extol the merits of meditation, yoga, and other "mind-opening" practices; for others it lends credence to telepathy, clairvoyance, and life after death. Few believers interpret "ten percent" as an insurmountable limit; it's more of a licence to fantasize about the unlimited possibilities of whatever potential human movement one has just taken up.

My guess is that this false factoid does not raise a scepticism flag because it sounds like a neutral pronouncement of science, barely different from "20 percent of air is oxygen." In fact, the 10 percent statement is sometimes attributed to...who else? Albert Einstein.

Conspiracy Theories

Those who believe that Princess Diana was murdered are also more likely to believe that she faked her own death. Those who believe that Osama bin Laden was already dead before his reported death in a 2011 American raid are also more likely to believe that he is secretly alive—or so a recent study has reported, confirming that some people are just constitutionally more inclined to believe in conspiracy theories. They usually believe in many conspiracy theories, not just one, and may even claim belief in logically contradictory theories.

Paranoia matters, as it informs opinions on issues that affect us all. In 2014 psychologists Stephan Lewandowsky, Gilles E. Gignac, and Klaus Oberauer reported a survey involving several conspiracy theories. True or false:

- The Apollo moon landings never happened and were staged in a Hollywood film studio.
- The US government allowed the 9/11 attacks to take place so that it would have an excuse to achieve foreign and domestic goals (e.g., the wars in Afghanistan and Iraq and attacks on American civil liberties) that had been determined prior to the attacks.
- The alleged link between second-hand tobacco smoke and ill health is based on bogus science and is an attempt by a corrupt cartel of medical researchers to replace rational science with dogma.

- US agencies intentionally created the AIDS virus and administered it to black and gay men in the 1970s.

The subjects were also asked whether they agreed or disagreed with the following statements:

- The potential for vaccinations to maim and kill children outweighs their health benefits.
- Humans are too insignificant to have an appreciable impact on global temperature.
- I believe that genetically engineered foods have already damaged the environment.

Those who believed in flat-out conspiracy theories were also more likely to agree with the above statements (the first two are wrong, and the third is unproved). Unlike the typical conspiracy theory, these beliefs affect everyday behaviour, both in the voting booth and outside it. Should I vaccinate my kids? Are hybrid cars worth the extra cost? Which tomato do I buy? The one-in-five rule casts a long shadow.

Five
___

The Low-Information Electorate

"It's hard to think of a major policy dispute where facts actually do matter," liberal economist Paul Krugman wrote in the *New York Times*. "It's unshakable dogma, across the board."

"The Democratic party's electoral majority is currently sustained by low-information voters and people who are unlikely to be persuaded by data that contradicts their own political narrative," said conservative scholar Jeremy Carl in the *National Review*.

Krugman faults "a big chunk of America's body politic" that "holds views that are completely at odds with, and completely unmovable by, actual experience…If you've gotten involved in any of these debates, you know that these people aren't happy warriors; they're red-faced angry, with special rage directed at know-it-alls who snootily point out that the facts don't support their position."

"Many liberals have a deeply ideological view," said Carl, "one in which certain 'truths' must be accepted to show one's moral virtue while genuinely inconvenient truths are ignored…it is hard to have a rational argument with a fanatic about the subject of his fanaticism."

Carl and Krugman are complaining about the same problem. Most voters are poorly informed to begin with, and they cherry-pick evidence to support their preconceived views. Conservatives and liberals never tire of talking about how spectacularly dumb the great mass of liberals and conservatives are...*because it's true.*

Throwing Darts at the Ballot

In 1992 the well-respected California judge Abraham Aponte Khan lost an election to a virtually unknown challenger who had been rated "unqualified" by the Los Angeles County Bar Association. The challenger's name was Patrick Murphy. He won because the name Murphy sounded less "foreign" than Khan. The all-American Judge Murphy later resigned over allegations of money laundering and chronic absenteeism.

In 2006 judge Dzintra Janavs, rated "exceptionally well qualified" by the bar association, lost an election to Lynn Diane Olson, who ran a Hermosa Beach, California, bagel store.

"You know the most frightening thing about judicial elections?" asked Parke Skelton, a consultant who worked for former Los Angeles mayor Antonio Villaraigosa. "Eighty percent of the people actually pick someone."

Consultants such as Skelton must be mavens of voter ignorance. They know that the news media don't cover judicial races. These contests are boring. Nobody cares except a handful of attorneys. Ergo even the best-informed voters know next to nothing about the judges on the ballot. Most judicial races are nonpartisan, so voters don't even have party affiliation as a pretext for their choices; they're left to pick names almost at random. This state of affairs turns the ballot into a highly effective psychological experiment in hidden bias. It doesn't do such a good job of electing competent judges.

The long twilight of the newspaper business has left many voters without a consistent source of local news. News channels and online aggregators overwhelmingly favour the high-profile national races that rack up clicks. It takes a gaudy candidate or scandal to divert eyeballs from the usual suspects. But look at a typical ballot. There may be several dozen races, and a half dozen at most have gotten decent reportage, anywhere.

I asked a national sample of American adults (not just "likely voters") to name the holders of fourteen elected offices—national, state, and local. The survey also invited participants to write in the names of any officials whose offices were not on the list.

Essentially everyone can name the president, and 89 percent were able to name the vice president (a higher percentage than some surveys have reported). Sixty-two percent could identify at least one of their state's US senators. Slightly less than half could name both. Fifty-five percent knew their district's congressperson.

Governor was another easy call. Eighty-one percent knew their state's chief executive. Barely half of those who said they lived in a

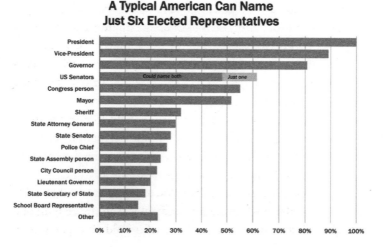

**A Typical American Can Name
Just Six Elected Representatives**

municipality with a mayor or city manager were able to name that official, though.

Those six offices were the limit of the typical citizen's knowledge. Not even a third of respondents could name the current holders of any of the other offices. That includes all the representatives to the state and city legislatures, where much of the business of government gets done.

I also asked participants to describe their political preferences on a five-point scale from "very conservative" to "very liberal." I found no correlation between these answers and knowing the names of elected officials.

There is, however, a correlation between knowledge and intelligent decisions. A voter who does not know the *name* of a mayor or state assembly person is unlikely to know much else about her, such as the issues she ran on and any accomplishments, failures, or criminal convictions that would bear on a bid for re-election. Can't fight city hall? Most people couldn't find it with a GPS.

The Myth of Character

A popular credo is that one should evaluate candidates by "character," without placing too much emphasis on education or knowledge of the issues. The last thing a politician wants is to be pegged as an intellectual. Many excel at projecting quite the opposite image.

The cult of character can override ideology. In every election we hear of swing voters who say they will decide between two ideologically different candidates based on character, likeability, or simply being the "better" man or woman for the job.

UCLA political scientist Lynn Vavreck has found that split-ticket voters—those who vote for candidates from more than one party—are less informed than those who hold to a party line.

Vavreck surveyed an impressively large sample of forty-five thousand Americans, asking them to identify well-known politicians by office. She compared survey results to voting patterns. Those who fell in the bottom third of political knowledge stood a twelve percent chance of voting for senatorial and presidential candidates from different parties in the 2012 election. Among the best-informed third, the chance of a split ticket was only four percent.

Under-informed voters were also more likely to describe themselves as undecided on hot-button issues such as immigration, same-sex marriage, and increasing taxes on the wealthy, a finding that fits in with the notion of a "mushy middle." Political pollsters recognize that many who identify themselves as moderates are really just those who "don't know."

We hope that voters in the middle supply a reality check to partisanship and help promote the compromise necessary to a democratic society. There *are* voters who hold strong, well-reasoned political convictions that happen to lie in between those of the two main parties. There just aren't too many of these voters, it seems.

"It is tempting to think that something as important as control of the Senate lies in the hands of voters who carefully pick and choose which candidates to vote for in each race on the ballot, but this seems unlikely," Vavreck wrote. "It is more likely that split-ticket voters are buffeted by idiosyncratic factors, like incumbency status, recent campaign advertising, and the tone and share of news coverage candidates receive."

Op-ed writers hate campaigns that focus on scare tactics and trumped-up scandals over policy. But politicians run such campaigns because they work. Low-information voters are most likely to be persuaded by political ads appealing to the lowest common denominator, and they're most likely to swing elections that can be swung.

The Voting Lottery

Los Angeles is a capital of voter ignorance and apathy. By inscrutable tradition, the city holds municipal elections in the spring of odd-numbered years. In 2013 only twenty-three percent of the city's registered voters showed up to elect Eric Garcetti mayor of USA's second-largest city. A 2014 Los Angeles school board election had an eight percent turnout rate.

One index of Los Angeles's desperation is a 2014 proposal by the city ethics commission to establish a voting lottery. Every voter would automatically be entered in a lottery to win cash prizes, perhaps as much as $25,000. The plan, dubbed Voteria, might succeed in increasing turnout. But unless someone also finds a way to educate the voters about municipal candidates and issues, the benefits are doubtful.

Economists have long argued that voting is an irrational act. The chance of your one vote swinging an election is minuscule and presumably cannot justify the minor bother of voting, much less the effort it takes to become truly educated on candidates and issues. Rational people, it's said, ought to be rationally ignorant (especially on down-ticket races that don't get discussed at dinner parties).

But people vote anyway. Since economists don't like to be contradicted, they call that the "paradox of voting." One way to think of it is that democracies are like casinos. They exploit human irrationality—and, come to think of it, there aren't many firmer foundations than that. There are enough "irrational" voters to channel the wisdom of crowds and select candidates who are in tune with public sentiment and who are, usually, not all that bad.

How big is the crowd whose wisdom we're relying on? An Ipsos MORI survey asked people around the globe to estimate the percentage of their fellow citizens who had voted in the last election. All fourteen nations polled significantly underestimated the percentage of voters *except* for the United States. On average, Americans guessed that fifty-seven percent of Americans had voted. That was almost exactly right.

It's hard to say whether the United States deserves a trophy or a booby prize. The actual percentage of voting Americans (fifty-eight percent) was the second lowest of the fourteen surveyed nations. Only Poland had a smaller share of voters.

Hey, maybe Americans don't vote, but at least they're realistic about it. The US does have a strong voting ethic. As Election Day approaches, citizens are bombarded with subtle and unsubtle directives to vote. Of course, political parties have incentives to get out the vote among populations they believe are likely to vote their way, but non-partisan patriotic pitches also abound. VOTE. It doesn't matter whom you favour or how much you know…just *vote*!

My survey asking Americans to name their elected representatives also asked whether they had voted in the most recent (2012) presidential election. The 2012 voters were far better informed; they were almost twice as likely to be able to name state and local office holders as those who didn't vote.

So perhaps it's inadvisable to twist non-voters' arms to vote absent some way of educating them as well. Such pressure all but ensures that many reluctant voters will be picking candidates the way they pick lotto numbers. And that's a voting lottery we don't want.

Name Your Representatives

Try naming your local or county councillor, your Member of Parliament, and your Member of the European Parliament.

A 2014 Opinium/*Observer* survey found that barely half the public (fifty-two percent) could name their MP. It was downhill from there—just thirty-one percent could name one of their local or county councillors, and only eleven percent knew their MEP.

Part Two

The Knowledge Premium

Six

Putting a Price Tag on Facts

William "Bud" Post was a drifter and grifter, convicted of passing bad cheques and otherwise earning quick cash in odd jobs as a carnival cook and truck driver. In 1988 his bank balance stood at $2.46. Post then made the one brilliant financial move of his life. He pawned a ring to buy lottery tickets.

One of them hit the jackpot—$16.2 million of Pennsylvania lotto loot. This was quickly followed by Post's second-best financial move, opting for twenty-six yearly payouts rather than a lump sum.

A couple of weeks after the drawing, Post collected his first annual cheque of $497,953.47. He had already spent most of it. He'd bought a private plane and an alcohol licence for himself and had leased a restaurant and a used-car lot for his two brothers.

Three months after that first cheque cleared, Post was in debt for half a million.

A year later, Post decided it was time to buy his dream house. This turned out to be a $395,000 fixer-upper mansion in Oil City, Pennsylvania. Then things got complicated. A brother hired a hit man to kill Post and his (sixth) wife, hoping to inherit. The hit man failed, and the brother was arrested. Post himself fired a rifle at his wife and took a shot at a bill collector (resulting in a restraining order and an assault conviction).

Post's former landlady, who was also his occasional girlfriend, sued him for a share of his jackpot. She had bought the lottery tickets for Post, and her story was that Post had agreed to share any winnings. Post strenuously denied this. A judge shrugged at the "he said, she said" testimony and ordered Post to give the plaintiff one-third of his winnings.

Post said he didn't have the money. His home was a money pit, and everything had been mortgaged to the hilt. The judge froze the lotto payments.

Post began selling off his possessions as his home fell into ruin. The *Washington Post* reported:

> Visitors to his crumbling mansion in Oil City noted plywood-covered windows, missing shower stalls, a swimming pool filled with debris, an old car on blocks in the weedy yard and a malfunctioning security system that chirped six times every 60 seconds.
>
> A dishevelled Mr Post ambled around his 16-room home without his false teeth, because he said they made his head hurt.
>
> "I was much happier when I was broke," he moaned.

Speaking of broke, Post declared bankruptcy. He sold his dream house for sixteen cents on the dollar ($65,000) and auctioned off the lottery's future payments.

That left him with a tidy $2.65 million. Show of hands: can anyone see where this story is heading?

Post blew those still-substantial assets on two homes, three cars, two Harley-Davidson motorcycles, a truck, a camper, and a sailboat.

He said he intended to use the sailboat to start a charter-fishing business in the Gulf of Mexico.

Post was arrested on that sailboat for the long-standing assault conviction. He served a short prison sentence. When he came out, he was nearly destitute. Post survived on food stamps and a $450 monthly disability cheque until his death in 2006.

William Post's sad tale resonates. We all cling to the belief that love, health, and happiness can be realized through a combination of luck, work, education—and, above all, money. Post was the Dunning–Kruger exemplar, a man who knew next to nothing about budgeting, investing in real estate, or starting a business and consequently believed these things to be easy. It may be true that money can't buy happiness, but ignorance all too often leads to unhappiness.

In the coming chapters, I will explore how factual knowledge (and ignorance) relate to personal well-being.

The connections are often quite strong. For instance, I surveyed 445 Americans about a list of ten general-knowledge questions spanning history, geography, civics, science, literature, art, and personal finance. This allowed me (actually, it allowed a statistical software package) to test whether there was a correlation between knowledge and income in my sample. There was. The people who knew more assorted facts made more money. To explain that further, I'll need to make a digression into statistics (that I promise to keep brief).

The (In)Significance of Statistical Significance

The one thing most people know about statistics is that polls and surveys are not entirely accurate. You're picking people at random and hoping that they're representative of the general population. So there's a "margin of error."

How do we determine that margin? Here's an example: one of the questions in my trivia quiz asked people to name the capital of Brazil. The correct answer, Brasilia, was chosen by 36.6 percent of the sample. But what we really care about is the percentage of the whole US population that would have got the correct answer. We don't truly know that, because I didn't ask everyone in the country, just 445 reasonably random people who participated in an Internet panel. Statistics tell us that, with a random sample of 445, the margin of error on 36.6 percent is plus or minus 4.5 percent, so the actual population value is likely to be in the range of 32.1–41.1 percent.

We're also interested in correlations, a more subtle concept. As I mentioned, the people who did better on the quiz tended to make more money. This is potentially an interesting finding, but again, how sure can we be that it reflects the overall population?

Suppose I had polled ten random volunteers, and one of them turned out to be a billionaire who is also a trivia nut. That alone would force a sort of correlation between trivia knowledge and income, but it would be statistical "noise" and might not signify anything.

This is a matter that statisticians worry about a great deal. They express their concern with a p (probability) value. The p value is, in plain language, the chance of a result occurring purely by chance. It's the probability of a false positive. Since we prefer meaningful results and not false positives, the smaller the p value, the better.

By convention, a p value of no greater than .05 (five percent, or one in twenty) is said to be "statistically significant." To express it another way, you want to be at least ninety-five percent confident that a given result is not just a glitch. Of course, all "statistical significance" really means is that the data support a conclusion to a reasonably high probability. There is nothing magical about the five percent threshold, and it is no guarantee of truth. It is, however, the usual threshold for publication in academic journals. Given the incentive to publish or perish, cynics say that achieving a $p=.05$ threshold is like rolling a twenty-sided die. Repeat an experiment enough times and you should get something to publish! (This practice is known as *p* hacking.) A .05 *p* value is also widely, though not universally, adopted by pollsters and journalists in reporting survey results.

Back to my trivia quiz. The correlation between the number of correct answers and reported household income had a *p* value of <.001, meaning that the probability of a false positive was less than one in one thousand. As you now know, a low *p* value is not, by itself, proof of a meaningful result. But when it's <.001, at least you can say that the *p* value leaves nothing to be desired. (And with that I will say no more about *p* values. For those interested, *p* values for the surveys conducted for this book are given in the endnotes. All the correlations reported will be significant, most of them well exceeding the .05 threshold.)

Now it's time to trot out another important rule of statistics: *correlation does not prove causation.*

My favourite demonstration of that is the Spurious Correlations website, which catalogues impressive and entirely meaning-less statistics. From 1999 to 2009, for example, the number of swimming-pool drownings correlated with the number of Nicolas Cage films released. In the same period, the age of Miss America winners correlated with the number of murders by steam, hot vapours, and hot objects.

Goofy coincidences like these are easy to find in our data-rich age. Tests of statistical significance do not necessarily filter them out. Anyone who looks long and hard enough for correlations will find them.

That's why it's a good idea to focus on correlations that make some kind of sense. There is an obvious explanation for a connection between factual knowledge and income: education.

Those who know a lot of facts are likely to have spent more years in school. Those who are well educated make more money. That, after all, is the unsubtle sales pitch for training courses and

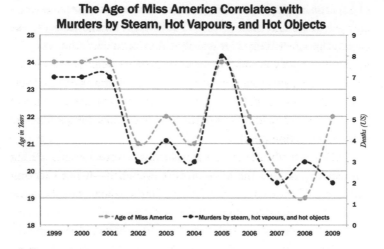

The Age of Miss America Correlates with Murders by Steam, Hot Vapours, and Hot Objects

student loans. An Oxbridge or Ivy League degree translates into cash (as has been endlessly chronicled).

This raises the question of whether knowing facts is a uniquely good predictor of income or whether it's just a tip-off to how much formal education one has (that is, whether knowing facts is a "surrogate" for education).

Statisticians often want to tease out the effects of more than one predictive factor on a given outcome. Among the most widely used tools are *linear regressions*. Despite the opaque name, it's a simple idea. Suppose you suspect there's a connection between the number of cronuts people eat and their weight. Can you use cronut consumption to predict weight? One way to find out is to collect individual data on weekly cronut consumption and weight. Then get some graph paper and make a dot for every individual in the data set (a scatter chart). Each dot's position indicates a given person's cronut consumption (on the *x* axis) and that same person's weight (on the *y* axis).

Should it turn out that there is a correlation—that the people who eat a lot of cronuts are heavier—the chart would show a cloud of dots running upwards, from lower left to upper right. In a clear-cut case, you could use a ruler to draw a trend line through the dot cloud. That line is a linear regression. You could use it to make predictions. Should you want to know the likeliest weight for someone who eats fourteen cronuts a month, you would draw a line up from fourteen on the cronut axis until it intersects the diagonal trend line. Then you'd read off the predicted weight, on the weight axis, at the intersection point.

Conceptually, this is what statistical software does in creating a linear regression. The code doesn't eyeball it—it has exacting mathematical procedures for fitting a line to data—but the basic idea is pretty much what I've just described.

Things get more interesting when you add more than one predictive factor into the mix. Your weight predictions would be more accurate if you took the sex of the subject into account, since men are usually heavier than women. For this you would need to make a three-dimensional scatter chart, something hard to manage on graph paper. It's no problem for statistical software, though.

So-called *multivariate regressions* are the main technique of big data. A customer of gender x who bought y and lives in postcode z is more likely to buy a, click on b, and vote for c. One of the things these models do is to gauge how useful each particular factor is for prediction. When you have a lot of factors, you often find that some are redundant. A model that incorporates postcode does not need to also include county of residence (a postcode gives the county and describes the place of residence more precisely). Software can recognize that.

We understand why a postcode is more informative than a county is. Usually the overlap between factors is less clear-cut and lacks an obvious reason. Any number of different factors may tell us some of the same things, but each may also convey some unique information. In that case a model gains predictive power by including multiple factors.

Because the connection between years of formal education and income is generally acknowledged and—we think—understood, it's useful to add it to any model that predicts income. I did that with the model for scores on my ten-question quiz. The quiz scores remained relevant—statistically significant as a predictor of income—even when educational level was added to the model. That means that factual knowledge is not simply a surrogate for educational level.

Another relevant factor is age. Middle-aged people make more money, on average, than young people—and also have had more years to be exposed to facts. This could produce an apparent correlation between knowledge and income, but the real story might be that those who have racked up seniority on the job have higher incomes.

So I did a regression with age, education, *and* quiz score as factors. Knowledge was still a highly significant predictor of income. People who are knowledgeable make more money, even when education and age are held constant.

The income difference between the more knowledgeable and the less knowledgeable is impressive. To make that concrete, I'll use a hypothetical thirty-five-year-old American with exactly four years of university as a benchmark (four years being the normal length of an American bachelor degree). The statistical model predicts that such a person who missed every question on my trivia quiz would have an average household income of $40,360 a year. A person of identical age and educational level who answered all ten questions correctly would have an income of $94,959. That's almost $55,000 a year more—or if you prefer, 2.35 times as much.

I should explain that no one actually scored zero—the questions were fairly easy—and only a few scored 100 percent. Of those who did, there weren't any who were *exactly* thirty-five years old and had *exactly* four years of university. The statistical software looks at all the data points and measures how income varies with all three factors. It uses that to predict, in a straight-line sort of way, the most likely income for any given set of factors.

There is, then, a large income difference attributable to knowledge and *not* to education or age. The difference is all the more remarkable because this is household income, and the person answering the questions may not be the household's primary earner. That would dilute the connection between knowledge and income, yet it's still detectable and large.

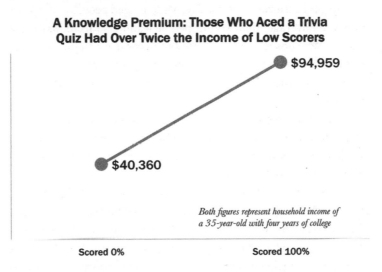

A Knowledge Premium: Those Who Aced a Trivia Quiz Had Over Twice the Income of Low Scorers

$94,959

$40,360

Both figures represent household income of a 35-year-old with four years of college

Scored 0%   Scored 100%

Cause and Effect

We know that general factual knowledge and income are correlated, but (as we learned in the case of Miss America and the "hot object" murders) correlation doesn't equal causation. There are three possibilities here:

A. Broad knowledge of a certain body of facts causes high income.

B. The reverse: high income causes people to acquire that broad knowledge.

C. Knowledge and high income each share a common cause or causes.

Possibility A proposes that the economic benefits of education go beyond having a diploma. The graduate is expected to know stuff. She must possess knowledge necessary to her work and a lot more besides.

Jack and Jane went to the same schools and graduated in the same year with the same grades and degree. Jane remembers her year one discussion of Mesopotamia, while Jack has long forgotten it (and a lot more of what he was taught). Though Mesopotamia is immaterial to Jane's line of work, her general intellectual range impresses co-workers. She is often surrounded by people of similar education and is expected to understand a joke about Virginia Woolf or Schrödinger's cat. The mere perception that Jane is smart could lead to a high starting salary and a fast climb up the ladder of success.

Not only that, but Jane's broad knowledge could also have additional, more substantial advantages. A manager needs to know enough about fields other than her own to communicate with colleagues. A marketer needs a grasp of popular culture. Broadness of knowledge is the sort of thing that distinguishes the engineer who remains an engineer from the one who gets an opportunity to move into management. Not knowing that Pluto is a dwarf planet is a mark of a pointy-haired boss who can't command the respect of the engineers.

This is one sketch of how knowledge *might* cause high income. There are other possibilities, not mutually exclusive. It could be that those who carry a lot of facts in their heads are better innovators. Their store of knowledge enables them to see analogies that others miss and to formulate creative solutions to problems.

Another explanation is that those who learn and retain a lot of general knowledge may also learn and retain a lot of knowledge about handling money. That could lead to better budgeting, saving, and investing, which could over time lead to high net worth and income. Still another explanation is that well-informed people tend to marry well-educated and financially secure spouses, resulting in high household income.

These scenarios would be instances of possibility A. But maybe we've got it backwards. It could be that high incomes cause broad knowledge (possibility B). The wealthy may have more leisure to follow the news, read books, listen to podcasts, and take classes. Meanwhile, those struggling to get by have less money and time to spend on non-essentials. They are more likely to be working a second job, less likely to have a nanny, and therefore less likely to have time for self-education.

The third possibility, C, is that another factor or factors causes *both* broad knowledge and high income. It's not hard to think of candidates for this third factor. Start with the observation that wealth is, in a sense, hereditary. Affluent kids have tutors and go to prestigious schools. They have the benefit of their mum and dad's subsidies on their first apartment's rent and their first house's down payment. Their parents have connections to help their careers, and they may inherit wealth.

In this case the causative factor would be wealthy parents. Having a rich mum and dad (back then) causes wealth (right now). The wealthy parents also cause, via tutors and schools, broad knowledge. This could easily produce a correlation between knowledge and income that persists even when you factor out years of formal education and age, for the rich kids may have benefited from a family emphasis on learning and have gone to better schools.

Another possibility is that the causative factor is simply memory. Those who happen to be born with a good memory retain more facts. It could be that memory is also useful in many careers, accounting for a high average income.

There are other cognitive factors that might be relevant. Many successful people credit curiosity (humblebrag for "intelligence"?) as a factor in their success. Others credit ambition, grit, and self-discipline. Education is a child's first career. Those with an innate drive to succeed may first express this by excelling in schoolwork—which involves learning facts. The same drive could lead to high-paying careers in later life, along with a lifelong habit of learning.

I will revisit this topic later. My best guess is that there is some truth to all these possibilities. Factual knowledge causes high income, is caused by it, and shares causes with it. Unfortunately, you don't get to choose how wealthy your parents are or whether you're endowed with mental superpowers. But we can all make an effort to learn.

Money and Happiness

Looking at income differences is the crassest way of "valuing" knowledge. It has some advantages, though. Money is quantitative. A survey subject asked to report his or her income has only to remember a number, whereas one asked to rate his or her health or happiness on a scale of 1 to 10 has to invent a number. Not everyone aspires to be rich, but no one really wants to be poor. Income can thus be a rough gauge of how well someone is achieving his or her life goals. There is an extensive body of research showing that income correlates with happiness, health, and longevity—at least up to upper-middle-class income levels. A 2010 article by Princeton psychologist Daniel Kahneman and economist Angus Deaton found, not surprisingly, that the middle class is happier than the poor. They also found that there is a point of inflection somewhere around

$75,000 (£50,000) a year. Happiness increases with income up to that level, and then it flatlines. Beyond that people report being no happier. *If I were a rich man*, we think...but, as William Post discovered, *it ain't necessarily so.*

Measuring happiness is tricky, though (one point of the Kahneman–Deaton paper). There is as yet no smartwatch or brain scan that will reveal how happy someone is. The only practical way to gauge happiness is by asking people how happy they feel. Pollsters and psychologists have been doing that for quite some time. As with surveys in general, the results depend a lot on the exact wording of the question.

Some of my surveys include a commonly used question testing happiness:

> Some people are generally very happy. They enjoy life regardless of what is going on, getting the most out of everything. To what extent does this describe you?

The answer is expressed on a rating scale. This wording seems to encourage candour. Answers to it have been found to track with extended psychological evaluations and other evidence of happiness.

I included this question in the trivia quiz I just discussed and found that factual knowledge *didn't* correlate with happiness. Oh, there was a slight positive trend, but it wasn't even close to being statistically significant. I've repeated this (non)finding several times. It does seem that general knowledge has a robust connection to income but not to happiness. What other positive life outcomes correlate with knowledge? What kinds of knowledge might offer the biggest bang for the buck? I'll examine these questions in the coming chapters.

Trivia Matters

You may be wondering what sort of questions have the power to predict income. Here are some examples from the survey I just discussed:

- Who was Emily Dickinson—a chef, a poet, a designer, a philosopher, or a reality-show star?
- Which happened first, the US Civil War or the Battle of Waterloo?
- What artist created this painting? (Shown was Picasso's 1928 *Painter and Model*.)
- Which nation is Cuba? (Respondents had to locate it on a map.)

These questions belong to the category we loosely call trivia not because the information is unimportant but because it seems to have nothing to do with basic survival or making money. And yet the statistics say it has a lot to do with making money.

Answers: Dickinson was a poet; the Battle of Waterloo was first. The Emily Dickinson question was easiest, with ninety-three percent answering correctly. About 70–75 percent knew the answers to the other questions.

Seven

Elevator-Pitch Science

QVC host Shawn Killinger and designer Isaac Mizrahi were at a loss for words. How could they describe the hideous seafoam-green blouse they were expected to pitch to the home-shopping public?

KILLINGER: It almost kind of looks like what the earth looks like when you're a bazillion miles away from the planet moon.

MIZRAHI: Yes!…From the planet moon.

KILLINGER: Isn't the moon a star?

MIZRAHI: No, the moon is a planet, darling!

KILLINGER: The sun is a star. Is the moon really a planet?

MIZRAHI: The moon is a planet, honey. It's a planet—

KILLINGER: Don't look at me like that! The *sun* is a *star!* Is the sun not a star?

MIZRAHI: I don't know what the sun is. We don't know what the sun is…You have to Google the moon, okay? The moon is such a planet I can't even stand it!

Posted to YouTube, this exchange went viral. It fit perfectly into a familiar narrative—that the public is pig-stupid about basic science.

We have mixed feelings about science. Parents and politicians alike view science, technology, and math (STEM) education as the path to prosperity—and a panacea for every economic problem, from outsourcing to the stagnation of middle-class wages. Politicians have vowed to slash humanities instruction so that every child can learn coding. Yet our affection for science has limits. Many adults pay little attention to developments in science beyond the latest tech gear. A politician who proposed to base all policy decisions on scientific facts would be a hard sell to some of the electorate.

The National Science Foundation runs periodic surveys tracking basic science knowledge in the United States, Europe, and Asia. True or false: The centre of the earth is very hot…All radioactivity is man-made…It is the father's gene that decides whether the baby is a boy or a girl…pretty easy, right? Here are some results from a survey conducted in European Union nations.

	Percentage of People Who Answered Correctly
The continents have been moving their location for millions of years and will continue to move. (True)	87%
The centre of the earth is very hot. (True)	86%
Human beings are developed from earlier species of animals. (True)	70%
Does the earth go around the sun, or does the sun go around the earth? (Earth around sun)	66%
It is the father's gene that decides whether the baby is a boy or a girl. (True)	64%
All radioactivity is man-made. (False)	59%
Lasers work by focusing sound waves. (False)	47%
Electrons are smaller than atoms. (True)	46%
Antibiotics kill viruses as well as bacteria. (False)	46%

Before you decide whether this glass is half empty or half full, consider that a group that guesses randomly on a true-false test can expect to score fifty percent. Fifty percent is effectively zero, the score consistent with sheer ignorance. I direct your attention to the final three questions, which *less* than fifty percent of Europeans answered correctly.

This survey had 24,895 participants, implying a likely error margin of about 0.63 percentage points either way. Thus the four lowest figures really are under fifty percent as projected onto the general population.

Ignorance Is Global

Europeans did relatively well on the evolution question. Seventy percent agreed that humans developed from earlier species. When the same question was posed to Americans, only forty-four percent gave the correct answer. When it comes to evolution, it's not easy to distinguish American ignorance from American piety. Because some regard these scientific ideas as challenges to traditional faith, they've taken on cultural and political dimensions.

Gallup has been polling American beliefs about evolution since 1983. In all that time, belief in divine creation of human beings has been the popular favourite and hasn't budged by more than a few percentage points. Gallup frames the question as multiple choice, with three options. One is, "God created human beings pretty much in their present form at one time within the last 10,000 years or so." In the 2014 survey, forty-two percent agreed with that.

Another thirty-one percent picked the poll's middle option: "Human beings have developed over millions of years from less advanced forms of life, but God guided this process." Just nineteen percent took the strictly secular position that humans evolved and that "God had no part in this process."

The Gallup results aren't inconsistent with the National Science Foundation results. They simply demonstrate how much wording matters. The Gallup question may provide a better window into the minds of average people when they think about evolution. Over half of those who accept Darwinian evolution prefer to think of it as an agent of divine will. And of course there's the substantial portion of the population for whom the world is young and dinosaurs didn't make it on to Noah's ark.

Each time such results are reported, op-ed writers lament anew the state of science education. It is customary to jump to the conclusion that knowledge is in decline and the industrialized West is falling behind the rest of the world. It is far from clear that either conclusion holds.

Surveys often find that young people know more about science than their elders. That reverses the pattern often seen in other areas of knowledge and refutes any alarmist theory that kids just aren't learning anything these days. The NSF surveys also show that ignorance of science is global. On average, the European Union participants got sixty-three percent of the NSF questions correct. That was the best score of the tested regions. The EU beat South Korea (sixty-one percent) and America (fifty-eight percent) by modest margins, and Japan (fifty-one percent), China (thirty-seven percent), and Russia (thirty-three percent) by substantial ones. Russia gets the booby prize—a majority answered incorrectly on every true-false item.

America's score on the evolution question was tied with Russia's (forty-four percent for both nations). All the other nations did vastly better. The score was seventy percent for China and seventy-eight percent for Japan.

Gallup found that the proportion of US secular Darwinians had doubled since 2000. Of course, it was only able to double because it was so small to begin with, hovering around ten percent from 1982 to 2000 and then zooming to nineteen percent in the years leading up to 2014. The gain came at the expense of those who chose the middle option of divinely directed evolution.

In 2013 the Pew Research Center reported that the percentage of Republicans believing in evolution had dropped eleven percentage points (to forty-three percent) in just five years. During the same period Democrats' belief in evolution had increased, to sixty-seven percent. Pew also found that Americans have become less familiar with the word *creationism* in the past decade. Notwithstanding red-state textbooks, creationism museums, and sneering media coverage of the same, many who believe in creationism don't know the word for it.

I've already mentioned the problem people have in grasping very large numbers. Science often deals in the astronomically large or microscopically small. I asked a survey group, "How old is the earth?" The answer is known with some precision: 4.54 billion years, plus or minus a percentage point, according to geologists. My question didn't need an exact answer, just a power-of-ten range, such as "1 billion–9.99 billion years old." That would have been the correct choice, but only twenty percent picked it.

Don't blame the creationism museums. There are some who accept Bishop James Ussher's conclusion (based on a study of the

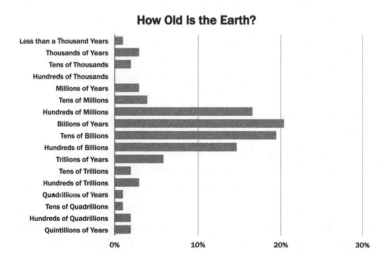

How Old Is the Earth?

King James Bible) that the world was created in 4004 BC. The relevant range—1,000–9,999 years—got less than three percent of responses. More overshot than undershot the right answer. Many must have been picking a large number, almost at random, without a basis in science or scripture.

The poet may think that any mortal contemplating his place in the scheme of things would be curious about something so fundamental as the age of the earth. The pragmatist can counter that this fact has no practical importance. What an amazing age, in which cosmic mysteries can be revealed to all and ignored by almost all!

Science and Fiction

In 2015 Jay Branscomb posted to Facebook a photo of Steven Spielberg sitting next to a dead triceratops—a *Jurassic Park* publicity image. Branscomb added the caption: "Disgraceful photo of recreational hunter happily posing next to a triceratops he just slaughtered. Please share so the world can name and shame this despicable man."

The post was shared more than thirty thousand times, racking up thousands of outraged comments. Outraged, that is, that Spielberg had shot a dinosaur. Doubtless many were trolling or playing along with Branscomb's fun, but much of the indignation appeared sincere. For one thing, not everyone knows the word *triceratops* or can recognize one from a realistic CGI picture. These people saw a dead exotic animal that looked vaguely familiar (maybe from nature documentaries). One of my surveys found that fifteen percent of the public believes that early humans and dinosaurs coexisted. That's not the same as believing they're coexisting *right now*, but it is an alarmingly wrong idea held by an alarmingly large group.

Science fiction has made dinosaurs, cloning, black holes, and quantum theory familiar if not comprehensible. There is a considerable industry of TV shows, radio segments, podcasts, blogs, and museum programmes presenting science facts in fun, accessible ways. Much of the public is engaged by science, but how much do they retain?

One thing that people have down pat is the planets. The average person I surveyed could name 6.9 of the 8 generally recognized planets in our solar system. Mercury and Neptune were most often omitted from the list. A modest twenty-five percent incorrectly named Pluto. Only four percent named the sun, and—QVC viewers or not—only two percent understood the moon to be a planet.

Asked for "the second-brightest star in the sky," less than a quarter gave a defensible answer. To answer that question, you have to know, first of all, that the sun is a star. Obviously it's the first-brightest star in the sky. You also need to know that Sirius is the brightest of the fixed points of light in the night-time sky. That makes Sirius the best answer. Only eighteen percent chose it, though.

You might object that most people don't think of the sun as a star. The second-brightest night-time star is Canopus (which is not

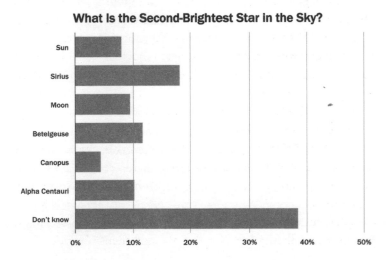

What Is the Second-Brightest Star in the Sky?

readily visible from much of the northern hemisphere). But only four percent picked that.

More notable is how many gave completely indefensible answers. Nine percent believed that the moon is a star. Eight percent chose the sun...implying they think there's a star brighter than the sun somewhere in the sky.

"We are made of star-stuff," said Carl Sagan. This distinction does not mean, however, that we have much insight into those star-forged atoms making up our bodies and our world. I asked a survey sample how many elements there are. Most of the answers ranged from 40 to 180. At the time of the survey, 118 elements were generally recognized, but only thirty percent picked an answer close to that. A similar percentage chose a "don't know" response.

Plastic is the ubermaterial of our age. What's it made out of? I offered these multiple-choice options and asked for the best answer.

A. Hydrogen, carbon, and inert gases.
B. Silicon, oxygen, hydrogen, and nitrogen.
C. Carbon, hydrogen, oxygen, and nitrogen.
D. Rubber, vinyl, and cellulose.
E. Natural gas and ethyl alcohol.
F. Amino acids, phosphorus, water, and methyl alcohol.

Answer C is the best. Just thirteen percent chose it.

The most difficult question on a science-knowledge poll conducted periodically by the Pew Research Center has been, "Which gas makes up most of the earth's atmosphere?" This is presented as multiple choice, with hydrogen, nitrogen, carbon dioxide, and oxygen as the options. Year after year, only twenty percent of those surveyed choose the correct answer (nitrogen). Oxygen is the most popular answer.

Unscientific Method

In 2014 the Ohio General Assembly considered a bill to revoke Common Core standards. One provision of the bill required that science instruction thenceforth avoid "political or religious interpretation of scientific facts" and "focus on academic and scientific knowledge rather than scientific processes."

There is a case to be made that a classroom, like a Christmas dinner, is not the place to challenge political and religious beliefs. What raised eyebrows was the proscription on teaching "scientific processes." Schools were to teach science without scientific processes? Uh-huh.

Representative Andy Thompson, one of the bill's sponsors, cleared up the mystery, explaining that the bill was simply a way of bringing creationism into the curriculum. "In many districts," he said, "they may have a different perspective…and we want to provide them the flexibility to consider all perspectives, not just on matters of faith or how the Earth came into existence, but also global warming and other topics that are controversial."

A journalist asked whether this meant teaching intelligent design. "I think it would be good for them to consider the perspectives of people of faith," Thompson replied. "That's legitimate."

In other words, the point of science class is to teach what people of faith believe but not what scientists believe or why they believe it. The bill's sponsors had convinced themselves that scientific facts are okay while scientific *thinking* is subversive.

With that in mind, I posed this survey question:

"What's the best way to see whether a new drug works?"

A. Send out free samples and have the users fill out an online form.

B. Give the drug to half of a group of volunteers, and give the other half a fake pill. See which group does better.

C. Analyse the drug to see what it's made of and whether it contains any ingredients known to cure or prevent disease.

D. Try the drug on chimpanzees. If it works on them, it will probably work on humans, as chimps share ninety-nine percent of our DNA.

E. Form a hypothesis and test it by giving the drug to a group of volunteers. If it works on most of the volunteers, it is likely to work on the general public.

Option B is the only one that describes the all-important notion of a control, central to scientific method and, indeed, critical thinking. It is the best answer here, and a respectable fifty-nine percent chose it.

Compare that to the miserably low scores on basic scientific facts. More people grasp the scientific method than understand the most basic things revealed by it—such as the name of the gas comprising most of the air we breathe.

This likely reflects educational priorities—the mandate to teach skills and critical thinking, not facts. The scientific method *is* an extremely important thing to teach (and that's one reason why the Ohio bill was so misguided). But facts matter, too. Without them, students can have only a superficial conception of science, heavy in catchphrases that are not deeply understood.

That is clearly the case with physics:

"Which is the best description of the 'uncertainty principle' in physics?"

My survey question offered these answers:

A. It's uncertain whether an electron will have a positive or negative charge.

B. The momentary position and speed of a subatomic particle cannot both be known with complete certainty.

C. The more we know about anything, the less we know.

D. The speed of light is fundamentally uncertain, depending on the frame of reference of the observer.

E. Many deterministic systems are, for practical purposes, unpredictable because small changes in their initial state lead to large changes in later states.

"Uncertainty principle" is a potent catchphrase. It expresses, or sounds like it expresses, the anxieties of our uncertain world. But only answer B comes close to describing the way physicists use the term. Thirty-one percent picked that answer.

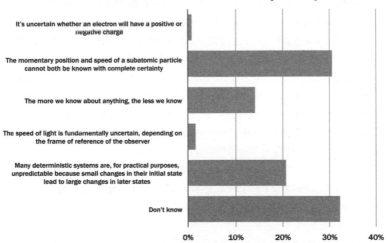

Which Best Describes the Uncertainty Principle?

Twenty-one percent confused the uncertainty principle with chaos (described in answer E). Both have received much attention in popular media, and they might be reduced to the same elevator pitch: things are unpredictable. Each asserts a completely different kind of unpredictability, however.

For a question asking people to choose "the best short description of Albert Einstein's theory of relativity," the options were:

A. Everything is relative, including perceptions of space and time.
B. The speed of light does not depend on the observer's motion, and gravity is due to the "curvature" of space and time.
C. The speed of light varies according to the motion of the observer, and time is the fourth dimension of space.
D. The speed of light is relative; the universe began in a big bang and has been expanding ever since.
E. Speed and position are relative and cannot be known simultaneously with complete certainty.
F. Energy is a form of matter ($E=mc^2$), and matter can be converted to energy by accelerating it to the speed of light.

Einstein applied the word *relativity* to two very different theories, one about physics at velocities near the speed of light (the special theory of relativity, 1905) and the other about the nature of gravity (the general theory of relativity, 1915). Answer B gives a reasonable shout-out to the content of both theories. But only seven percent picked it.

By far the most popular answer was F, chosen by forty-seven percent. I specifically wrote this answer to be meaningless, like the exposition in a bad science-fiction movie. It appears that many saw $E=mc^2$ and figured that the text surrounding it must be right.

Which Best Describes the Theory of Relativity?

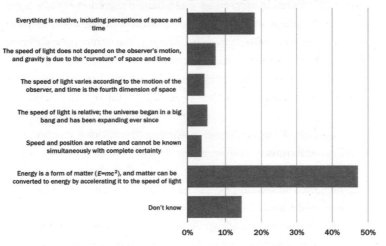

Everything is relative, including perceptions of space and time

The speed of light does not depend on the observer's motion, and gravity is due to the "curvature" of space and time

The speed of light varies according to the motion of the observer, and time is the fourth dimension of space

The speed of light is relative; the universe began in a big bang and has been expanding ever since

Speed and position are relative and cannot be known simultaneously with complete certainty

Energy is a form of matter ($E=mc^2$), and matter can be converted to energy by accelerating it to the speed of light

Don't know

Both the uncertainty principle and relativity questions had options that might be called pseudo-philosophical bastardizations: "The more we know about anything, the less we know"; "Everything is relative, including perceptions of space and time." Both were fairly popular answers, chosen by fourteen and eighteen percent respectively.

Many missed the linchpin of relativity, which is that the speed of light is a constant, *not* depending on the motion of the observer. It was this completely unexpected finding (in the Michelson–Morley experiment) that led Einstein to imagine a world in which time and space are relative. Two of the relativity answers, C and D, contradict this key premise.

Admittedly, relativity and quantum theory are difficult topics. You wouldn't expect non-physicists to understand them deeply— and they don't. People have an elevator-pitch conception of science, structured around a few misunderstood catchphrases and equations.

Some say our culture and educational system steer women away from careers in science. I ran a science-literacy survey asking a set of eight questions on biology, chemistry, physics, astronomy, and computer science. Results were strongly correlated with the sex of the respondent, with men scoring higher. The men averaged sixty-six percent right on the survey, versus fifty-five percent for women.

These results are typical, but they need to be viewed in the context of a much wider body of research. An experiment conducted by Joyce Ehrlinger and David Dunning gives a more nuanced picture. They asked men and women to estimate their scientific-reasoning ability. On average, the women rated themselves lower than men. Then the subjects were given a quiz testing scientific reasoning—and afterwards they were asked to estimate how well they performed on it. Overall the women scored the same on scientific reasoning, yet they had a lower opinion of their performance than men did. Finally, the researchers invited the men and women to participate in a science competition for prizes. The women were less likely to participate, and their decisions correlated not with how well they did on the quiz but with how well they *thought* they did. This experiment was designed as a none-too-subtle allegory of what may be happening in our educational system. The results hint that the "science gap" exists only because we *believe* it exists.

My survey found no significant correlation between science knowledge and income. There definitely *is* a cultural perception that a scientific education leads to a bigger salary. So why no correlation? Scientists and engineers account for about 4.8 percent of the US workforce. Reformers who think it's all about the STEM pay cheques should take note of that. My survey was primarily testing the income "value" of science knowledge for the ninety-five percent majority of non-scientists. For them science knowledge may not be so valuable, at least not in monetary terms.

This is a good time to bring up another rule taught in statistics classes, one far less well known than "correlation does not prove causation." It is the flip side of that rule: *lack of correlation does not disprove causation*.

An extraterrestrial statistician visits earth and tries to find out what causes humans to have babies. The ET might find that there is very little correlation between having sex and having babies (given the vagaries of fertility, birth control, and other factors). Yet any earthling would insist that sex causes babies—and is the *only* thing that causes them. The ET would of course be wrong to conclude otherwise.

One reason why studies fail to show a correlation is that the sample size isn't big enough. How big should a sample be? Well, that's the thing—you never know. My survey on science knowledge was big enough to show a highly significant gender gap. It's possible that a larger survey would have found a correlation to income as well. It's also possible that it wouldn't.

Lack of correlation doesn't disprove cause, but it should inform further thinking and research. Recently several large and well-designed studies showed no correlation between eating eggs and having high cholesterol. This was received as good news for the British Egg Industry Council and anyone who eats a full English breakfast. It could hardly be otherwise. A study that might have shown a correlation didn't. When all you know is that a study didn't find a correlation between A and B, there's a good reason to dial down expectations of A causing B.

Flunking the Turing Test

Here are two science questions I asked. I was surprised by how easy the survey volunteers found the first one and how difficult they found the second one.

1. What is the second digit of pi
(the first digit to the right of the decimal point)?

$$\pi = 3.\_4159\ldots$$

2. What is the best description of the Turing test?

A. The traditional oral test required of PhD candidates in the sciences, originated at Cambridge University in the 1700s.

B. A way of determining how closely two individuals or species are related by matching mitochondrial DNA sequences.

C. A statistical test, used in evaluating new drugs, that compares the effect of a drug to a placebo.

D. An experiment in which a human poses questions to an unseen being in order to decide whether it is a computer or a human.

The correct answers are 1 and D.

Seventy-one percent got the pi question right. People were just as good at naming the third digit of pi (seventy percent knew it was 4). This question had a correlation to income, with those who knew the missing second digit earning $32,000 (£21,000) more a year per household than those who didn't.

The contemporary world has caught up with Alan Turing's visionary 1950 thought experiment. Versions of it are used in spam filters: it's a cliché of *Dilbert* cartoons and science fiction, and Turing-test tournaments have proved that not-so-intelligent machines are better at fooling humans than anyone expected. Despite that, only thirty percent of the survey sample knew what a Turing test is.

Eight

Grammar Police, Grammar Hippies

I live near a restaurant with a hand-painted sign promising CUBAN FOOD AT IT'S BEST! (Sic; it should be "its," not "it's.")

There are two philosophies about how to react to the "sic" moment—call them the grammar-police way and the grammar-hippie way. The former holds that dictionary spellings and the pithy advice of Strunk and White remain relevant ideals in a post-grammatical age. An expensive sign shapes customers' first impressions of a business, and it ought to be correct. Food preparation, like grammar, is a discipline with a set of unforgiving rules. Don't follow the rules, and the sauce curdles, the crème is sour, and the chicken comes with a side of salmonella poisoning. That misplaced apostrophe betokens a restaurateur who doesn't sweat the details.

The grammar-hippie view is that grammar is a crowdsourced hallucination. Language is fluid, and the vernacular always trumps elitism. Text messages, tweets, and status updates thumb-typed on a bumpy subway ride point to the future (such as it is) of spelling and grammar. Nobody's going to avoid a restaurant because of a punctuation error.

I have friends who can't tolerate signage errors. They bitterly recount such grammatical atrocities at the dinner table and fantasize about turning vigilante—going out in the middle of the night to correct the errors with a paintbrush. Grammar vigilantism exists in both the real and virtual worlds. Software engineer Bryan Henderson has reportedly made more than 47,000 Wikipedia edits, all correcting his very personal pet peeve: the use of "comprised of" instead of "composed of."

Menus and the Grammar Wars

Menus are a battlefield of the grammar wars. "Restaurant people are not writers," said Gregg Rapp, a menu consultant. "For a chef, doing a menu is like writing a term paper." Errors of spelling and usage turn up on menus because most non-chain restaurants now print their own. Instead of sending copy to an old-fashioned printing shop that employs a human proofreader, menus are banged out on a laptop.

"I don't expect chefs to be writers, just as they don't expect me to make my own puff pastry," wrote the *Washington Post*'s Jane Black. "But given the existence of spell-checkers (the writing equivalent of frozen puff pastry dough), the number of errors is surprising."

The question is, how many customers notice? In 2013 the food-ordering service GrubHub examined users' search terms for misspellings of menu items. Most GrubHub customers use a mobile app and are struggling with virtual keyboards. Neither stray keystrokes nor autocorrect can account for the commonest misspellings, though. Italian foods particularly flummox Americans.

Over seventy percent got *fettuccine* wrong, most opting for *fettucine* and *fettucini*. It's not unusual for misspellings to be more common than correct spellings, both in online menus and recipes and in searches by hungry citizens. According to Google Trends, the

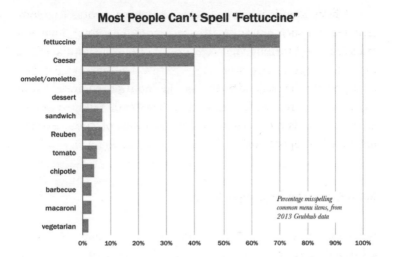

Most People Can't Spell "Fettuccine"

fettuccine	
Caesar	
omelet/omelette	
dessert	
sandwich	
Reuben	
tomato	
chipotle	
barbecue	
macaroni	
vegetarian	

Percentage misspelling common menu items, from 2013 Grubhub data

0% 10% 20% 30% 40% 50% 60% 70% 80% 90% 100%

misspelling *ciabbata* is four times as common as the correct *ciabatta*; *osso bucco* is 2.5 times more common than the proper *osso buco*.

Pizza Margherita is said to have been named for a Queen Margherita. Many spell it as they would the name of a tequila cocktail. *Caesar*, as in the salad, is misspelled forty percent of the time. *Mesclun* appears as *mescaline* with alarming frequency. Celebrity chef Guy Fieri has been known to pronounce *mascarpone* as "marscapone," and that spelling has appeared on his Food Network show's titles.

I once worked for two magazine publishers who were unsure whether spelling and grammar mattered. Line editors and proofreaders added to overheads. Does a reduction in spelling and usage errors translate into more magazine subscriptions, more ads? They suspected not.

As one of the editorial staff, I felt it *had* to matter. I was just guessing, of course, as were the publishers. I was realistic enough to know that readers were not going to complain about bad editing. I instead had the hazy theory that spelling and grammar made a subliminal difference in people's perceptions of the magazines. You can tell a cheap suit or a cheap toupee a block away, and you don't have to know anything about tailoring or hairpieces. I supposed that readers would intuit the quality of editing and that it would shape their opinions of the content.

Do correct spelling and grammar actually affect consumer judgements and decisions? To find out, I ran three surveys testing the value of spelling and grammar in business contexts. One presented the menu of a fictitious sandwich shop and asked people to answer a few questions about it: How appealing is the food selection? Would you try this place? How much would you be willing to pay for lunch here?

Unbeknownst to them, each survey participant was randomly assigned to a group that saw one of two versions of the menu. In one version, the spelling and grammar were scrupulously correct. In the other, I packed in every common misspelling and error I could manage. Here's what the incorrect version of the menu looked like.

REAL FOOD AT IT'S BEST

LOCALLY SOURCED SALADS

ALTHOUGH WE PAIR OUR DRESSINGS, YOU MAY CHOOSE YOUR OWN VINAGRETTE: HOUSE, LEMON OR OLIVE OIL & BALSAMIC

ORGANIC CEASAR SALAD WITH GRILLED CHICKEN 9

THAI FETTUCINE SALAD WITH LEMONGRASS, BASIL, AND GRAPE TOMATOE 9

MESCALINE GREENS WITH EDAMAME, CRANBERRY & CANDIED WALNUT 10.5

SHITAKE MUSHROOMS WITH GORGONZOLA DOLCE, AVOCADO, BACON & EGG ON SPRING MIX 12

SANDWHICHS

ORGANIC CHIPOLTE CHICKEN WITH LINGONBERRY CHUTNEY ON RAISIN WALLNUT 9

ORGANIC TURKEY BREAST WITH BRIE, PEAR, TOMATOE, HONEY & FIG COMPOTE ON WHEAT 9.75

TURKEY RUEBEN SALAD WITH GRANNY SMITH APPLE & OLIVE TAPENADE ON WHEAT 8.75

ORGANIC CAGE-FREE DENVER OMLETT ON CIABBATTA 8

PULLED PORK BARBAQUE, GRUYERE, PICKLES & MUSTARD ON FOCCACIA 10

PROSCUITTO & FRESH FIG WITH RICOTTA, HONEY & BALSAMIC REDUCTION ON RAISIN WALLNUT 11.75

VEGITARIAN SANDWHICH: HUMMUS, ROASTED VEGGIES & DRIED TOMATOE W. BASIL PESTO ON 5 GRAIN 9.5

DESERTS, SIDES & MORE

CHOCOLATE MARSCAPONE POUND CAKE 8

CHEESE PLATTER: SELECTION OF FOUR FINE CHEESES WITH DRIED FRUITS, NUTS & BREAD BASKET 15

DAILY HOT OR COLD SOUP CUP 4 .5/ BOWL 6 SMALL BAG OF CHIPS 2.25 MINI VEGAN 5.5

COFFEE 2.5 TEA 2.5 SPARKELING WATER 3.5 SOFT DRINKS 3.5

PRICES SUBJECT TO CHANGE WITHOUT NOTICE BASED ON MARKET FLUCTUATIONS & GAS PRICES... THE GOOD STUFF COSTS MORE! AVAILABILITY ON SEASONAL ITEMS FLUCTUATES BASED ON SEASON

My survey did not ask anything about spelling. I wanted to see whether bad spelling would have an effect, maybe an unconscious one, on bottom-line perceptions of the sandwich shop.

Nope. By every criterion the misspelled menu was rated the same as the correct one, to within statistical margins of error. People were equally likely to try the sandwich shop, to rate its food as healthful, and to judge its prices fair.

The chart shows the error bars. In all cases they overlap extensively, providing not the slightest evidence that the errors made any difference. And I'm talking about errors such as *sandwhichs*, *barbaque*, and *vegitarian*. When it comes to spelling and grammar, we're willing to cut restaurants a good deal of slack.

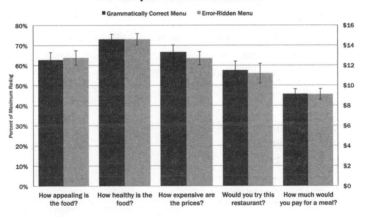

**Menu Errors Made No Difference
in Perceptions of a Restaurant**

Blaming Autocorrect

"Trust is something I know has to be earned, whether your a husband, a father or a congressman." That was from a press release issued by Louisiana congressman Vance McAllister, apologizing for one sin (adultery) while committing another (using "your" for "you're").

Autocorrect has become the scapegoat for such errors of usage. Software that was supposed to free our minds from petty details is now committing errors in our stead—and sometimes offering a convenient excuse. How much grammatical knowledge does the average person have today? To find out, I wrote a short article into which I crammed as many egregious usage errors as I could manage. It became the basis of another survey. This time the participants were told to look for grammatical errors. Each person saw not my error-ridden template but a randomized permutation of it in which about half the errors were replaced with their correct counterparts. Participants were asked whether highlighted phrases were correct or incorrect.

The survey covered confusion over *your* and *you're*, *it* and *it's*, and *there* and *they're*. It also contained errors such as these:

- "Throws of passion" (instead of *throes*, meaning "violent struggles")
- "Mother load" (should be mother *lode*, as in a vein of ore)
- "A complete 360-degree turn" ("a 180-degree turn" is generally meant: 360 degrees would be a full revolution, meaning no net change of direction)
- "Daring-do" (should be *derring-do*, meaning "courageous action")
- "Bemused" as a synonym for "amused by someone else's inappropriate reaction" (the word properly means "puzzled")

I found that a third of the public accepts *its* for *it's*. People are better at distinguishing *there* from *they're* and *your* from *you're*. Only about fifteen percent okayed the wrong versions.

Nearly two-thirds marked *who* as correct in a construction in which it should have been *whom* (say the grammar police). This well demonstrates the obsolescence of *whom*, a word that almost never naturally occurs in speech or any native-digital medium. (On this I'm with the grammar hippies.)

How Many Spot These Usage Errors?

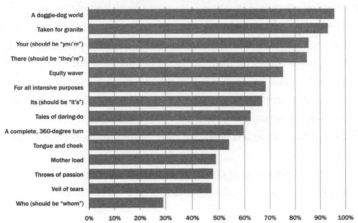

Just over half marked "throws of passion" as correct. Nearly as many fell for other common usage errors. English teachers can take heart that the vast majority recognized "taken for granite" and "doggie-dog world" as wrong.

Derring-do is a fossil term going back to Chaucer. The confusion with the familiar soundalike *daring* is understandable. In fact, *daring-do* was more likely to be marked correct than the correct version was (38–26 percent). Each participant saw one version of the article only, and they evidently weren't confident that either *derring-do* or *daring-do* was correct.

That many suffer from lack of grammatical confidence was one of the survey's main findings. I threw in a few extra uncontroversial correct usages to get a baseline. One was "viral story." Only sixty-seven percent marked it as correct. Perhaps this reflects the (justified) expectation of trick questions. Even so, it tells us that grammar is an area in which many people feel inadequate.

But not inadequate enough to double-check their spelling. Businesses today produce more public and internal communications than ever through more mediums than ever, including social network streams, websites, videos, and slide shows. Spell-check notwithstanding, misspelled words seem as common as ever in business documents, and the writers who have the most to gain from spell-check are often the ones least likely to use it. Many business documents are created in slide-show, spreadsheet, e-mail, and media-editor apps rather than with a word processor, and users don't always turn on or know how to use spell-check in programs that aren't primarily about text.

I polled a sample on the spelling of words that are commonly misspelled in business documents. The survey was multiple choice, which ought to be less challenging than spelling a word from scratch. Yet only about half the sample was able to pick the correct spelling of words such as *embarrass*, *consensus*, and *prerogative.*

It's a small club that understands *supersede* to be correct—barely ten percent. Eighty-three percent wanted to spell it *supercede.*

Back to my original question: Do grammar, correct usage, and spelling matter any more? Well, they don't—and can't—when you're

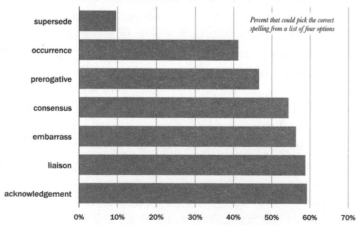

Words Often Misspelled in Business Writing

speaking or writing to the less grammatical half of the population. But few communicators set out to exclusively address the grammatical underclass.

I found no correlation between spelling or grammar and age, income, or even education. Of course, my data can only speak for the spellings and usages I tested, which were mostly those that graduates routinely get wrong. Few English classes get around to warning about oft-botched constructions such as "mother lode". Those under the age of thirty were about as good (i.e. bad) at spotting old-fashioned errors as those who were older. Though income also failed to show a significant correlation with spelling, the trend was positive, with better spellers earning more.

Here's one example that does matter: using *your* for *you're*. Those who recognized this usage as wrong earned $23,000 (£15,000) more per year, in household income, than those who didn't. The your-you're distinction involves words in everyday use, and only fifteen percent of the sample got it wrong. That makes the error pretty glaring to an eighty-five percent majority.

A reasonable conclusion is that while it's important to avoid obvious errors, there is scant advantage to knowing fine points of usage. Mistakes such as *daring-do* and *supercede* fail to correlate with income.

If you use a word correctly in a professional report, and there's no one to know you used it correctly, what's the point? Clearly, much depends on your audience. For a doctoral dissertation, or a proofreader's CV, the standards are going to be higher. Corporate and political communications intended for a wide audience should be scrupulously correct, if only to avoid grammar-police threads on comment boards. But as we now know, restaurateurs have a free pass. We expect chefs to know how to make quenelles, not spell them.

Been There, Done That, Got the T-Shirt

In 2014 the US Federal Bureau of Investigation drew ridicule for having compiled a list of 2,800 acronyms and abbreviations used in text messages, Facebook, and, yes, Myspace. It was an Urban Dictionary for the oblivious, paid for with tax money. The list contained a handful of abbreviations that are actually used and known to almost everyone (except some FBI agents). They were accompanied by thousands of obscure or obsolete abbreviations that the Feds somehow dredged up. BTDTGTTSAWIO, we're told, means "been there, done that, got the T-shirt, and wore it out."

The FBI effort demonstrated two points. One is that the life of online abbreviations and slang is short. The other that is those who use abbreviations like BTDTGTTSAWIO don't care whether anyone understands them. Maybe they're hoping someone will ask.

I surveyed the understanding of some typical acronyms and abbreviations, slang, and trendy words using a multiple-choice format with four options for each item. LOL ("laughing out loud") is understood by practically everyone. Almost every other common

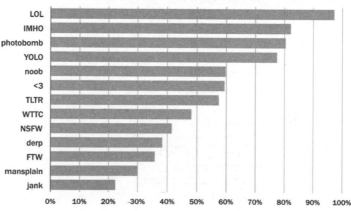

How Many Understand Slang, Abbreviations, and Trendy Words?

text-message or tweet-friendly acronym is not. About twenty percent of my US sample couldn't identify such common acronyms as YOLO and IMHO ("you only live once" and "in my humble opinion"). About forty percent didn't recognize <3 (a heart sign, meaning "love") or TLTR ("too long to read," the preface for posting an online rebuttal anyway).

As expected, there was a strong correlation between knowledge of acronyms or slang and youth. Still, the comprehension rates weren't anywhere near universal, even among those under thirty. One in five Millennials couldn't define the seemingly ubiquitous NSFW ("not safe for work"), and less than half of all adults could.

Perhaps thanks to breezy journalists who overuse neologisms that have been added, with press-release fanfare, to the online *Oxford English Dictionary*, a few terms were widely understood in my survey, including *photobomb* (eighty percent) and *noob* (sixty percent). Sadly, the genuinely useful *mansplain* was recognized by a mere thirty percent.

There has been debate about whether the informal written language of our mobile devices is destined to supplant that of print. Not in doubt is that language choices convey subtle messages of their own. Your reader is smart enough to pick up on that—and so is Google's autocompletion function.

Google	how can an individual
	how can an individual **become famous**
	how can an individual **improve performance at work**
	how can an individual **be tax exempt**
	how can an individual **buy stocks**
	Press Enter to search.

Google	how can u
	how can u **get herpes**
	how can u **get pregnant**
	how can u **get hiv**
	how can u **order a ladder**
	Press Enter to search.

GIF or JIF?

So the message is that language savvy doesn't affect our financial prospects? Not quite—I found one important exception.

I tested words likely to be mispronounced in business meetings, asking volunteers to pick the most standard and correct pronunciation from a list of four options. A quarter didn't know that *segue* is a two-syllable word. Somewhat more than half got *cache*, *Wednesday*, *hyperbole*, *espresso*, and *Linux* correct (as "cash," "WENZ-day," "hy-PER-bow-lee," "es-PRESS-o," and "LIN-ucks"). Well over half don't know that *niche* is pronounced "neesh."

The pronunciation of *GIF* is a topic of controversy. The acronym refers to Graphics Interchange Format, a 1980s file structure that has endured and become synonymous with short animations. Most pronounce it with a hard *g* (as in *graphic*). Informed sources say they're wrong. The preferred pronunciation is "jif," like the peanut butter.

Why? Because Steve Wilhite, the format's inventor, said so. "The *Oxford English Dictionary* accepts both pronunciations," Wilhite said in 2013. "They are wrong. It is a soft 'G,' pronounced 'jif.' End of story."

You Might Be Mispronouncing These Words in Business Meetings

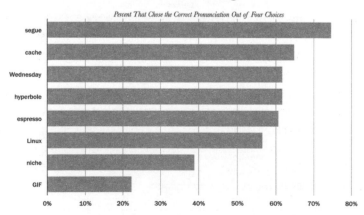

Percent That Chose the Correct Pronunciation Out of Four Choices

Only twenty-three percent of my sample chose "jif" as correct. (By the way, PNG files are pronounced "ping.")

I was surprised to find that correct pronunciations *do* correlate with income, and the effect was large: a $55,000 (£36,000) a year household-income difference between those who did best and worst on the survey. Why does pronunciation matter while spelling doesn't? My guess is that correct pronunciation is a measure of knowing educated people, and this tracks more closely with income than merely being educated. It's who you know, not what you know.

Modern Language

Can you pick the right spelling: *acomodate*, *accomodate*, *accommodate*, or *acommodate*?

What do WTTC and GTM mean?

Which is the correct way to say *mischievous*: "miss-chive-us," "miss-chee-vee-us," "miss-chive-ee-us," or "miss-chuh-vus"?

Just thirty-two percent spelled *accommodate* correctly.

WTTC and GTM mean "welcome to the club" and "giggling to myself." If you understand that, count your knowledge of pop acronyms as being better than half the respondents'.

Americans generally manage to squeeze four syllables out of *mischievous*: "mis-chee-vee-us," a pronunciation that adds a completely imaginary *i* (which often finds its way into the spelling, too). The British, along with US purists, consider the proper pronunciation to be "mis-chuh-vus." Only twenty-nine percent of Americans picked that in my survey.

Nine

Nanofame

São Paulo called out the riot police. That's how big and boisterous the crowds waiting to see Jérôme Jarre were. A hemisphere away, thousands showed up at an Iceland mall to see Jarre, convincing security that a terrorist attack was under way. "One way to describe Mr Jarre's life now is to think back to the Beatles in the 1960s, when throngs of women screamed at the mere sight of the band," wrote *New York Times* reporter Nick Bilton. "That may seem like an exaggeration, but when I took a walk with him around Union Square last week, he was stopped every few feet by squealing teenagers who begged to take a selfie with the 6-foot-3 Frenchman. Some girls were brought to tears; others proclaimed they 'couldn't breathe' at the mere sight of him."

Jérôme Jarre is a Vine celebrity, famous for six-second videos viewable on a smartphone app. One difference between Jarre and the Beatles is that everyone knew who the Beatles were. Jarre is an example of *nanofame*. The nanofamous have an avid, mostly teenage audience and primarily appeal to one sex only. They are unknown to almost everyone over twenty-five. Most adults cannot explain what Vine is, much less name a Vine celebrity.

Some of the nanofamous have agents and make tonnes of money. Jarre recently turned down a $1 million contract to promote an "unhealthy food." YouTube celebrity PewDiePie, a twenty-something Swede, has twenty-seven million subscribers and earns a reported $4 million in ad sales per year. In a multiple-choice survey with five options, just twenty-three percent could identify PewDiePie as the host of a YouTube series.

Nanofame is part of a continuum. Force of habit compels us to judge anyone who has a TV series as "famous." But with five-hundred-plus channels, there are thousands of actors, TV chefs, and reality stars who are major celebrities to the one percent of the public that watches their shows and nonentities to everyone else. *Game of Thrones* got abundant coverage in the media, but only two percent of the American public have seen a single episode. "*Californication* has been on for 19 years and I've yet to meet anyone who watches it," quipped a member of the public on Twitter.

TV stars are actually near the top of today's food chain. One rung down are the lesser celebrities of budgeted online media, such as those who appear in the offerings of Netflix, Amazon Studios, and Yahoo. In its purest form, nanofame is zero-budget and app-specific. Vine is said to have more than two hundred "celebrities" with at least a million followers. In the future, everyone will be famous on a social network you've never heard of.

America Is Confused About Hip-Hop

"Hi, Kanye!"

That was celebrity art dealer and scenester Jeffrey Deitch greeting a luminary at Art Basel Miami Beach, the billionaires' art fair. The luminary wasn't, however, Kanye West. It was Sean "Diddy" Combs. The gaffe made global news, and Deitch was left to explain how he could have made such an unhip mistake. He insisted he was a good friend of both Combs and West.

Kanye West has not been shy about claiming the spotlight. Much of the world has not been paying attention. I ran a survey asking Americans to identify hip-hop stars from headshots. The respondents—a sample drawn from people of all ages who are not necessarily hip-hop listeners—did best at identifying performers who had reality shows and/or were white. Seventy-seven percent recognized Snoop Dogg, and seventy-two percent knew Eminem. Sixty percent could identify Kanye West, a bit less than recognized Pitbull (sixty-two percent).

The survey was multiple choice, and quite a few respondents gave wrong answers for West rather than picking "don't know." Four percent thought he was Jay Z, and two percent said he was Chris Brown. That confusion was typical—for black hip-hop artists. It's tough to escape the conclusion that, for a large segment of the public, hip-hop artists are more or less interchangeable. A few more examples:

- Seven percent think Kendrick Lamar is A$AP Rocky.
- Four percent think A$AP Rocky is Lil Wayne.
- One percent think Lil Wayne is Drake.
- Four percent think Drake is Chris Brown.
- Four percent think Chris Brown is Kendrick Lamar.

It will come as no surprise that knowledge of popular music is an age test. Answers on this survey correlated strongly with age—or, rather, with youth. The hip-hop survey was one of just a few in which the more knowledgeable made less money, on average. Data-crunching showed that the income difference was almost entirely a result of the age effect, though.

Age thirty-three is a Rubicon in popular music. A recent Spotify data analysis put it starkly: most people stop listening to new music sometime in their early thirties.

When Spotify looked at its music-streaming data, it found that teens listen to contemporary and popular music almost exclusively. As listeners age, their tastes expand. They spend more time listening to obscure bands and album tracks that were not hits. As the years go by, some take up jazz or world music or classical. But somewhere around age thirty-three, most stop listening to contemporary hits at all. The phenomenon even has a name—taste freeze. Men are more susceptible to it than women. Another fun fact: become a parent, and your "music relevance" takes a hit equivalent to ageing four years.

Industry observers hold that streaming has promoted the age segregation of music tastes. Radio has less power, now that we're all DJs. We create playlists to share with friends who are the same age and like exactly the same things.

The Coachella Valley Music and Arts Festival, held in Indio, California, is conceivably the most influential showcase for new and established performers in rock, indie, hip-hop, and electronic music. Shortly after Coachella 2015, I ran a survey asking Americans whether they had heard of the most popular and widely reviewed acts.

Most 2015 Coachella Acts Were Less Known to the Public Than Søren Kierkegaard Is

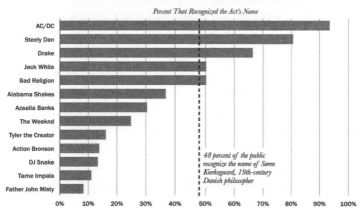

Percent That Recognized the Act's Name

48 percent of the public recognize the name of Søren Kierkegaard, 19th-century Danish philosopher

Only three Coachella 2015 acts significantly topped fifty percent name recognition. All three were outliers—the boomer oldies AC/DC and Steely Dan and the ultra-commercial Drake. The hipper Coachella acts failed to match the name recognition of, say, Danish philosopher Søren Kierkegaard (whom forty-eight percent could recognize by name). "Music relevance" is not something that most American adults have much of.

Pricing the Endorsers

The changing nature of celebrity matters to marketers, who continue to pay staggering sums for endorsements. Hip-hop's royal couple, at least to corporate advertisers, is Jay Z and Beyoncé. Jay Z earned $20 million for promoting Samsung Galaxy phones. Beyoncé signed a multi-year contract with Pepsi for $50 million in 2013. Even those numbers are dwarfed by the sports world, where nine-figure deals are reported with some regularity. Though dinged by scandal and fading performance, Tiger Woods still has a $100 million contract with Nike and gets a trickle of new endorsement deals. David Beckham has a lifetime deal with Adidas for $150 million. That's one of a portfolio of endorsement contracts that includes Armani, Diet Coke, H&M, and Samsung. It is estimated that Beckham rakes in $20 million a year just from endorsements.

These corporate sponsors are betting that celebrity is still a common language, a way of cutting through the ad clutter. But the massive payouts make sense only to the extent that consumers recognize the celebrity doing the endorsing.

I did a survey testing facial recognition of the biggest-money endorsers, as far as I could determine them from press accounts. Participants were asked to identify the celebrity—this survey was fill-in-the-blank, and spelling didn't count.

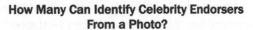

How Many Can Identify Celebrity Endorsers From a Photo?

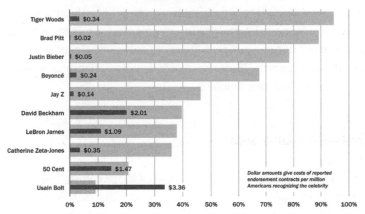

Tiger Woods — $0.34
Brad Pitt — $0.02
Justin Bieber — $0.05
Beyoncé — $0.24
Jay Z — $0.14
David Beckham — $2.01
LeBron James — $1.09
Catherine Zeta-Jones — $0.35
50 Cent — $1.47
Usain Bolt — $3.36

Dollar amounts give costs of reported endorsement contracts per million Americans recognizing the celebrity

Only four endorsers were recognized by more than half the public. They were Tiger Woods, Brad Pitt, Justin Bieber, and Beyoncé. With a ninety-five percent recognition rate, Woods is more recognized than all but a few US presidents and movie stars. The notoriety that cost Woods tens of millions in further endorsement contracts probably also boosted his recognition among those who aren't golf fans.

There were huge differences in recognition among the endorsers. Only nine percent were able to identify Olympic runner Usain Bolt, and only twenty-one percent could name 50 Cent. Incidentally, 50 Cent makes the list of top endorsers because he acquired equity in Formula 50, a vitamin-water brand that was sold to Coca-Cola.

I also estimated the cost of the reported endorsements per million Americans who recognize the celebrity doing the endorsing. For instance, T-Mobile is said to have paid something like $40 million to Catherine Zeta-Jones to do advertisements. About thirty-six percent of the public can identify Zeta-Jones. T-Mobile's cost for the Zeta-Jones contracts, per million recognizers, comes to about thirty-five cents.

This calculation leads to per-million-recognizers costs ranging from a few pennies to a few dollars. Some of the variation makes sense. Brad Pitt was by far the cheapest (two cents per million recognitions) because his endorsement career was limited to a single, much-hyped advert for Chanel No. 5, at a fee of $6.7 million. That's not the same as agreeing to wear a Chanel cap on every red carpet.

Usain Bolt and David Beckham were the most expensive in prorated terms ($3.36 and $2.01 respectively). Both are global celebrities, and athletes are usually marketing shoes and gear to fans who are far more likely to recognize professional sports stars than the general public is.

Other differences are not so easily explained away. Adverts for phone networks and soft drinks try to appeal to just about everyone. Why is Catherine Zeta-Jones's endorsement worth seven times Justin Bieber's? Why is Beyoncé's worth almost twice Jay-Z's? It's hard to escape the conclusion that valuing a celebrity endorsement is not an exact science, and some companies overpay greatly.

Ten

Is Shrimp Kosher?

I know Weinstein's parents were upset, Superintendent,
but I was sure it was a phony excuse. I mean, it sounds
so made up: "Yom Kippur."

—Principal Skinner on *The Simpsons*

Between sitcoms and co-workers, you'd think people would have a
baseline understanding of Jewish culture. This is not the case. Most
of the public cannot say how many candles a Hanukkah menorah
has (nine), identify when the High Holidays occur (September–
October), or say what day of the week the Jewish Sabbath begins
(Friday). Only half are aware that shrimp isn't kosher.

The ignorance isn't mutual. Jews can answer simple questions
about Christian holidays and customs about as well as Christians
can. In fact, a 2010 Pew Research Center survey reported that
Jews outscored Christians in answering a set of thirty-two general
religious-knowledge questions. The group that knew the most about
religion was made up of atheists and agnostics.

The Pew survey covered not only the Judeo-Christian tradition but also the world's other major religions. (Is the Dalai Lama
Buddhist? Only forty-seven percent of the US population can answer
that question correctly.) Atheists and Jews were especially better
informed about world religions than Christians were, and Christians

were often hard put to answer questions about their own faith. Here's one of the Pew survey questions:

> Which of the following best describes Catholic teaching about the bread and wine used for Communion?
>
> A. The bread and wine actually *become* the body and blood of Jesus Christ.
> B. The bread and wine are *symbols* of the body and blood of Jesus Christ.

The correct answer, since the 1551 Council of Trent and repeatedly confirmed by Catholic leadership, is A. Overall, forty percent got this right, a less-than-impressive result considering there are only two possible answers. It seems that many judged A to be a wacky, jump-the-shark answer that couldn't possibly be right. Indeed, only fifty-five percent of Catholics answered correctly. For Hispanic Catholics, it was forty-seven percent.

Stephen Prothero, a professor in Boston University's religion department, has been polling people about their religious knowledge

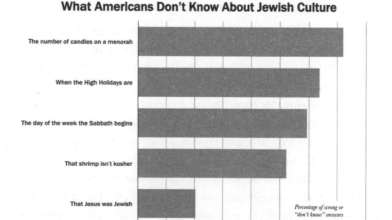

What Americans Don't Know About Jewish Culture

Percentage of wrong or "don't know" answers

for years. He began after noticing how little incoming students knew. Prothero found, for instance, that just sixty-three percent of BU students could say what the Golden Rule is. On average his students were able to name 4.6 of the Ten Commandments. Boston University is a historically Methodist-affiliated college that claims seven Nobel laureates among its faculty and alumni. Probably BU's students are better informed about religion than their peers are.

Yet according to Prothero's research,

- most Americans cannot name the first book of the Bible (Genesis);
- about half the public can't name any of the four Gospels;
- only one in three know who delivered the Sermon on the Mount (Jesus);
- fifteen percent of teenagers cannot name even one of "the five major world religions" (only five percent can name all five); and
- one in ten agreed with the statement "Joan of Arc was Noah's wife."

"Americans are both deeply religious and profoundly ignorant about religion," Prothero wrote. "Atheists may be as rare in America as Jesus-loving politicians are in Europe, but here faith is almost entirely devoid of content."

When George W. Bush ran for president in 2000, he battled the perception that he was not an especially deep thinker. A journalist asked him to name his favourite philosopher. Bush's answer was "Jesus Christ."

It was Susan Sontag who supplied the wry disclaimer: "Bush didn't mean, and was not understood to mean, that…his administration would actually feel bound by any of the precepts or social programmes expounded by Jesus." Yet Bush's answer was probably both honest and politically astute. Like many believers today, Bush sought to spin the leader of his faith as a great thinker and thereby downplay the gulf between old-time religion and a modern secular world.

Sontag wrote that American religion is more about the idea of religion than about religion itself. We expect our leaders to be men and women of faith, though the content of that faith matters a good deal less. This attitude parallels the conviction that voting is more important than knowing anything about the candidates one is voting for.

Recent Pew polls have found that believers in "God or a universal spirit" are an overwhelming majority, constituting about ninety-two percent of Americans. That finding is typical. Not so typical was that the Pew researchers asked people how certain they were of God's existence. As we've seen, a survey that asks about doubt tends to find it. In this case, only sixty-nine percent (of all respondents, believers and not) were "absolutely certain." The remainder picked the options "fairly certain," "not too certain," "not at all certain," and "don't know" to describe their states of belief. The expressions of agnosticism accounted for about twenty-three percent of the public, a figure that dwarfs the two percent who said at the outset that they didn't know whether God exists and the six percent who said they didn't believe in God. Agnosticism is largely a matter of asking a follow-up question.

You may wonder why children score so poorly on maths tests, but there's no mystery about their ignorance of religion. It's barely taught in schools. Paradoxically, children are usually given some exposure to Islam, Buddhism, Hinduism, and the extinct faiths of the ancient Mediterranean as part of their history or social studies curriculum. But most schools in the industrialized West shy away from teaching Christianity and Judaism. These are left to be taught at home, in Sunday school, and in Hebrew school, places where there is little incentive to discuss other religions.

It is, then, a simple thing to demonstrate ignorance in religious matters. Tougher to say is whether it matters. Is it important for a Mormon to know about Hinduism? Must a Catholic know about her own church's doctrine of transubstantiation if she's perfectly happy not knowing? "No matter what the results," said the 2010 Pew survey report, "we would not give the public an 'A,' an 'F' or any other grade because we have no objective way of determining how much the public should know about religion."

Though there is literature offering evidence that the faithful are happier than non-believers, I did not find any correlations between religious knowledge and self-reported happiness. Nor were there correlations between religion and income or relationship status.

But there are other reasons for acquiring religious knowledge. Prothero (who served as an adviser for the Pew survey) makes two distinct cases: first, that religious literacy is essential to overall cultural literacy. Many of our ethical controversies, from abortion to stem-cell research, are framed as religious disputes. So are many of the globe's conflicts. Everyone, non-believers included, will be at a loss to understand the news without some grounding in religion. Draw a blank at "Adam and Eve," "Mecca," or "Zen-like" and you will have trouble following political speeches, talk-show chatter, and iced-tea ads.

These are fair points. The question is how much you *really* need to know just to keep up with the news and literate conversation. I suspect the answer is "more than has sometimes been demonstrated in religious-literacy surveys but not very much more."

Prothero's second thesis is that religious knowledge civilizes us; that it's an inherently positive influence, leading to better, more humane decisions. It's not hard to think of compassionate people who knew a lot about religion (and/or have deep religious belief). It's also hard *not* to think of obvious counterexamples, such as the fifteenth-century Spanish inquisitors and the twenty-first-century ISIS executioners.

The "religion as civilizing force" argument reminds me of the way PE teachers say that playing team sports builds "character." Is there any evidence for that? What is character, exactly? What the teachers are really saying is that they've *heard* that team sports build character, maybe from other PE teachers. It's the kind of claim they like to repeat because it sounds better than admitting that hardly anyone will find time to play any after graduation.

"Religious knowledge is not necessary to be a good citizen," wrote journalist Mark Oppenheimer. "It's just necessary if one wants to be an educated person. It enriches our lives. That's blessing enough." That is a good way to look at the value of any kind of factual knowledge.

Guest List for the Last Supper

Name everyone present at the Last Supper (or as many as you can).

What nationality was Gautama Buddha: Chinese, Indian, Japanese, Korean, or Mongolian?

The guest list for the Last Supper is not something you'll find in any of the four Gospels. Renaissance depictions of the event, such as Leonardo's, assumed it was Jesus plus all twelve disciples. The traditional list thus runs: Jesus, Peter, Andrew, James the Greater, James the Lesser, John, Matthew, Philip, Thomas, Bartholomew, Judas, Jude, and Simon. The median respondent in my survey could give only four names. Nearly a third omitted the guest of honour. Seventeen percent were unable to name anyone.

The Buddha was Indian or, in modern terms, Nepalese. If you answered correctly, you did better than sixty-nine percent of survey participants.

Eleven
─────

Philosophers and Reality Stars

"**A**ll art is quite useless," Oscar Wilde wrote. In provoking the Victorian bourgeoisie, Wilde hit on the paradox of cultural literacy. It is nearly impossible to prove the value of cultural literacy to those who just don't get it. Today mobile devices are transforming what we learn and retain of the traditional humanities. I surveyed knowledge of philosophy, literature, art, and film and looked for any evidence that such knowledge was not so useless in terms the bourgeoisie understands: high incomes.

In one set of surveys people were simply asked, "Who is ____?" The blank was a cultural figure, high or low, and there were five possible occupations, such as "inventor" and "artist." The participant had to pick one.

This chart presents a subset of the results: Western philosophers versus reality-show stars. Aristotle and Plato were about as recognized as the two most famous Kardashians. René Descartes, the proponent of dualism, was considerably less familiar to survey participants than child beauty contestant Honey Boo Boo. Nietzsche, who said God is dead, was trumped by Snooki Polizzi, who asked,

Nietzsche is Less Famous than Khloé Kardashian

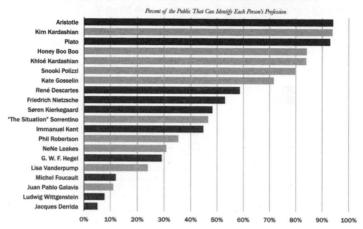

Percent of the Public That Can Identify Each Person's Profession

where's the beach? Three times more people recognized the name Lisa Vanderpump (*The Real Housewives of Beverly Hills*) than recognized Ludwig Wittgenstein (*Tractatus Logico-Philosophicus*). Other prominent philosophers trailed cast members of *Jersey Shore* and *Duck Dynasty*.

The Canon

Educators have long sought to broaden the canon of the humanities. They've still got work to do. "Name an artist, novelist, poet, playwright, architect, or film-maker who lived all or most of his/her life in Latin America." I posed that simple demand to a demographically balanced group of Americans. The challenge was to name just *one* creative figure from *any* Latin American nation, a person who could be of the present day or of centuries past.

Only thirty-one percent could do it. The most popular correct answer was Frida Kahlo, mentioned by twelve percent of respondents. Gabriel García Márquez accounted for another six percent.

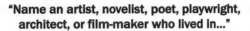

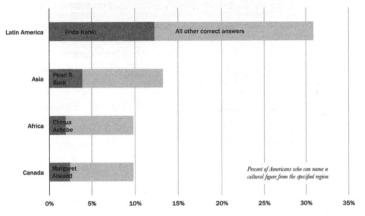

"Name an artist, novelist, poet, playwright, architect, or film-maker who lived in..."

Latin America — Frida Kahlo / All other correct answers

Asia — Pearl S. Buck

Africa — Chinua Achebe

Canada — Margaret Atwood

Percent of Americans who can name a cultural figure from the specified region

0% 5% 10% 15% 20% 25% 30% 35%

I tried the same question for Asia. Thirteen percent could supply a correct answer.

The most popular response was Pearl S. Buck, an American novelist who lived in China. I didn't want to count that as correct, but I had to. Buck accounted for almost a third of the correct answers. No other creative Asian came anywhere close to that. Indians and Middle Easterners were rarely mentioned. Almost all the answers referred to Chinese or Japanese visual artists. Hayao Miyazaki and Osamu Tezuka (contemporary anime film-makers) got as many mentions as Akira Kurosawa and Katsushika Hokusai did.

A mere ten percent could name an African artist, writer, or other cultural figure. Chinua Achebe was most often cited, by two percent of the survey sample. Answers leaned heavily towards white South Africans and those who spent part of their lives in Europe, the United States, or Australia.

Finally I tried Canada. It's not a continent, but Canada has a unique relationship to the United States, so close and yet so culturally invisible. Americans were no better at naming a Canadian creative figure than they were at naming an African creative figure. There were more wrong answers given for Canada than for any other region. Many survey subjects named Canadian-born entertainers who spent their careers in the United States, including Mike Myers, William Shatner, and Lorne Greene. As the question didn't ask for actors, these responses were counted as incorrect. The most-named Canadians were writers Margaret Atwood and Alice Munro.

Don't assume that Americans know much about their own nation's masters of nuanced prose, either. As far as I can determine, no living intellectually "serious" novelist, short-story writer, or poet is known by name to a clear majority of the US public.

Forty-seven percent of my sample knew that Toni Morrison was an author. That was enough to make Morrison a rock star among living literary figures. She was tied with Joyce Carol Oates; all other tested authors were less recognized.

There are of course commercial novelists (Stephen King, J. K. Rowling, George R. R. Martin) who are widely recognized, along with a large number of long-dead icons whose works are taught in school (from Shakespeare to Capote). In my survey Kurt Vonnegut

Most People Don't Know Who These People Are

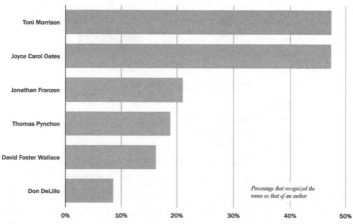

Percentage that recognized the name as that of an author

had fifty-three percent recognition. But famous living—or even recently deceased—literary writers seem to be rare to non-existent.

The apex of pop fame for a contemporary novelist is, perhaps, playing himself or herself on *The Simpsons*. Jonathan Franzen and Thomas Pynchon both did that. But only twenty-one percent knew or guessed who Franzen is. It was nineteen percent for Pynchon.

What happens in Mark Twain's *Adventures of Huckleberry Finn*? I posed that question, offering a laundry list of answer options, some correct and others incorrect. Survey participants were instructed to click all that applied.

A majority could name only two facts: that Huck runs away from home and that the epithet *nigger* is used repeatedly.

Other widely remembered passages were Tom Sawyer whitewashing the fence and Tom and Huck attending their own funeral. These occur in *The Adventures of Tom Sawyer*, not in *Huckleberry Finn*.

Twenty-eight percent were unable to name even one event that occurs in one of the greatest nineteenth-century novels.

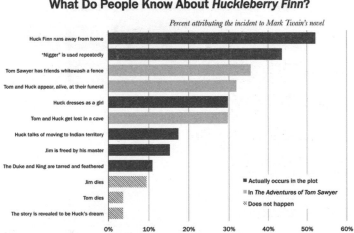

What Do People Know About *Huckleberry Finn*?

Percent attributing the incident to Mark Twain's novel

As gauged by attendance at art fairs, attendance at museum shows, and auction prices, interest in contemporary art has never been greater. Little of this interest has filtered down to the general public. One survey presented images of iconic works of contemporary art and asked participants to name the artists who made them. In every single case, "don't know" was the most common multiple-choice response.

To get a baseline, I also tested *Mona Lisa*, *The Starry Night*, and *Guernica*. Most were able to connect them to Leonardo da Vinci, van Gogh, and Picasso. It is worth pondering, however, that nearly one in five failed to identify the painter of *Mona Lisa*. The image must have been familiar, but knowing who painted it is another thing.

Critics routinely lament the publicity and money thrown at Jeff Koons and Damien Hirst, said to be more popular with the public and zillionaires than with thoughtful audiences. Actually, Koons and Hirst are *not* that popular with the public, assuming that recognition is a precondition for popularity. Just one in five could identify Koons as the artist of *Balloon Dog*, and only ten percent could connect Hirst's *The Physical Impossibility of Death in the Mind*

Few Can Identify Contemporary Artists from Their Work

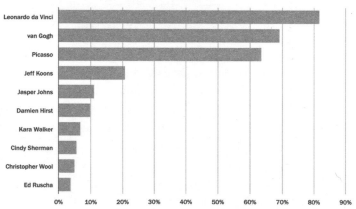

of Someone Living—a tiger shark suspended in formaldehyde—to the artist. Nearly three-quarters drew a complete blank, choosing "don't know."

Few contest the seriousness of Jasper Johns. And yet only eleven percent of people could identify Johns as the painter of the classic *Flag*. Recognition went downhill from there. A Kara Walker installation (*Presenting Negro Scenes Drawn Upon My Passage Through the South...*), one of the most reproduced photographs from Cindy Sherman's *Untitled Film Stills* series, Christopher Wool's *Apocalypse Now* (auctioned for $26 million in 2013), and Ed Ruscha's *Burning Gas Station* barely registered. The differences in recognition rates among these celebrated living artists are not statistically significant.

What *is* significant is that some wrong options were chosen more frequently than the right ones. More were ready to believe that *Flag* was painted by Andy Warhol than by Johns; that Annie Leibovitz, Diane Arbus, or Ansel Adams shot the Sherman photo (a self-portrait, by the way); and that Roy Lichtenstein did Ruscha's burning gas station. This must be a visual counterpart to Churchillian drift. In the popular mind, contemporary art is ascribed to a few big names.

Another conclusion: the wisdom of crowds doesn't apply to contemporary art.

I've noted the importance of pronunciation in business contexts. The same issue imposes a kind of caste system at cultured gatherings. Someone who pronounces André Gide's last name as "Jide" or "Guide" is not likely to be taken seriously, no matter how well reasoned his observations are. (It's "Zheed," and only about eleven percent of Americans know that.) Gide is an example of a "shibboleth name," as one blogger put it—a name "by which the privileged judge their inferiors."

Certainly there are many cultural luminaries whose names a majority of the public cannot pronounce correctly. Even English

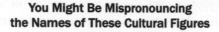

You Might Be Mispronouncing the Names of These Cultural Figures

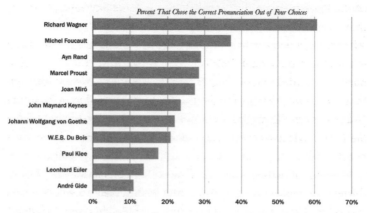

Percent That Chose the Correct Pronunciation Out of Four Choices

names can be trouble for Americans. More than three-quarters don't know that John Maynard Keynes's last name is pronounced "Canes."

Some names are so widely mispronounced that there is a semi-official "American" pronunciation, not strictly correct in the famous person's native tongue, but a signifier that one is a relatively well-educated American. Accepted pronunciations include "Richard VOG-ner," "Michel Foo-COE," "Ine Rand," "Marcel Proost," "Wahn Me-ROW," "YO-han Wolfgang von Ger-tuh," "W. E. B. Duh-BOYZ," "Paul Clay," and "Leonhard OY-ler."

Knowing these pronunciations correlated with income as strongly as pronouncing the business meeting terms properly did.

Spoiler Alert

Of course, it's easy enough to "cheat" at cultural literacy. Consider the case of films and TV shows. Binge viewing and the ready availability of films for downloading have complicated the notion of a spoiler and indeed what it means to have experienced a film or show.

Most people who took my survey knew that the serial killer in *Psycho* is Norman Bates dressed as his dead mother; that the Planet of the Apes is earth; that Darth Vader is Luke Skywalker's father; that Bruce Willis's character is dead throughout *The Sixth Sense*. Almost forty percent knew that Brad Pitt's character in *Fight Club* is a multiple-personality projection of Edward Norton's unreliable narrator. A third or less knew that *Citizen Kane*'s Rosebud is a sled; that *The Crying Game*'s female lead is a transsexual man; that *The Usual Suspects*' Kevin Spacey is Keyser Söze; that the original *Friday the 13th* movie inverts *Psycho* by revealing its slasher to be not Jason but his mum.

As proof that nobody knows what happens in *Memento*, only thirteen percent endorsed the interpretation, widely accepted by cineastes, that amnesiac Leonard had already killed his wife's assailant.

These figures, though they may seem low, demonstrate how expert we have become at faking cultural literacy. A back-of-the-envelope estimate based on box-office figures suggests that about 10 percent of the movie-going public saw *The Empire Strikes Back*, 2 percent saw *The Crying Game*, and 1.2 percent saw *Fight Club*.

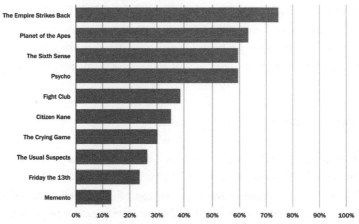

How Many Know the Spoilers to These Movies?

That's in cinemas. Rental and TV viewings would increase the proportions, while multiple viewings by fans would trim them. Either way, it's all but inevitable that most of those who answered correctly in my survey had *not* seen the movie. The spoilers are out there, in the cultural air we breathe. They're in the collectible soft-drink cups, TV parodies, comment boards, and other second-, third-, and *n*th-hand sources.

The ability to cobble together an understanding of high and low culture from the detritus of contemporary media may be a worthwhile skill. It is a skill we're acquiring, anyway. Novelist Karl Taro Greenfeld wrote:

> Every few weeks, my wife mentions the latest book her book club is reading, and no matter what it is, whether I've read it or not, I offer an opinion of the work, based entirely on…what, exactly? Often, these are books I've not even read a review or essay about, yet I freely hold forth on the grandiosity of Cheryl Strayed or the restrained sentimentality of Edwidge Danticat. These data motes are gleaned, apparently, from the ether—or, more realistically, from various social media feeds.
>
> What was Solange Knowles's elevator attack on Jay Z about? I didn't watch the security-camera video on TMZ—it would have taken too long—but I scrolled through enough chatter to know that Solange had scrubbed her Instagram feed of photos of her sister, Beyoncé. How about this season of *Game of Thrones* and that non-consensual intercourse in the crypt? I don't watch the show, but I've scanned the recaps on Vulture.com, and I am prepared to argue that this was deeply offensive.…
>
> It's never been so easy to pretend to know so much without actually knowing anything.

That prompts the question of whether faked cultural literacy is good enough. Is it still important to have a deep acquaintance with a set of ideas, books, artworks, and films judged important by our culture?

Traditional high culture is commanding a smaller share of the collective attention than it has in the past. It's not necessarily that we're dumbing down; it's just that there are more modes of cultural expression commanding our attention. This is surely one factor in the low levels of traditional cultural knowledge that the surveys revealed.

Cultural literacy was a good predictor of educational level. But I found surprisingly little correlation between cultural knowledge and income. That may be an "arts effect." The more culturally literate are more likely to have taken an arts subject, and therefore tend to earn less than others with similar education levels.

Of course, money is hardly the only or best yardstick here. The value of experiencing great works of literature, art, and film goes without saying to anyone with a soul capable of appreciating such things. What may be changing is the notion that everyone has to experience the same great works. Canons are dissolving, and predictions of cultural doom have not come to pass. Cultivated taste is more diverse than it's ever been. For the less cultivated, a superficial literacy cribbed from the cloud is enough to get by in the world—and it's time to stop pretending otherwise.

Who Was Vladimir Nabokov?

Would you say Vladimir Nabokov was an athlete, an author, a businessperson, or a philosopher?

Only thirty percent recognized the author of *Lolita* and *Pale Fire*. This was a strong predictor of educational level but not of income.

Twelve

Sex and Absurdity

Mississippi teachers have a unique use for the Peppermint Pattie (a disc of peppermint cream covered in chocolate). It is removed from its wrapper and passed from hand to hand around the room to demonstrate that (as one Mississippi parent put it) "a girl is no longer clean or valuable after she's had sex."

Welcome to sex education in the Deep South. Mississippi has one of the highest teen pregnancy rates in America. Parents expect sex education classes of some kind, but a vocal group demands that those classes teach abstinence. That part isn't a Mississippi phenomenon by any means. Gilbert Herdt, founder of San Francisco State University's Department of Sexuality Studies, reported that the US federal government has spent almost a billion dollars on abstinence-only education programmes in schools, despite evidence that such programmes decrease knowledge of sex, contraception, and STDs.

The problem is that the literal facts of life are insufficient to sell hormone-charged teens on abstinence. So in the South, particularly, schools are selectively supplementing facts with fibs, urban legends, and outright lies. One parent said the Mississippi curriculum boiled down to: "If you have sex, you will get AIDS. And you're going to die."

A recent study of Texas schools' sex education programmes found that "two of the curricula didn't contain a single fact." Among the pro-abstinence factoids taught in Texas schools are that "touching another person's genitals can cause pregnancy" and "half of gay male teenagers have tested positive for HIV."

Alice Dreger, a mother and former clinical professor of medical humanities and bioethics at Northwestern University, recently attended her son's abstinence-only sex education class and live-tweeted the madness.

> The whole lesson here is "sex is part of a terrible lifestyle. Drugs, unemployment, failure to finish school—sex is part of the disaster"
> She's now telling story of a condom box in which EVERY SINGLE CONDOM HAD A HOLE.
> "We are going to roll this dice 8 times. Every time your number comes up...pretend your condom failed and you get a paper baby." JESUS!!!
> Paper babies are being handed out to EVERYONE. They have ALL HAD CONDOM FAILURE AND THE WHOLE CLASS IS PREGNANT.

Clearly many of these schools are failing to teach kids about sexuality—and about diet, exercise, health, and medicine, for that matter. The Internet has been touted as a great equalizer. Operating without judgement, it dispenses sex and health information twenty-four hours a day. Young people learn the facts of life from their smartphones, and their parents use Google to decide whether a condition warrants a doctor visit. Here is a classic case of outsourcing memory and information to the cloud. How well is that working?

One survey asked young people aged eighteen to twenty-five about sexual health and contraception. Women were better informed than men. Nearly all the women (ninety-six percent) were able to identify the "form of contraception [that] protects against sexually transmitted diseases AND pregnancy" as a condom. Eighty-seven percent of men got this easy question right, but they were more likely to choose patently wrong answers such as "birth-control pills" and "oral sex."

Men were risk-takers. They more often thought that balloons and plastic wrap were "acceptable substitutes" for a condom (seventy-one percent of those choosing this dicey response were male).

True or false: To prevent conception, an IUD must be inserted each time a woman has sex. Fourteen percent of women, and twenty-seven percent of men, said this was true. (Wrong!)

Ignorance on sexual topics is nothing new. Back in the 1950s, doctors doing epidemiological studies on STDs often had male patients fill out questionnaires asking whether they had been circumcised. Two physicians, Abraham M. Lilienfeld and Saxon Graham, wondered how accurate those questionnaire responses were. To find out, they had men fill out questionnaires and then drop their pants so that the doctors could verify the circumcision status. It turned out that thirty-four percent of circumcised men did not know they were circumcised. They said they weren't circumcised, but actually they were.

This isn't an artefact of the repressed Kinsey era. I asked a survey sample of both sexes to estimate the percentage of American men who have been circumcised. This isn't a statistic you'd expect anyone to know with accuracy, but you *would* expect young people to have observed or inferred that most American men have been circumcised (seventy-nine percent, by one study).

The survey estimates ran the gamut, with no meaningful knowledge gap between the sexes. A reasonable guess is that men and women in the US just don't have a clear idea of what an uncircumcised penis looks like.

But knowledge of female anatomy is sketchier yet. "The vast majority of my female students have no idea how big their clitoris is, or how big the average clitoris is, or what types of variations there

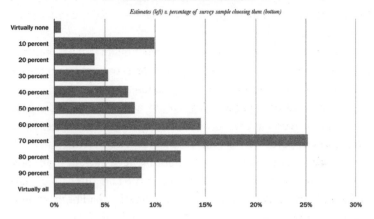

What Percentage of American Men Have Been Circumcised?

Estimates (left) v. percentage of survey sample choosing them (bottom)

are among women," said Nancy Tuana, who teaches a course on sexuality at Pennsylvania State University. "Compare this to the fact that most of my male students can tell you the length and diameter of their penis both flaccid and erect, though their information about the average size of erect penises is sometimes shockingly inflated—a consequence, I suspect, of the size of male erections in porn movies."

The Internet is a more effective dispenser of porn than of fact. That's one reason to curb expectations about the digital realm's value as a sex-ed teacher of last resort. It is, however, playing that role. In 2006 San Francisco inaugurated a programme that lets teens text questions about sex, anonymously, for prompt answers from health-care professionals. Such programmes have since become a mainstay of Southern states.

Fringe Medicine

Have you heard about Agenda 21? It's the top-secret programme, funded by the Rockefeller and Ford Foundations, to battle overpopulation. They're paying the agriculture company Monsanto to develop genetically modified foods that slowly kill the people who eat them.

Everything in the previous paragraph is completely false. But Agenda 21 is a popular falsehood among conspiracy theorists. A 2014 survey conducted by J. Eric Oliver and Thomas Wood, published in *JAMA Internal Medicine*, described Agenda 21 and asked people whether it was for real.

Twelve percent believed it was true. Forty-six percent were undecided. Add that to the believers, and more than half the public gave some credibility to the claim that two of the nation's most prominent philanthropic organizations are engaging in mass murder, aided by a company that sponsored half a dozen attractions at Disney theme parks.

Speaking of Disneyland, the happiest place on earth became a measles hot zone in early 2015, thanks to anti-vaccine parents. Oliver and Wood found that one in five believed the vaccine-autism legend to be true and only forty-four percent rejected it as false.

They also reported that thirty-seven percent believed the Food and Drug Administration was suppressing natural cures for cancer. Twenty percent—a perfect "one in five"—believed that "health officials know that cell phones cause cancer but are doing nothing to stop it because large corporations won't let them."

Oliver and Wood reported that those endorsing health- and medicine-related conspiracy theories were more likely to use herbal supplements, organic produce, and alternative medicine. They were less likely to get an annual check-up, use sunscreen, and get a flu shot. In one of the most amusing turns of phrase to be found in *JAMA Internal Medicine*, Oliver and Wood concluded that these correlations persisted even after controlling for "socio-economic status, paranoia, and general social estrangement."

The Metapolitics of Gluten

Using a "gluten-free" label is like printing money. It can be slapped on practically anything, including foods that never had gluten in the first place. No one blinks. There's no need to tout the benefits of a gluten-free lifestyle (claims that might incur regulatory scrutiny). The public already knows about gluten, or thinks it does. A recent Consumer Reports National Research Center survey found that about a third of the US public was trying to cut down or eliminate gluten. Sixty-three percent believed that a gluten-free diet "would improve physical or mental health." A less scientific Jimmy Kimmel survey found that many gluten avoiders hadn't a clue what gluten actually is.

Gluten-free is a triumph of marketing, not medicine. Doctors hold that less than seven percent of the public have coeliac disease or an authentic gluten sensitivity that would justify eliminating gluten from their diets.

Well, it can't hurt to cut out gluten, right? Maybe it can. Gluten-free products often substitute rice flour for wheat flour, leading to increased exposure to arsenic, which is not only a slow poison but also a carcinogen. Some research links gluten-free diets to weight gain and obesity.

Whatever its effects on your health, there's no question that going gluten-free can be a hazard to your wealth. Products labelled gluten-free command premiums of fifty percent or more. "Perception is reality," said food marketing consultant Richard George, "and if consumers believe gluten-free products are better, then logic no longer matters."

The most popular gluten-free-labelled snack is crisps. Crisps are made from potatoes—duh—and have never contained gluten, which is found in wheat and barley. But without the gluten-free label, consumers might not know that potato chips are...health food?

I asked young people between the ages of eighteen and twenty-five, "What is the best description of gluten?" Answer options were: a protein, a carbohydrate, a sugar, an additive, or a fat. Only thirty percent chose the correct answer, protein. The sample was confident of its mostly wrong answers, for only seven percent picked "don't know."

The most popular answer was carbohydrate (thirty-six percent). Had I asked for a chemical definition of a carbohydrate (or a protein or a fat), I am sure that most would have had a hard time answering. But nearly everyone must be aware that protein has a benign reputation, while carbohydrates are perceived as downright deadly. No-carb diets and low-carb foods abound. Nobody goes on a no-protein diet, and you see foods advertised as a "good source of protein." If gluten is bad for most people—and twenty-three percent agreed with that statement—then it's likely to be a carbohydrate. Or so some may have reasoned.

Gluten is a paradigm of knowledge and ignorance in our media-rich age. People actually know a lot about gluten—not about its chemistry but about its role as a cultural signifier. Most understand that:

- gluten-free items are sold in hipster coffee shops, artisanal bakeries, and shops like Whole Foods;
- gluten-free baked goods may not taste the same or as good as those containing gluten;
- gluten-free foods are more expensive than foods containing gluten;
- gluten-free is "upmarket";
- gluten-or-not is a cultural divide—those who believe gluten is bad are usually diet-conscious, health-conscious, and concerned about the environment; and
- asking for gluten-free products will, in some settings, identify you as someone who *cares.*

All the above are facts about the contemporary sociology and politics of gluten. We absorb that kind of information painlessly, more readily than facts about the clinical effects of a low-gluten diet.

Which is the real definition of *gluten*?

"Reality is that which, when you stop believing in it, doesn't go away," said science-fiction writer Philip K. Dick. His witticism is of a distinctively modern sort. The notion of objective facts, existing independent of human culture and belief systems, is relatively new. Until recent centuries, what those around us believed was the primary reality. Hearsay *is* a better guide to truth than nothing at all. When your Palaeolithic ancestor heard through the grapevine that a certain berry was poisonous, that would have been reason enough to avoid it. The common wisdom could be wrong, but why take the chance?

Today we are heirs to a global scientific culture whose empirical facts can be accessed from any mobile device. Yet we still relate most naturally to the social dimensions of knowledge; witness the popularity of "social networks." We learn which people to ask, to believe, and to trust. This still works pretty well, even with gluten. Those who don't know that gluten is a protein nonetheless know that some people think it's bad. From the standpoint of someone unable or too busy to plough through the research, this is itself informative—a form of crowdsourcing. What most people believe is not always accurate, but the crowd's opinion is usually better than a completely uninformed one.

Whatever your grasp of health and diet issues, there is some evidence of a link between general knowledge and good health. In several surveys I asked participants to rate their health on a scale of 1 to 10. I also asked them the number of friends they had, how satisfied they were with their sex lives, how much exercise they got, and whether they were single, married, in a long-term relationship, divorced, or widowed. There was scant evidence of a connection between general knowledge and any of these things *except* health and marital status.

In a few surveys, the most knowledgeable were most likely to be married. Living with another person and raising children are educations in themselves. Thus marriage may promote knowledge while being single may limit it.

The health question read: "Compared to others my age, I am in good health. To what extent does this describe you?" The people who correctly answered the most trivia questions reported themselves healthiest.

In one survey, the statistical model predicted that a hypothetical thirty-five-year-old with four years of university who got none of the questions right would have a health rating of 6.32 out of 10, while an equally educated thirty-five-year-old who got all fifteen questions right would have a health rating of 6.96. That's a ten percent difference. I can't say what that means in medical terms, as respondents' answers were subjective, but the difference was statistically significant.

Perhaps that brings a new perspective to the question I began with. Is the Internet a useful source of health information? The answer depends a lot on the user's ability to distinguish good information from bad. Young children often fail at this, and so do many adults. The online researcher not only needs to know some medical terms to type into a search box, she also needs to be able to assess the credibility and agendas of the websites that come up in the results. There is no simple prescription for doing that. The user must play detective, looking for clues such as spelling and grammar (often faulty on unreliable sites), errors of fact and misstatements of scientific reasoning, use of fringe-medicine buzzwords, appeals to magical thinking or fear, and even website design (which says much about the site's promoter and its intended audience). A broad spectrum of knowledge may be relevant, and that may be one reason (of many) why knowing facts correlates with health.

Trivia, the Best Medicine?

Who is associated with "I think, therefore I am"?

**What is the biggest object in the solar system—
the earth, the moon, the sun, Mars, or Jupiter?**

Though these questions have nothing to do with health, they are predictors of it. Those who answered correctly were healthier than those who answered incorrectly.

About thirty-eight percent connected "I think, therefore I am" to René Descartes. Seventy-one percent knew that the sun is the biggest object in the solar system.

Thirteen

Moving the Goalposts

Sports metaphors are considered a hallmark of accessible communication. Those explaining a merger, a tax bill, or string theory are advised to couch their content in the language of football or cricket, basketball or golf. Yet a sizeable segment of the public cannot answer even simple sports questions. One in five Britons (and over two-thirds of Americans) don't know the number of players on a football team (eleven). Roughly one in five Americans didn't know which sport awards the Stanley Cup (hockey) or which one is responsible for the expression "grand slam" (baseball).

You might guess that sports knowledge (or the lack of it) would break down roughly along gender lines. It actually doesn't make much of a difference. British men were more likely than women to know that the colour of a cue ball is white and the number at the top of a dartboard is 20. But on most of the questions I asked, there was no meaningful difference between the sexes.

Of course, the sports-challenged may get the gist of expressions such as "a sticky wicket," "moving the goalposts," and "saved by

Some Can't Answer Easy Sports Questions

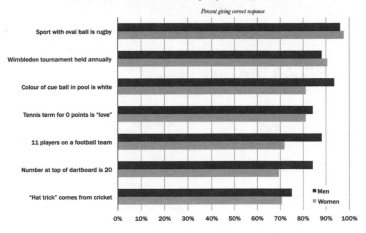

Percent giving correct response

- Sport with oval ball is rugby
- Wimbledon tournament held annually
- Colour of cue ball in pool is white
- Tennis term for 0 points is "love"
- 11 players on a football team
- Number at top of dartboard is 20
- "Hat trick" comes from cricket

■ Men
■ Women

0% 10% 20% 30% 40% 50% 60% 70% 80% 90% 100%

the bell" without knowing the precise meaning of these terms. But here's one potential reason to follow sports more closely: I found that sports knowledge correlates with income. At least, knowledge of sports trivia does. A linear regression model predicted that the average household income for those who scored zero on my UK sports quiz was £25,122 per year. For those who got scored 100 percent, it was £50,920 per year. A US sports survey found a similarly large income difference.

This appears to be an exception to the pattern we've seen so far, wherein general knowledge correlates strongly with income but knowledge in specific areas, such as science and spelling, does not, or does so only weakly.

What makes sports so special? One possibility is that we're seeing evidence of the gender gap. In both Britain and the US, women earn about eighty percent of what men earn in similar jobs. If women as a group know less about sports, that could account for a difference in income. That is, it could account for up to a twenty percent income penalty for not knowing anything about sports. It couldn't account for the twofold difference seen here. And, as I've

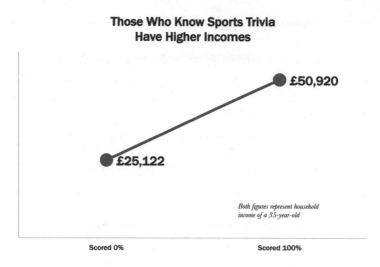

**Those Who Know Sports Trivia
Have Higher Incomes**

● £50,920

●£25,122

*Both figures represent household
income of a 35-year-old*

Scored 0%   Scored 100%

already mentioned, there wasn't that much of a gender gap in sports knowledge.

I added gender to the statistical model anyway. It showed that gender had only a minor effect on income, and this effect was not significant. It was indeed sports knowledge that was the main predictive factor.

Given that this survey took household income rather than individual income into account, it could be that married people—women especially—are more likely than singles to know about sports. One single-fact correlation was particularly strong: Americans who knew that a shortstop plays between second and third base were much more likely to be married, suggesting that some may start following baseball because a spouse does or their children do.

Many married households have two breadwinners, so this could account for some of the income difference—but again, not as much as the data showed.

Another hypothesis is that sports are so pervasive in our culture that the (easy) questions on my quiz amounted to a test of general rather than specialized knowledge. You will not learn grammar or quantum physics just by paying attention to what's said at the water cooler. You *can* learn about sports that way.

To test this, I prepared a second, more difficult sports quiz, adopting questions from Internet quizzes that were intended to be challenging for hard-core fans. The questions covered baseball, American football, and basketball (only) and dealt with specific professional players and fine points of the rules. Examples:

- Which player is on the NBA logo? (Julius Erving, Jerry West, Magic Johnson, Tim Duncan, or Wes Unseld)
- Which of these Hall of Famers never pitched in his career? (Cy Young, Babe Ruth, Don Larsen, Tony Gwynn, or Catfish Hunter)
- Which of the following had the nickname Snake? (Don Beebe, Jerry Stovall, Kenny Stabler, Preston Dennard, or Rick Mirer)

I reasoned that these were not the sorts of facts a non-fan would pick up by osmosis. (Correct answers: Jerry West, Tony Gwynn, and Kenny Stabler.)

Answers to this difficult quiz failed to show a correlation to income. And just to make sure the first result wasn't a fluke, I reran the US version of the "easy" sports quiz with a different random sample, again finding a correlation between score and income. On this second run I included a happiness question and found a strong correlation there, too. Those who did best on the easy sports quiz rated themselves about fifty percent happier, on a scale of 0 to 10, than those who did worst.

The easy quiz was not just easier; it was also broader, asking about additional sports (hockey, tennis, "soccer") and confirming that breadth of knowledge, as opposed to depth, is the best predictor of income.

I found, however, no evidence that sports fans are healthier, or spend more hours per week exercising, than non-fans. It appears that many fans' engagement with sports begins and ends on the couch.

"The Greatest Hitter Who Ever Lived"

This is what I mean by an easy sports question: Which is held every year—the Commonwealth Games, the Olympic Games, the Championships, Wimbledon, the FIFA World Cup, or the Rugby World Cup?

About eleven percent of Britons didn't know the answer (Wimbledon).

As with presidents, we eventually forget even the greatest of athletes. Who was Ted Williams—an athlete, an author, a business person, or politician? Fifty-nine percent of Americans knew he was an athlete (a Boston Red Sox Hall of Famer and "the greatest hitter who ever lived"). They made an average of $23,000 (£15,000) per year more than those who didn't know who Williams was. But those over sixty years old accounted for half the correct responses and much of the income difference. Only twenty-three percent of those under the age of thirty knew or guessed who Williams was.

Fourteen

Marshmallow Test

Gloria C. MacKenzie, an eighty-four-year-old Florida woman, won $590 million in a 2013 Powerball lottery. That's right—more than half a billion dollars. An economist might say that a $590 million payout is absurd—it would make more sense to award fifty-nine prizes of $10 million apiece. But economists are not much for playing the lottery. Lottery boards engineer the payouts to appeal to those who buy tickets, and they have found that stratospheric jackpots boost lotto sales. Raising the chance of winning doesn't.

Fantasy drives today's lottery marketing, said the Tennessee lottery president, Rebecca Paul Hargrove. "'What made me play?'... You pay $1 and then for three days you can think about that question. Would I share with my brother-in-law? No! I don't like that brother-in-law. But I would share with my neighbour's nephew." It's not enough for a lottery ad to say that a winner could take a nice vacation. They show winners buying a jet or an airline, an island or a castle. Odds aren't part of the pitch.

I asked a British sample to estimate the chances of a given

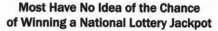

Most Have No Idea of the Chance
of Winning a National Lottery Jackpot

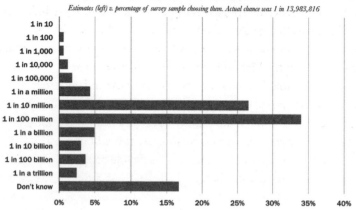

Estimates (left) v. percentage of survey sample choosing them. Actual chance was 1 in 13,983,816

ticket winning a National Lottery jackpot. The survey question was multiple choice with power-of-ten options.

I half-expected to find naive optimism. Why would people play the lottery unless they had an unrealistically rosy notion of the odds? The actual chance of a given ticket winning the National Lottery jackpot is 1 in 13,983,816. Thus "1 in 10 million" was the best of the survey's available answers. But more guesses fell on the pessimistic side of reality. There was the usual wide spectrum of responses, with common answers ranging from one in a million to one in a trillion. It's not that the public thinks lotto odds are better than they are. It's more likely that the fantasy is the payoff, and the odds aren't something that ticket buyers think much about.

It could be that lotto players differ from the general public in estimating odds. But a 2010 survey found that fifty-nine percent of British adults had bought tickets for the National Lottery Draw in the previous year. There isn't that much difference between "lotto players" and "everyone."

If any type of specialized knowledge correlates with income, you might expect that personal finance would, and you'd be right. I made a list of six questions regarding compound interest, inflation, and taxes as they relate to average workers and savers. At any given age or educational level, those who answered the most questions correctly had the highest incomes and most savings.

Household incomes for a thirty-five-year-old with four years of university varied by about $18,000 (£12,000) per year, depending on quiz score. Though the difference is less than we saw for one of the sports or general-knowledge quizzes, it is still impressive.

What is money if not a means to achieving happiness? Financial literacy correlated with that, too. The highest scorers rated themselves twenty-four percent happier on a four-point scale than the lowest scorers did.

Does financial literacy cause wealth, or vice versa? Wealthy people have good reason to educate themselves in subjects like mortgages, taxes, and retirement savings—topics that can be pretty boring otherwise. In that sense, you could say that wealth causes financial literacy.

Scores on a Financial Literacy Quiz Predict Income

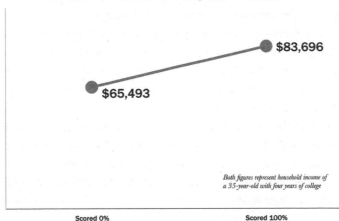

$83,696

$65,493

Both figures represent household income of a 35-year-old with four years of college

Scored 0%   Scored 100%

But financial savvy is not just for the wealthy. Inflation is a special concern for workers whose wages haven't kept up with rising prices and for retirees living on a fixed income. They deal with it every time they go to the market or fill up a gas tank. One survey question asked:

Which is better for someone on a fixed income: a three percent inflation rate or a seven percent inflation rate?

A. Three percent is better.
B. Seven percent is better.
C. The inflation rate doesn't matter in this situation.

This is about as easy as an inflation question can possibly be. Seventy-five percent gave the correct answer, A. Let's hope the other twenty-five percent have someone more knowledgeable handling their money for them.

The sub-prime mortgage crisis of 2007–2009 led to finger-pointing from the right and left. Conservatives said that home buyers who took out mortgages they couldn't afford were irresponsible. Liberals said the lenders promoting too-easy mortgages were exploitative. Sometimes overlooked is that many borrowers just don't have the basic knowledge necessary to make good decisions. A 2010 study by the Federal Reserve Bank of Atlanta established that poor numerical skills (measured by ability to answer simple survey questions) correlated with being unable to pay a real-world mortgage. Borrowers who did poorest on simple financial maths questions were more often late with their payments, more likely to default, and more likely to be foreclosed upon than other respondents. This was true regardless of income, ethnicity, and other demographic factors.

The Federal Reserve Bank's questions were even simpler than the ones I asked. Here's one:

In a sale, a shop is selling all items at half price. Before the sale, a sofa costs $300. How much will it cost in the sale?

It's not surprising that someone unable to answer this question would be in a poor position to understand the ins and outs of balloon payments and negative amortization. From that perspective, moral judgements such as "irresponsible" and "exploitative" may be missing the point. In the absence of basic maths skills, financial responsibility is a hollow concept.

Olivia Mitchell and Annamaria Lusardi, of the Wharton School and the George Washington University School of Business respectively, have been studying the connection between financial literacy and wealth for some time. They estimate that a third of US wealth inequality can be attributed to a "financial knowledge gap." The more knowledgeable save more and invest more intelligently than the less knowledgeable.

"The Most Powerful Force in the Universe"

One of my survey questions was a notable predictor of income, wealth, and happiness.

Suppose you put $1,000 in a tax-free account that earns seven percent per year on this investment. How many years will it take to double your original investment, to $2,000?

A. Between 0 and 5 years.
B. Between 5 and 15 years.
C. Between 15 and 45 years.
D. More than 45 years.

This looks like a maths question. It's not, really. You don't need to know how to calculate the answer, nor do you need to know the "rule of 72." A glance at the list of choices shows that only a ballpark estimate is required. This isn't an algebra question so much as a test of having an intuitive, practical grasp of compound interest. Those who do have that knowledge will know that it takes, very roughly, ten years to double your money at a realistic rate of return (seven percent is more or less realistic). That means B has to be the right answer.

"The most powerful force in the universe is compound interest." Internet quote mills sometimes attribute that statement to Albert Einstein; others attribute it to Bill Gates. I wouldn't bet that either said it, but the wisdom is sound. The achievements of human effort follow an arithmetic series: 1, 2, 3, 4, 5, 6… Debts and investments are different. They grow as geometric series: 1, 2, 4, 8, 16, 32…which means that compounding trumps mere labour. Wealth flows to whoever uses compounding to his or her advantage.

In economist Thomas Piketty's analysis, compounding is the basis of income inequality. The rich get richer off investments, and regular people's wages can't keep up. The power of compounding is also the axiom underlying almost all real-world financial advice. In our credit-mad society, the cash-strapped take out payday loans at outrageous rates, max out credit cards, struggle with student debt, and take out too-expensive mortgages. Compound interest keeps poor people poor. It's also why financial planners say it's important to begin saving early. A worker who starts saving at age twenty-one has a shot at earning more return on his investments than the sum total of his lifetime wages. Compounding is the basis of all truly great fortunes. Successful entrepreneurs do not work ten thousand times longer or harder than everyone else. Instead they find a way to grow their businesses exponentially—for a few years.

Fifty-nine percent of my sample got the compounding question right. That's more than can find Venezuela on a map and about as many as can recognize a photo of Kanye West. But there were striking differences between those who answered correctly and those who didn't. The group with the correct answers reported $32,000 (£21,000) more personal annual income, more than twice as much in savings, and rated themselves fifteen percent happier.

Some research implies that it is financial security—more than getting and spending—that accounts for the correlation between money and happiness. A high income cannot itself confer security. There are multimillionaires who spend everything they make and worry about losing it all (remember William "Bud" Post). There are thrifty schoolteachers and cops who have a cushion of savings giving them a measure of security in an uncertain world. Financial behaviour may also reflect habits of character that factor into happiness. Those who can get their spending under control and manage to put something away are also more likely to have the self-discipline needed to make wise decisions.

You've probably heard of psychologist Walter Mischel's famous "marshmallow test." Mischel presented small children, between four and six years old, with a diabolical choice: the child could have *one* marshmallow and eat it immediately, or he or she could hold off eating it for fifteen minutes and be rewarded with a *second* marshmallow. The initial marshmallow was kept in view and within reach during the torturous fifteen minutes.

Some of the kids crammed the marshmallow into their mouths instantly. Others fell into Hamlet-like indecision, tugging at pigtails and kicking in frustration. Still others played "Odysseus and the marshmallows," covering their eyes and turning away from the sweet's siren song.

Mischel timed the children with a stopwatch. The average time before giving in to temptation was six minutes.

Mischel's daughters attended the school where many of the original marshmallow experiments were held. As the years passed, they noticed differences between the kids who had eaten the marsh-mallows right away and those who had waited: the latter were often more successful in later life. They had better grades and went on to better schools. They seemed happier, less troubled.

The other group, those who had eaten the marshmallows early in the fifteen minutes, often did poorly in school and relationships, and they had more problems with alcohol and drugs.

Mischel and his colleagues began doing follow-up studies on the original marshmallow-test class. They found an impres-sive correlation between how long a child had put off eating the marshmallow (in minutes and seconds) and quantitative measures of later-life success, such as SAT scores. The set of children who ate the treat early grew into adults with higher rates of obesity, borderline personality disorder, crack cocaine use, and divorce.

Life is a succession of marshmallow tests. The dieter is put-ting off a sugar rush now, not for the paltry reward of two treats in a few minutes but for the long-term prospect of being slimmer, healthier, and more attractive. The budgeter skips today's frivolous impulse purchase to save for a new car or the kids' education. The health-conscious endure a cornucopia of deprivations and annoy-ances (jogging, flossing, and salads; using a condom and maintaining a gym membership; having regular check-ups and remembering to take medication) in order to be more fit months and decades into the future.

No one is saying that you should always defer gratification. Hence a rich vein of folk wisdom: *You only live once. A bird in the hand is worth two in the bush.* The key thing is to be able to strike a balance. It's not clear why some are better at impulse control and long-term planning than others. But those who seek to master these skills are more likely to learn, remember, and take to heart certain relevant facts. Knowing approximately how fast money compounds is one of those facts. It is, like the speed of light in physics, one of the foundations of the financial universe. It is not just something that the already wealthy make it their business to know: it is also the kind of information that motivates people to pare down debt and build up savings in the first place.

Learning facts of no obvious immediate relevance is a marshmallow test. It requires a modicum of self-discipline for a pay-off that is uncertain and usually long delayed. Those who do that well might be more likely to be good long-term planners in financial matters as well.

Exit Interview

The elements of personal finance are practical wisdom of a most important kind. This is not an area where the uninformed can just look up the "right answers." Though there is plenty of excellent personal finance information online, it's lost in a sea of bogus pitches. And someone who's spending too much on credit card interest does not necessarily know there's a problem until she's Googling a bankruptcy attorney.

Schools at least *try* to teach kids about sex. They don't always bother to teach kids about money. But individuals today, more than those of previous generations, are expected to make complex financial decisions by themselves. "An uneducated individual armed with a credit card, a student loan and access to a mortgage can be nearly as dangerous to themselves and their community as a person with no training behind the wheel of a car," wrote John Pelletier, director of the Center for Financial Literacy.

The sub-prime mortgage crisis spurred calls for teaching personal finance in schools. The same crisis left governments out of cash and legislators unwilling to fund new initiatives. A 2013 report found that only seven US states required high school students to be instructed and tested in personal finance. Though some schools have instituted financial literacy instruction on their own, the subject is more often a casualty of our metrics-happy age, when teachers are pressured to teach to standardized tests.

Universities are no better. One US report mordantly observed that "financial literacy in college often consists of exit interviews... reminding students to repay their [student] loans that average $26,600 in 2011."

So okay, we need to teach financial literacy in schools—right? Some impressive studies have already poured cold water on that idea.

Business professors Lewis Mandell and Linda Schmid Klein tracked Midwestern US high school students who had taken a well-regarded full-semester elective course in personal finance. One to four years later, the students were no better at answering finance questions than were their classmates who had not taken the course.

This can't come as a shock to anyone who's read this far. All students take geography and history and English—and you see how that works out.

Mandell and Klein had the former high school students evaluate their financial behaviour as adults. They were asked whether they'd had a cheque bounce, whether they made credit card payments on time, and to rate their level of thrift on a five-point scale. The reports of those who had and hadn't taken the finance course were statistically indistinguishable.

A clever study conducted by Shawn Cole and Gauri Kartini Shastry, of Harvard Business School and the University of Virginia respectively, mined three decades of census data. During that time frame, several US states made financial literacy classes mandatory, allowing the duo to conduct a natural experiment on financial knowledge with millions of participants. The census "long form," sent annually to a randomly selected group of households, asks for investment income, which can serve as an index of savings and effective investment decisions. The researchers wondered whether the states that had instituted financial literacy instruction would show increases in investment income relative to the states that hadn't.

They found no correlation. High school finance classes didn't promote smarter investing. Cole and Shastry did not go so far as to say that we should abandon teaching personal finance in high school. But one message is clear: don't expect miracles.

For a teenager, discussion of credit cards, mortgages, and retirement savings can seem remote, not to mention mind-numbingly tedious. Perhaps there is more room to hope that adult learning could have a positive effect. Those who have credit problems, are filing for bankruptcy, or are applying for a reverse mortgage are often required to take counselling in the belief that this will promote better decisions. But aside from these special cases, often limited to those who have already made some serious mistakes, few adults receive personal finance education. Those who most need such education may be the least likely to seek it out, online or elsewhere.

In a free society, even one as obsessed with money as ours, there is little prospect of educating every adult on personal finance. It's up to each individual to take the initiative to learn—but this is one form of adult education that's likely to pay off.

The Only Lottery You'll Ever Win

You win a lottery and decide to invest the money. Which of these options is the *safest* way to invest?

A. Put all the money in one stock.

B. Put all the money in two stocks.

C. Put all the money in an index mutual fund that invests in stocks of the five hundred largest companies.

The only "lottery" the average working person has much chance of winning is the stock market—specifically the tax-deferred stock investments possible in retirement accounts. Letting savings compound, untaxed, in the stock market over decades is a de facto requirement for financial security. But the market is full of risks. The main way of reducing them is diversification. Seventy-three percent gave the best answer to the first question, C. This question was strongly correlated to saving. Those who gave a wrong answer reported an average of $50,000 (£33,000) in household savings. Those who answered correctly averaged $351,000 (£231,000), seven times as much.

Fifteen

The Value of Superficial Learning

It's time to take a deep breath and stand back. What have we learned about the practical value of knowledge? A connection between income and financial literacy, which my surveys did show, is understandable. But some of the other results I've shared may seem arbitrary and puzzling. I found strong correlations between income and performance on quizzes of general knowledge. There were also correlations between income and specialized areas of knowledge, among them sports and pronunciation. Several topics I mentioned in the first part of the book were also predictors of income: the map test, the UK citizenship exam, and being able to name elected representatives. But results on science, celebrities, and spelling were ambiguous. I found no indication at all of a connection between income and knowledge of grammar, slang, sex, or religion.

We are used to thinking of an informal hierarchy of knowledge, one in which rote memorization of maps or sports trivia would presumably rank near the bottom. We are told that knowledge of history and literature is the mark of a good education and, usually, a good job; that science, technology, and maths majors make good money. In many ways our society rewards specialists, not generalists.

And yet, although almost all tested areas of knowledge *did* correlate with years of formal education, the most provocative finding is that general factual knowledge has an effect above and beyond educational level in predicting income.

There are a number of ways of accounting for that. One is that survey performance reflects the quality of education. There is a difference between having a degree from Oxbridge and the same degree from a less distinguished university. We know that graduates of prestigious universities tend to make more money. If they also know more, that could explain a correlation between knowledge and income, even when the years of education are the same. Note that the higher income enjoyed by a graduate of a prestigious university might be attributable to that school's cachet in the marketplace, the social connections the student made in university, or having a family with the money and connections to facilitate admission to Oxbridge in the first place. Knowing more facts than graduates of less prestigious schools might have little to do with it.

An alternative possibility is that the correlation reflects the quality of the student. Some students buckle down and learn; others coast. The survey results could reflect how engaged the participants were with learning, in school and beyond. If that's the case the results certainly suggest that it pays to be engaged and to retain what you learn.

Lifelong attitudes to learning are likely an important factor. In effect, one question the data-crunching posed was: What do high-income people know that low-income people of the same educational level don't know? The answer might be: Material not in the curriculum. Personal finance and sports trivia are not emphasized in school. Nor does schooling help an adult long out of school name her current elected representatives or locate nations that have only recently come into existence.

The map test is as much about current events as schoolbook geography. Essentially everyone can find Spain, Russia, and Australia. The variance in survey scores comes mainly from new nations and obscure ones not emphasized in geography classes. There are maps in newscasts, infographics, history books, apps, and airline ads. The map test is a measure of paying attention—and, as the poet John Ciardi put it, "We are what we do with our attention."

Paying attention may be a good two-word description of what is driving the income correlation. It is most reliably measured by an assortment of general-knowledge questions that are neither too difficult nor too easy. Someone who scores low in general knowledge is probably not paying much attention to the outside world, whereas someone who scores high has been absorbing a lot, resulting in broad (if superficial) contextual knowledge.

A set of spelling questions, say, is likely to be less informative. Knowing how to spell "prerogative" correlates strongly with knowing how to spell "consensus" or "supersede." It's basically the same group who knows how to spell frequently misspelled words. Yet of course there are many brilliant people who can't

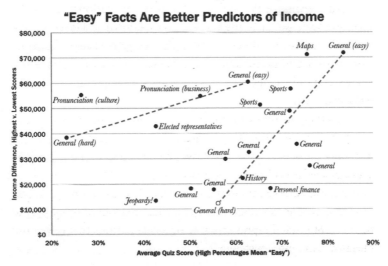

"Easy" Facts Are Better Predictors of Income

spell, and some have quite encyclopedic knowledge otherwise. For that reason, a focused set of questions—on spelling or any other narrow topic—is less likely to achieve statistical significance as a predictor of income.

Easy questions seem to be better predictors than hard ones. Here's a scatter chart showing performance on quizzes of general and specific knowledge. Each black dot represents a survey. The horizontal axis shows how difficult the survey was, measured by the average percentage of questions answered correctly. The vertical axis shows the income advantage of the highest scorers over the lowest scorers. As usual, we're looking at the projected income difference between a thirty-five-year-old with four years of university who got all the questions right versus a thirty-five-year-old with four years of university who missed all the questions.

For instance, a map test that included rather easily identifiable nations such as Russia, Japan, and Turkey had an average score of seventy-six percent (dot at upper right). Performance on this quiz was a good predictor of income, with high scorers reporting about $71,000 (£47,000) more household income per year than low scorers.

In the lower part of the chart, at left centre, is a set of ten fairly difficult questions taken from a TV quiz show (*Jeopardy!*). These questions were harder—the average score was only forty-three percent correct—and the income difference was less: $13,000 (£8,500) a year.

The connection between difficulty and income difference is certainly noisy, but the cloud of dots generally runs from lower left to upper right, implying that the easier the question, the stronger the connection to income.

To test this idea, I sent out some linked surveys. Everyone in a randomized group answered a set of "easy" questions and a set of "hard" questions on an identical assortment of topics. This method eliminates most of the variables, as distribution of income, education, and other demographics remained constant within the sample. The only variable was the difficulty of the questions.

The chart's dashed lines join surveys sharing the same set of participants. Both lines slope upwards. For each of the two randomized groups, the easier set of questions was associated with a greater income difference than the harder set. (The difficult survey at bottom centre is shown as a hollow dot, as it was not statistically significant. Both of the easy surveys, and the other hard survey, were highly significant.)

On a quiz show, answering difficult trivia questions is worth more money than answering easy trivia questions. Real life seems to be different. There's a real advantage to knowing what the crowd knows, but there are diminishing returns beyond that.

Another way of thinking about it is that there is an income penalty for *not* knowing widely known facts. A graduate who cannot identify Sputnik or Ernest Hemingway (two of the "easy" questions on the general-knowledge surveys) has not got much out of her education and lacks the level of cultural literacy that most of her fellow graduates have.

But there is not much of a prize for knowing little-known facts unrelated to one's work. I am not challenging the value of being an expert in *something*. Every professional has to be. But that's not what my surveys were intended to gauge or were able to gauge. They point instead to the value of a liberal education in the broadest sense of the term—and, above all, to the value of paying attention.

Chess Masters and Birdwatchers

The connection between knowledge and income raises questions about what causes what. Is it possible that knowledge enhances mental ability? This question has been studied in connection with the game of chess.

For several years the famed director Stanley Kubrick worked as a chess hustler in New York City parks. He spent up to twelve hours a day playing chess, earning about $20 a week. As Kubrick later explained,

> chess is an analogy. It is a series of steps that you take one at a time and it's balancing resources against the problem, which in chess is time and in movies is time and money.... You sit at the board and suddenly your heart leaps. Your hand trembles to pick up the piece and move it. But what chess teaches you is that you must sit there calmly and think about whether it's really a good idea and whether there are other, better ideas.

Chess figures in several of Kubrick's films. The chess game in *2001: A Space Odyssey*, between an astronaut and the homicidal computer HAL, is adapted from the 1910 match between Otto Roesch and Willi Schlag in Hamburg. The astronaut resigns, leaving HAL to retort, "Thank you for a very enjoyable game."

Chess plays an important role in the history of artificial intelligence. Since the dawn of the computer age, it has been used as a model of human expertise. Chess is a difficult game with simple rules. The rules are easily coded; the expertise is not. Knowing the rules does not make a human (much less an algorithm) a good chess player. Nor does knowing the history of chess and chess trivia or memorizing a few famous matches. What does a good chess player know that a poor one doesn't? Is chess ability an innate talent one is born with, or is it a skill that can be acquired through long practice? These questions have engaged chess players since the game began, and psychologists and computer scientists as well.

Dutch chess master Adriaan de Groot, who represented the Netherlands in the Chess Olympiads, was also a psychologist. He asked expert and novice chess players to document their thought processes and was surprised to find that there weren't many overt differences. You might think that the master players would have looked ahead by more moves or have evaluated more potential moves than the beginners did. They didn't. Instead the expert players had better instincts. They spent more time analysing promising moves and less time analysing lousy moves. The beginners did the opposite. The mind of a great chess player has more efficient code, not a faster processor.

De Groot is best known for a remarkable experiment. He showed players chessboards set with configurations of pieces from actual games for five seconds. After that brief viewing, the players were asked to reproduce the boards' configurations from memory.

The master players were incredibly good at this. They reproduced the exact positions of every single piece with virtually 100 percent accuracy. Lesser players were hopeless, often with accuracies of 20 percent or less.

De Groot then conducted a telling variation on the experiment. He showed players chessboards set at random—arbitrary configurations of pieces that had not and probably could not have arisen in play. This time the masters were no better than the novices. All struggled to remember the location of even half a dozen pieces.

Good players are better at remembering *realistic* board configurations only. They do this by recognizing patterns they've seen before—gambits and sacrifices and strategies. Artificial intelligence pioneer Herbert A. Simon, who repeated de Groot's experiments, maintained that good players categorize the board's configuration into "chunks," facilitating memory.

This strategy is not limited to chess. A novice birdwatcher sees only a blur of colour and feathers. He is unable to categorize the bird he sees; he does not know which features are diagnostic and which are irrelevant. The novice struggles to remember everything about the bird—an impossible task—in order to consult a field guide. An expert immediately recognizes an immature female golden oriole and need only remember that categorization. In broad outline this analysis applies to anything we do with deliberation and imagination—running a business or a marathon; designing an app or a wedding; understanding a frightened child or a TED talk. By recognizing familiar patterns we make sense of a complex whole.

No one is saying that the ability to remember a chess position is the only distinction of a master player—or even the most important distinction. That ability is necessary but not sufficient. As Kubrick had it, chess is a game of opportunity costs. It is not enough to conclude that a move is a good one. The master player must always be asking, is there a better move? Critical thinking is paramount, but memory lays the groundwork: a player who must constantly keep looking back at the board just to recall where the pieces are *now* will be severely handicapped in that weighing of options.

It is natural to ask whether the ability to categorize/memorize a chessboard, acquired from long practice, constitutes knowledge, skill, or talent. Maybe the best answer is that the question is wrong. *Knowledge, skill,* and *talent* are labels we have made up to describe mental processes that we don't deeply understand. They may not have much to do with the cognitive ground truth.

Chess is popularly caricatured as the epitome of logic and thus the proper domain of Deep Thought, HAL, and other soulless entities. But as the game is played by humans, it is no less an exercise in intuition and the unconscious. Good players acquire the ability to recognize chessboard configurations that occur during play. Logic has nothing to do with this: it's more like recognizing a familiar face in a crowd. No one is born knowing the inner game of chess. Chess masters acquire their intuitions by learning many "facts" and also by knowing how those facts fit together globally. Learning facts is one way we build intuitions, and these are the fundamentals of so-called skills and talents.

Eureka Moments

In the early 1950s, Bette Nesmith Graham was a divorced single mother who took a job as a secretary at Texas Bank and Trust. The bank had just outfitted its offices with IBM Selectric typewriters. They came with one big drawback. The Selectrics used a carbon film ribbon that produced crisp type that was impossible to erase. A single error meant that an entire page had to be retyped.

Bosses, who were men, didn't care. Women's labour was cheap, so much so that Graham supplemented her meagre income by painting Christmas decorations for the bank's windows. The exercise reminded her of something she'd once learned: artists painted over their mistakes rather than erasing them.

And that's what led Graham to her eureka moment. She realized she could paint over typing errors rather than erase them. She mixed white tempera paint in her kitchen blender and put it in a little bottle. Whenever she made a typo, she blotted it out with a brush, waited a few seconds for it to dry, and typed over it. Marketed as Liquid Paper, the invention became one of the bestselling office supplies of the late analogue age. In 1979 Graham sold her company to Gillette for $47.5 million.

"Imagination is more important than knowledge," Albert Einstein wrote in 1931. But it's also true that the latter undergirds the former. What we call imagination often involves making a connection between two facts—seeing the relevance of a painter's solution to a typist's problem, say. Einstein was interested in a branch of mathematics with no practical value—the non-Euclidean geometry of Bernhard Riemann. Physicists did not study Riemann because his work had no connection to physics. Einstein's greatest eureka moment was realizing that Riemann's geometry could be the basis of a new theory of gravity, one in which matter warps space and time.

In cases like this, knowledge and imagination go hand in hand. There was a generation of physicists working on a new theory of gravity and a tiny group of mathematicians who knew of Riemann's work. Einstein, and perhaps no one else, fell in the intersection of that Venn diagram.

There are many other examples of this phenomenon. Charles Darwin and Alfred Russel Wallace were both interested in the origin of species. Each had read a topical book on the origin of poverty, Thomas Malthus's *An Essay on the Principle of Population.* They both made the same connection and came up with similar theories of natural selection.

Aaron Copland knew American folk music along with Schoenberg's twelve-tone system. Picasso was among the first classically trained European artists to study African sculpture. Mark Zuckerberg knew how to code and also how much Harvard students used their printed student directory, the "face book."

We all confront problems in our lives and careers. In ways big and small, "irrelevant" knowledge can be a source of analogies, inspirations, and solutions.

Learning changes not just habits of thought but also brain anatomy. It's conjectured that London black taxi drivers learn more discrete facts than do practitioners of any other profession. This has recommended the profession to neuroscientists. They report that the posterior hippocampus, the brain's primary site for creating new long-term memories, enlarges during the process of studying for the drivers' Knowledge exam and remains larger than those of the public.

A 2015 report in *Nature Neuroscience* found that children of well-educated and well-to-do parents had a greater cortical area than children of less educated and less affluent parents. The cortical differences were particularly notable in regions of the brain connected to language, reading, and decision-making. The study didn't directly address the reasons, but explanations weren't hard to find. "Money can buy better education, homes in areas further away from freeways," said lead researcher Elizabeth Sowell. "It can buy guitar lessons. It can buy after-school programmes." The act of learning the guitar can lead to more capable brains and other advantages, even for those who do not intend to become professional guitar players.

One possible explanation for the connection between broad factual knowledge and income is that learning improves cognitive abilities that are useful in almost any task, including a career. Learning causes better brain function, which in turn causes higher income.

No one would claim that ride-sharing apps and Segways have made walking obsolete. Exercise is needed for the human body to function; whether it is also needed to get from point A to point B is beside the point. Our brains need the process of learning to function at peak performance. That facts can be looked up elsewhere doesn't change that.

Part Three

Strategies for a Culturally Illiterate World

Sixteen

When Dumbing Down Is Smart

We live in a Dunning–Kruger world. That the public is unaware of its own ignorance is a fact of life, one that needs to be taken into account by designers, marketers, and communicators. Consider the hamburger icon. You've seen it: it's a stack of three rounded bars ("patties"), like a Big Mac assembly schematic from McDonald's Hamburger University. The hamburger is an icon for summoning a menu or navigation bar. Invented as a response to the cramped screens of early smartphones, the hamburger has become ubiquitous and has migrated to desktop screens. It's a global standard—except that, for many, the hamburger is "mystery meat," says Web designer Eric W. Mobley. Novice users may not even recognize the hamburger as an icon. Its vaguely classical symmetry suggests a decorative bullet.

The hamburger is part of an evolving visual language that fills our real and virtual worlds. This language has its roots in twentieth-century design-school utopianism. Clean modern graphics would replace words in the multicultural, visually orientated world to come.

Exemplifying this ethos, the American Institute of Graphic Arts (AIGA) and the US Department of Transportation released a set of icons designed for airports and train stations in 1974. They include the familiar no-smoking glyph and the stylized men's-room and women's-room symbols that have perfectly circular heads. Many AIGA icons are models of lucidity, as long as you understand the concept of synecdoche (not a coat hanger but a cloakroom; not a martini but a bar).

Simultaneously with the AIGA effort, Xerox PARC engineers were developing the first computer interface using icons rather than typed-in commands. Xerox designers were influenced by ergonomic studies suggesting that users relate better to pictures than to words, an idea that would catch on commercially in the 1980s with the Apple Macintosh.

In today's world of small screens, there is less room for elaborate icons, and app designers favour simple, sometimes cryptic, pictographs. This philosophy assumes that users will experiment to learn how icons work.

I reproduced several standard icons in a survey to see how many people could recognize them. I expected that the hamburger would throw a few people, and it did. I didn't expect how poor recognition would be for some of the airport icons.

A mere five percent could correctly identify the AIGA symbol for "exit," and less than four percent identified the dollar sign within a circle as the sign for "cashier." The other multiple-choice options for that icon were "automatic teller machine," "bank," "currency exchange," and "expensive." The most popular guess was "currency exchange" (chosen by thirty-five percent).

My sample also failed to recognize icons that Web designers assume to be all but universally understood. A quarter of

How Many Can Identify These Airport Icons?

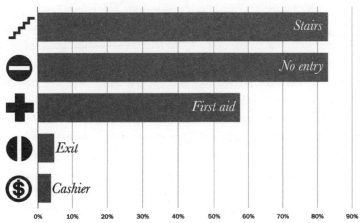

How Many Can Identify These Mobile Device Icons?

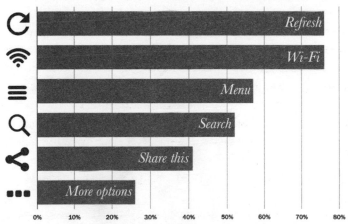

respondents didn't understand the Wi-Fi symbol. The hamburger eluded nearly half. (As usual, everyone in my sample was a computer and Internet user. In that regard, they would have been somewhat more digital-savvy than the population as a whole.)

The magnifying-glass icon for "search" also scored poorly (fifty-two percent recognition). This is one icon that depends on a literary allusion, to Arthur Conan Doyle's Sherlock Holmes. Notwithstanding an ongoing movie and TV franchise, many smartphone users may not be familiar with the character. Another problem is that a magnifying-glass icon is also used in graphics programs to indicate "zoom in" and "zoom out." This ambiguity was a big factor here, for "magnify" was the second-most-popular choice (thirty-six percent).

The least recognized of all the icons was the ellipsis—the three dots meaning "click here for more options." Barely a quarter were able to pick the right meaning. In practice, the ellipsis is often interchangeable with the hamburger. At least the hamburger looks something like a list of menu items. The ellipsis metaphor refers to punctuation—not always a strong suit of digital natives.

Icons are tools to help users do what they want to do. When people don't understand them, it's the designers, not the users, who deserve a flunking grade. Designers need to know what users don't know (even if users are unaware of this themselves) and factor that into their designs. App makers have more remedies than those creating real-world signage. An app can know whether the user is a newbie or a power user. It can also know the user's age. My survey showed, as expected, that young people are far more likely than old people to recognize icons. An app can label an icon with text for users likely to need it, then dispense with the label after that user gains experience.

Read the Label

Food and drug companies should also heed the public's cluelessness. A 2006 study in *Annals of Internal Medicine* asked adult patients to describe how they would take five common prescription medicines based on the labels. Serious errors were typical, and they were often of the Dunning–Kruger variety. Those who misunderstood the labels thought they understood them perfectly. The errors mostly came down to two things: botching simple maths and mixing up simple units of measurement.

Asked to explain the instruction, "Take one teaspoonful by mouth three times daily," many replaced "teaspoon" with "tablespoon." This mix-up accounted for just over half of all the errors.

Even among those who were able to recite the label instruction "Take two tablets by mouth twice daily" word for word, one-third did not measure out the correct number of pills they were supposed to take per day (four).

I did surveys testing the public's understanding of labels, including this nutrition label for ice cream. A large majority knew that "g" means "grams" and "Sat Fat" stands for "saturated fat"—the bad kind. But many had trouble applying label information. When the question required maths or drawing a logical inference, scores went south.

One of my questions asked, "If you ate the entire container, how many calories would that be?" Sixteen percent gave a wrong answer, and most of the wrong answers were way off. Another question: "Suppose you're on a low-carb diet that allows 15g of carbohydrates for a snack. How much of this ice cream could you have?" One in three respondents gave a wrong answer. "Pretend that you're allergic to penicillin, latex gloves, peanuts, and bee stings. Is it safe to eat this ice cream?" The answer is "no," as the label lists peanut oil as one of the ingredients. Eleven percent got it wrong.

I asked respondents about a medicine label containing the common warning, "Avoid alcohol." This laconic instruction means, "Don't drink any alcoholic beverage when taking this medicine." But eleven percent felt that "avoid alcohol" permits wiggle room. They wrongly interpreted it to mean, "It's okay to have a drink or two, as long as you aren't driving or operating machinery," or, "Don't drink to excess while taking this medicine" or admitted that they didn't know what the instruction meant.

Lists of side effects are another minefield of confusion. In the name of protecting consumers, US law requires drug companies to report any "temporally associated symptoms" that turned up in testing a new medicine. That means anything that happened to anyone while taking the drug or shortly thereafter. Side effects must be listed even if there was an equal or greater number of reports in the control group that got a placebo instead of the drug.

Nutrition Facts		
Serving Size		½ cup
Servings per container		4
Amount per serving		
Calories 250	Fat Cal	120
		%DV
Total Fat 13g		20%
Sat Fat 9g		40%
Cholesterol 28mg		12%
Sodium 55mg		2%
Total Carbohydrate 30g		12%
Dietary Fiber 2g		
Sugars 23g		
Protein 4g		8%

*Percentage Daily Values (DV) are based on a 2,000 calorie diet. Your daily values may be higher or lower depending on your calorie needs.
Ingredients: Cream, Skim Milk, Liquid Sugar, Water, Egg Yolks, Brown Sugar, Milkfat, Peanut Oil, Sugar, Butter, Salt, Carrageenan, Vanilla Extract.

The law thus throws correlation, causation, and common sense under the bus. There is a rationale for this. The law properly recognizes that a lot of money is at stake in testing new drugs. Doctors and drug companies have financial incentives to downplay side effects, and disclosing every potential side effect is a step towards transparency.

But transparency has side effects of its own. The disclosures are worthwhile only to the extent that average people can use them to make better decisions. Unfortunately human decision-making falters when confronted with small and hard-to-gauge risks of terrible outcomes. There will be people who won't take an antidepressant that could help them because suicide is listed as a side effect. To make any kind of an informed decision you would need to know the probabilities. Is the chance of suicide one in ten...or one in one hundred million? Is it actually less likely with the drug than without because the suicide rate was higher in the group getting a placebo? The label doesn't give that information.

Package inserts helped fuel the anti-vaccination movement. Anti-vaxxers tell parents to look at the measles, mumps, and rubella (MMR) vaccine insert, which does indeed list autism among the possible side effects, but not for the reason the crusaders claim. The recommended age for the vaccines happens to coincide with the age at which autism is most often diagnosed. That makes autism a "temporally associated symptom" that has nothing to do with causality. Not on the label is the fact that measles still kills about 145,000 people a year, nearly all of them in developing nations where children aren't vaccinated.

> "If it takes 5 machines 5 minutes to make 5 widgets, how long would it take 100 machines to make 100 widgets?"

This brain-teaser appears in the Cognitive Reflection Test that marketing professor Shane Frederick, then of MIT, published in 2005.

Frederick found that most people, including students at prestigious universities, get it wrong. It's not a hard question in any normal sense. The difficulty with this question and the others on Frederick's test is that they suggest an impulsive answer. The question's parallel wording all but ensures that "100 minutes" pops to mind. Many go with that first impulse...which in this case is wrong. The correct answer is five minutes. A machine takes five minutes to make a widget. More machines mean more widgets—but it still takes five minutes to make one.

Many medicine-label instructions are confusing in the same way. Tell someone to "take two tablets twice a day," then ask, "How many pills should you take a day?" The impulse answer is "two," and that's the usual wrong answer on surveys.

Frederick's research holds out little hope that better education is the solution. MIT students get an excellent education that includes two semesters of calculus...but many of them botched the widgets arithmetic. The only realistic remedy is to avoid medicine instructions that pose cognitive difficulties. This can be accomplished by following a couple of simple guidelines:

- Minimize the need to do even simple arithmetic. Whenever practical, a dose should be a single pill.
- Avoid ambiguity. In Britain, the "avoid alcohol" language has been replaced with "Do not drink alcohol while taking this medicine." This leaves no room for rationalizing.

Land of the Unhandy

For a good example of the Dunning–Kruger effect, look at practical knowledge of cooking and household management. All of us have a little knowledge of these things, and those who are truly misinformed tend not to know how misinformed they are. I asked a survey sample how long it takes to hard-boil a large egg. More than two-thirds failed to give an answer that was even in the ballpark (nine to thirteen minutes).

Now, of course the answer depends on whether you put the egg in cold or already boiling water. Either way, it takes about eleven minutes at boiling heat to cook an egg yolk all the way through. Someone who puts the egg in cold water and counts the time it takes to boil the water could come up with a figure like twenty minutes. But a third of the sample believed they could cook a hard-boiled egg in six minutes or less.

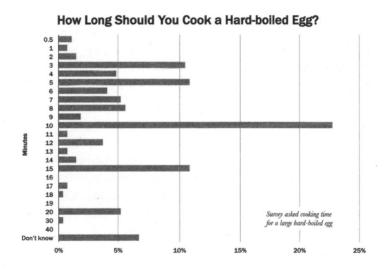

How Long Should You Cook a Hard-boiled Egg?

Survey asked cooking time for a large hard-boiled egg

Another question asked how long it takes to grill each side of a one-inch-thick steak until it's medium done. Five minutes would be a reasonable answer. Again the majority gave unreasonable answers. With steaks as well as eggs, more undershot rather than overshot the reasonable answer—expectations shaped by extensive experience with a microwave oven, perhaps?

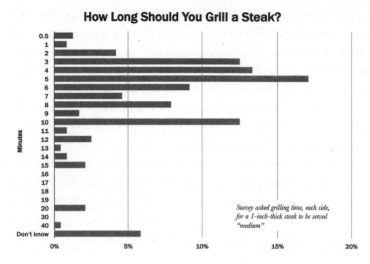

How Long Should You Grill a Steak?

Survey asked grilling time, each side, for a 1-inch-thick steak to be served "medium"

Name the ingredients in bread. This came with eleven options, among them flour, water, and yeast—without which it would be a challenge to make anything resembling bread. Eight percent thought they could make bread without flour; an equal number omitted yeast, and twenty-six percent left out water.

Everybody's heard that you should only eat oysters in a month with an *R* in it. Or is it a month without an *R*? Nearly half said they didn't know, and only thirty percent picked the correct answer, *with* an *R*. The rule of thumb skips the four warm months May through August, in which shellfish may accumulate toxins from red tides.

It's a well-to-do crowd that eats oysters. The income difference between those who knew and didn't know this rule was $24,000 (£16,000).

We're told that British and American cooks resist going metric because they don't know a gram from a millilitre. Guess what? They don't know a teaspoon from a tablespoon, either.

I asked a nationwide US sample how many teaspoons there are in a tablespoon. Barely half (forty-nine percent) gave the correct answer, three.

Asked how many tablespoons are in a fluid ounce, only twenty-four percent got it right (two tablespoons = one ounce), and answers ranged from one to sixteen. For the record, these right answers only apply in the US and UK. In Australia four teaspoons make a tablespoon, and a tablespoon is two-thirds of a fluid ounce.

We all know "bad" cooks who swear they follow recipes to the letter. I wonder how many culinary failures can be traced back to the measuring-spoon confusion.

How big is a two-by-four? I asked a survey sample whether that familiar lumber size was actually two by four inches, smaller than two by four inches, or larger than two by four inches. Anyone who's handy knows that it's thinner and narrower than claimed, 1.5 by 3.5 inches.

Forty-three percent of the sample took the question to be a case of, "Who's buried in Grant's Tomb?" They said a two-by-four was just that. Only thirty-eight percent said "smaller," and fourteen percent said "larger."

The sample did better with questions about tools that would be used in light indoor repairs. Shown a picture of a screw, ninety-one percent could identify the type of screwdriver needed (Phillips head). Sixty-eight percent could identify an adjustable wrench from a picture.

"About how often should you change the oil in your car?" This survey question was multiple choice, offering answers ranging from "every 500 miles" to "every 200,000 miles." By far the most popular answer was "every 3,000 miles," picked by thirty-eight percent.

How Often Should You Change a Car's Oil?

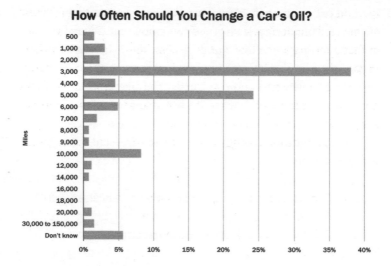

It *used* to be a rule of thumb that oil should be changed every three thousand miles. Around that time, it was also a rule of thumb that every computer needs two floppy-disk drives. In the past thirty years, motor oils and motors have improved, greatly increasing the recommended service interval. Most car manufacturers recommend oil changes at intervals of 7,500 or 10,000 miles (or else that you defer to on-board monitoring systems that calculate the recommended interval based on usage). One of the most popular motor oils, Mobil 1 Extended Performance, is guaranteed for 15,000 miles.

If the survey results are any indication of behaviour, consumers are changing their oil two or three times as much as they need to. Not only is that billions of dollars down the drain, it's also tonnes of oil down the drain, placing a needless burden on waterways and wildlife.

Ignorance doesn't just happen. Sometimes it's manufactured. That the three-thousand-miles credo is a profitable scam is an open secret in the industry. The trade publication *National Oil and Lube News* brims with advice about persuading customers to change their oil early and often. "Many people…know when to have their oil changed but don't pay that much attention to it. Take advantage of that by using a window sticker system [and] customers will be making their way back to you in a few short months." In other words, even the minority that knows to change the oil every ten thousand miles may not remember when the last change was. They defer to a window-sticker or e-mail reminders.

The publication recently offered these suggested messages for window stickers:

- Psst…this is your engine speaking. Change my oil please.
- Don't wait for the light, change the oil now.
- An oil change now is cheaper than a new motor later.
- Your wife called…don't forget to get your oil changed today.
- Diapers and politicians should be changed often… for the same reason.

David Langness, a former automotive service adviser, called the three-thousand-mile rule "a marketing tactic that dealers use to get you into the service bay on a regular basis. Unless you go to the drag strip on weekends, you don't need it."

It's not hard to learn the truth about oil changes. It's in your car's manual. Otherwise, Google, "How often should I change my car's oil?" You'll find plenty of good information and even a Wikipedia entry entitled "3,000 Mile Myth"—along with propaganda, of course. The thing is, you're not going to ask the question unless you already know that you don't know the answer. In my survey, less than six percent chose "don't know"—a fraction of the number who confessed ignorance on the boiled egg and grilled steak questions.

The Not-So-Smart Home

Not a joke: Do you know how to screw in a light bulb? Fifteen percent of my sample didn't. The question asked which way to turn an Edison screw bulb into an empty socket (the correct answer is clockwise).

Seventeen

Curating Knowledge

You've heard of The Onion, the news parody site. The Onion pays talented writers to produce fake news stories that are often brilliant. You may not have heard of The Daily Currant, Global Associated News, Mediamass, or National Report. All are Onion knock-offs. Known in the trade as spoof sites, they have a different business plan. Their content is largely reader-generated and not funny. They settle for deadpan conceptual prankery. Thus these sites spew steady streams of fake "news" that is not readily identifiable as satire. Spoof-site articles regularly get posted on Facebook. Every now and then a piece gets thousands of reposts, not because readers think it's funny but because they think it's *true*.

"Actor Adam Sandler is reported to have died shortly after a snowboard accident earlier today," read a recent Global Associated News story. Whereas The Onion may cleverly invert the clichés of journalism, Global Associated News simply uses journalese as camouflage for shareable falsehoods. "The actor was wearing a helmet at the time of the accident and drugs and alcohol do not appear to have played any part in his death," the story concluded.

That Sandler's falsely reported death had been tweeted 4,766 times and racked up 77,000 Facebook "likes" was probably the intended punchline.

Global Associated News specializes in fake celebrity death stories. Its partner in ghoulishness is Mediamass, known for refuting true A-list obituaries with the claim that they were hoaxes.

These sites play off the journalistic maxim that it is all but impossible to quickly determine whether a moderately famous person has just died. When a story says that aliens have landed in Piccadilly Circus and nobody else is covering it, you know it's fake. When one source says the star of a 1990s sitcom has just died, the claim is apt to be believed even though it hasn't made the bigger, more trusted sources.

The Internet "seems to make it harder, not easier, to determine the truth," said Dean Miller, former director of the Center for News Literacy at Stony Brook University. That may sound alarmist. We've always known that you can't believe everything you read. But Miller is taking audience habits into account. The Internet can make it easy to check out a story that seems fishy, but you're not going to check it unless you're suspicious. That requires a modicum of scepticism, contextual knowledge, and research skills. The people most lacking in those attributes believe they're pretty good at telling when a story is fake. They're the ones who post links to fabricated news, causing others to repost. The Dunning–Kruger effect goes viral.

The media visionary's pitch has always been that digital aggregators will improve the quality and relevance of news. Instead of being restricted by the narrow blinkers of a local newspaper or TV station, we can sample stories from around the nation and globe. One drawback is that stories online are effectively stripped of context—and sometimes the context matters. It does when we stumble upon someone's deadpan joke, not realizing we're the butt of it.

·

So where are we headed? Experiments say the Internet may be making us forgetful, overconfident, and oblivious. Some futurists and thought leaders spin the research into apocalyptic scenarios. The psychologists I've spoken with are a few degrees more cautious. Henry Roediger III, of the presidential forgetting studies, is often asked to comment on the ways digital devices are changing human memory and the mind. His candid answer is that (a) no one really knows and (b) "it might not be all that different" in the future.

What Google-effect experiments can't show is how we will adapt to new technologies over the long term (or how those new technologies will adapt to *us*). The human mind has a great capacity to recalibrate to a new normal.

For Roediger, the real novelty is novelty itself. There is so much more *new* information to process today, he observes, resulting in an unprecedented cognitive load. In a few generations, we have gone from a world of three TV channels to a world of five hundred channels and from a daily newspaper to multiple social-network feeds that update every second. It's not just a matter of remembering or forgetting: we are dealing with too much information to process it all.

The business of news gathering is co-evolving along with us. "I was in Paris, working for Reuters, when Sonia Delaunay died [in 1979]," journalist Brian Cathcart recalled. "I'd never heard of her. It was the middle of the night, and I wrote two paragraphs on her. In the morning my colleague, who knew much more, was able to follow up with a proper obituary. The point is, I was not then expected to know who Sonia Delaunay was. Today it would be gross incompetence to not come up with *hundreds* of facts about Sonia Delaunay in 20 minutes."

Today's news benefits from the speed and ease of online research. But this doesn't necessarily result in better-informed audiences.

The Fox News Effect

Fox News, carried in over 40 nations, is one of the globe's most successful news operations. Yet a 2012 Farleigh Dickinson University survey reported that Fox News viewers knew less about current events than those who didn't follow the news. Fox News viewers scored lower on current events quizzes than those who got their news from other sources, or no source at all.

The Farleigh Dickinson finding wasn't a fluke. Some of the surveys I conducted for this book threw in a question asking participants to indicate which American news and information sources they regularly followed. There was a list of more than thirty choices, spanning old and new media and presented in a different randomized order to each participant. With striking consistency, those who listed Fox News as a source of information scored lower on factual knowledge than those who didn't list Fox News. The difference wasn't small.

On most of my surveys Fox News viewers *did* manage to outscore those who didn't follow the news at all (though the difference was never statistically significant). But on all the surveys, Fox News viewers were significantly less informed than the audiences for the highest-scoring news sources.

Here is a typical example of the breakdown, involving a set of twelve questions spanning current events, geography, science, religion, and personal finance.

The chart shows the error bars (they vary widely because of the different audience sizes). Fox News viewers averaged fifty-seven percent correct. That was better than the no-news crowd but the lowest of all the actual news sources.

The most informed news audiences, scoring over sixty-five percent, included those who followed PBS, the *New York Times*, the *Wall Street Journal*, National Public Radio (NPR), and satirical cable news shows such as *The Daily Show*. These results also

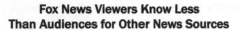

Fox News Viewers Know Less
Than Audiences for Other News Sources

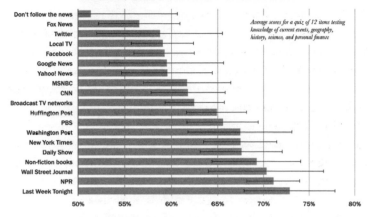

Average scores for a quiz of 12 items testing knowledge of current events, geography, history, science, and personal finance

confirmed the findings of the Farleigh Dickinson survey. *Last Week Tonight with John Oliver* scored highest of all in my sample (though again, that first-place rating is not significantly higher than the few below it).

These results are especially surprising given my simple though ham-handed methodology. I did not ask for a main source of news. No one was asked to identify himself or herself as a Fox News viewer per se. Should you think that the Fox News audience lives in a media bubble, you're wrong. The average Fox News viewer claimed to get news from 5.5 sources. That was higher than average (4.5 sources) for all survey participants. Fox News viewers were especially likely to say that they also got news from the major broadcast networks (forty-four percent), Facebook (forty percent), and CNN (thirty-one percent). Nearly one in five Fox viewers said they also watched the liberal news channel MSNBC.

Thus any effect of following Fox News was diluted. Some people watch Fox and listen to NPR and were counted in both averages. Despite that, the difference in knowledge between the average Fox News viewer and the average NPR listener was dramatic. It was as if watching Fox News was a jinx, diminishing one's ability to answer moderately difficult questions in almost any field.

I found that the Fox News audience was less likely to be able to name the capital of Canada or explain the uncertainty principle, to know the number of justices on the US Supreme Court or the religion of the Dalai Lama, to find South Carolina or Antarctica on a map, to know the names of their senators or the size of the federal budget, to recognize Pluto as a dwarf planet, or to know that Judaism preceded Christianity.

One question on which the Fox News audience did okay was the compound interest question. ("How long will it take to double your investment at seven percent return?") Sixty percent of Fox viewers got it right, a score in the middle of the pack—better than the audiences for many Internet news sources.

If we needed a reminder that our sources of news and information matter, here it is. In this chapter I will try to account for the knowledge gap between news audiences and explore what it tells us about staying informed.

The first thing to say is that the Fox News effect is a correlation that does not imply causation.

Consider another Rupert Murdoch–controlled news medium, the *New York Post*. Imagine that a study showed that *New York Post* readers are less informed than *New York Times* readers. Would anybody be surprised?

No one familiar with those newspapers would. The *Post* is a tabloid-format newspaper convenient for reading on public transportation. It has brassy headlines and a sports section outshining the *Times*' anaemic one. Advertisers are well aware that the average *Post* reader is less educated and less affluent than the average *Times* reader. Judging by the content, the average *Post* reader is engaged by local crime, human interest, celebrity gossip, and sports. The *Post* audience cares less about the national and international news, policy analysis, and arts coverage to be found in abundance in the *Times*.

My point is that knowledge differences between news sources inevitably reflect differences in audience demographics. The Fox audience may be less educated than others, and this would pull down knowledge scores. (Are there PhDs who watch Fox? Sure, but they aren't watching because they understand Fox to be an elitist network for the super-educated conservative. They're watching because they want to keep up with a channel that influences mass opinion.)

The Fox audience scored lower both on current events (that they must have learned, or failed to learn, from the news sources they followed) and on timeless facts that they might have learned in school. Fox News does not have much cause to mention the second digit of pi or to note that "veil of tears" is grammatically incorrect. But Fox News viewers were less likely to know these things, too.

Readers might be tempted to infer that liberal news sources have the most knowledgeable audiences. A counterexample is the *Wall Street Journal*, which has a very conservative editorial page. It scored as well as any other news source.

To some of its critics, Fox News is the confirmation bias network, reassuring viewers by telling them what they already believe. Fox News was created for a conservative audience that felt ignored and marginalized by the mainstream media. But if it's true that Fox News programming appeals especially to those conservatives who want validation of their beliefs and prefer not to hear anything challenging those convictions, that could limit the range of stories presented and help account for the Fox News effect.

Another common analysis is that Fox News lies. That's something like the idea that the tabloid press lies. Both the tabloids and Fox have a different definition of news from that of mainstream media, but nearly all of what they report as news is grounded in reality.

Whatever you say about journalists, they don't like to lie, and mostly they don't. But selective reporting is something else again. Today journalism is about survival of the fittest. Fox News has carved out its own niche, zeroing in on a subset of the news that resonates with its audience. This includes outrageous tales of little-guy victimhood at the hands of big government or intellectual elites; liberals who say and do wacky things; and conspiracy theories that some politician has mentioned, justifying their presentation as news ("True or false—you decide"). Often the red meat is more sizzle than steak. But it leaves less time for reporting stories that may be less emotionally engaging and more fact-based.

Another criticism of Fox News is that it blends opinion and entertainment with news and thus is less trustworthy as an information source. When people talk about Fox News they are often thinking not of the news operation but of the prime-time block of opinion shows—edgy infotainment with roots in conservative talk radio. The obvious challenge to this is *The Daily Show* and other news satires, shows that are 100 percent entertainment and 98 percent partisan, at least as plainly as anything on Fox. But both the Farleigh Dickinson study and my own found *Daily Show* viewers to be exceptionally well informed, and I found similar results with audiences of other satire shows.

Essentially every criticism of the Fox News template I've mentioned applies to these series as well. They appeal to liberals and strongly confirm progressive philosophies. The writers have to focus on a subset of the news that can be made funny to their audience— and this often means prioritizing stories about the crazy things that conservatives did or said, women or minorities wronged by bigotry, and corporate rapaciousness. All this presents a skewed impression of the world, much as Fox News does. But the satire shows' viewers are among the best informed and the Fox News viewers the least informed.

To summarize, the evidence says that the Fox News effect

- is not a result of Fox News viewers tuning out other sources of news and opinion (because they don't);
- is not caused by the network's conservative spin (compare with the *Wall Street Journal*); and
- is not a result of the blending of news, opinion, and entertainment (compare with *The Daily Show*).

The mystery remains—why are Fox News viewers so poorly informed?

National Public Radio listeners are among the most knowledgeable of media audiences. Like BBC Radio 4, NPR's news coverage is notable for having more foreign news than is usual for American media. It has a centre-liberal slant that must be described as subdued next to Fox News' bravado. NPR has an opinion show, *Left, Right, & Center*, that gives equal time to all three perspectives without making any look ridiculous.

Two important features of NPR may be too obvious to bear mentioning. It's *public*, and it's *radio*.

Because NPR is non-profit, ratings matter less than they do at a commercial network. There is not the same pressure to attract every possible listener. This gives NPR the freedom to be…well, what many consider boring. It covers political stories lacking a simplistic hook; it covers economics, sports, science, technology, and high culture. There is less celebrity news than elsewhere. NPR doesn't try too hard to push buttons or give listeners what they want.

That's not to say that NPR ignores its audience. But the network's funding model encourages listeners and donors to take the long view. Twice-a-year pledge drives ask listeners to consider how valuable their NPR station's programming has been to them over the previous six months. Much of the network's funding comes from philanthropic foundations that take an even longer perspective. That contrasts with the commercial model, in which audience sizes for every segment and show are known with precision and dictate ad prices.

Both NPR and Fox News were created for those who felt under-served by existing media. The mechanics of exercising choice are different, though. The Fox News viewer has a remote. Should a story not connect on a gut level, hundreds of other options are a button press away. Radio is different. Many listeners are driving a car and don't have the attention or inclination to station-surf. In many markets NPR stations have a near monopoly on serious journalism.

Radio is among the least customizable of media. There is no fast forward, no Sky+ box, no aggregation algorithm. The radio audience is a relatively captive one that listens to whatever the programmers decree. And in NPR's case, the programmers decree a reasonably balanced survey of the day's news. Spend an hour listening, and you'll learn a lot of material you wouldn't necessarily have chosen to learn.

You might say that NPR is like the diet at a spa. You eat what's put before you, and it's good for you. The experience of watching the news on TV is more like an all-you-can-eat buffet. You choose how to fill your plate. There's a lot of red meat on offer because that's what most people choose. There may not be much broccoli because few choose it—not when spare ribs and ice cream are available. The spa diet ends up being healthier, and the NPR listener ends up absorbing more facts than the Fox News viewer does.

"Don't watch the news," advised entrepreneur Bert Gulick. "If there's anything you need to know, someone will call you and tell you about it." Those words have become a rallying cry, seconded by motivational speakers and almost anyone who's successful or aspires to be. Empowered by new digital tools and a new culture of entitlement, we graze information the way whales graze plankton. We expect knowledge to find us, to end up in our filters.

Tech pundits have long touted the customization possible with digital media. Our social nets and news aggregators let us tailor information streams to our work and our off-hours interests as we presently conceive them. Increasingly, our sources of information are purged of the irrelevant, the dull, and the uninteresting.

My findings suggest that those who aspire to be well informed should not overdo the customization of news. Here's a chart showing the results of another general-knowledge quiz, consisting of fifteen questions. The results broadly agree with the survey shown in the bar chart. But this time, I've grouped the results by type of news medium to show how much the medium matters. Those who don't follow the news are among the least knowledgeable of all (far left). They are followed, in approximate ascending order of knowledge, by the audiences for TV news shows and news channels; Internet news aggregators, blogs, and social networks; radio news; newspapers and books; and, finally, satirical TV news shows in the *Daily Show* mould. The latter scored so much higher than other TV news sources that I broke them out separately.

Print and Radio News Audiences Are Better Informed

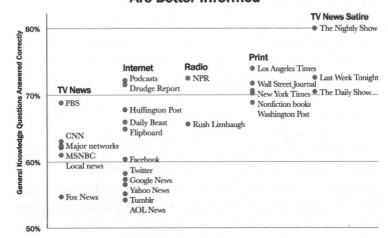

I mentioned being surprised to find the large differences in knowledge, given that almost everyone listed multiple sources of news. A closer look at the data shows a reason for that. Those who follow one "low-information" news source tend to follow others and are less likely to follow high-information sources. Those who follow one high-scoring source usually follow other high-scoring sources.

This isn't so unusual. It's like the observation that someone who has seen the *Spider-Man* films is likely to have seen the *Iron Man* films as well but may be less likely to have seen many Bergman films.

Consider the *Wall Street Journal*. Slightly more than half of *Journal* readers said they also read the *New York Times* (fifty-three percent). In contrast, only six percent of Fox News viewers read the *Times*. A quarter of *Journal* readers listen to NPR, while few Fox viewers do (twenty-seven versus eight percent).

In fact, about half of *WSJ* readers (forty-seven percent) watch Fox News. But the favour isn't returned. Only eleven percent of Fox viewers said they read the *WSJ*.

For nearly all its readers, the *Wall Street Journal* is a supplement. They read the *Journal* for financial news and seek general news somewhere else. That alone betokens a commitment to staying informed. So does the fact that there's a charge for reading the *Journal*, both online and in print.

Fox News viewers as a whole seem to be more casual in their news gathering. They do a lot of channel surfing and consult Facebook and other Internet sources. These are sources that, like Fox News itself, correlate with low knowledge levels.

Audience studies have shown a divide between viewers of twenty-four-hour news channels and viewers of old-fashioned prime-time news shows. The typical network news viewer watches the evening round-up and supplements it with rolling news now and then. The typical rolling-news viewer may watch several channels but is less likely to watch a big-three network's evening round-up. Rolling-news viewers may regard prime-time shows as quaint and obsolete. But those shows present a reasonable summary of the world in thirty minutes. Rolling-news viewers—who often spend more time watching news than their counterparts—miss the curated overview as they flip from channel to channel.

In general the audiences for new, highly customizable media scored lower than those of less customizable media. Among Internet sources, news aggregators such as Google, Yahoo, and AOL scored especially low.

Another approach to custom news is social networks. Facebook and Twitter use friends and trusted sources to suggest personally relevant content. They also use analytics to favour the posts most likely to appeal to the individual user. The social networks didn't fare much better than news aggregators.

It's not hard to see why. I did a quick tally of the hundred most recent links posted on my Facebook feed. Only about five of them were "real" news—major national or international stories that would be covered in a newspaper or on a network TV newscast. Another eleven were partisan clickbait, typically about a disturbing comment made by an obscure politician I'd never heard of. These exist to reassure one side of the culture war how terrible the other side is.

The remaining eighty-four stories were about what you'd expect—celebrity news and family news; funny videos and news of the weird. Most of it was fun. But I could no more get "real" news from Facebook than from Sky Sports.

There are unstated rules to posting on Facebook. You don't post just any old link; you post only those that will get an instant reaction from your friends. They've got to be shocking or funny or heartbreaking or *something*. As a news source, Facebook is Fox News squared.

Personal news aggregators, such as Flipboard and News, an Apple app, assemble customized news stories into a digital magazine. In Flipboard you can, for instance, see a slickly designed "newspaper" page made out of the news stories on your Facebook or Twitter account. (But maybe you don't want to.) Flipboard is addictive and more visually appealing than traditional news aggregators. Yet it, too, scored poorly in knowledge surveys.

Newspaper publishers are all too aware of the fact that social-network audiences consume news differently. Incoming links supply exposure—readers from all over the globe may discover a newspaper's articles and opinion pieces that way. Few such readers graduate to reading an original news site regularly. A Pew Research Center study found that those who navigate directly to a news site visit an average of twenty-five pages. Those who enter the same site via a Facebook or Twitter link visit fewer than five pages and spend less time on a page. The social-network users are scooping up the cherries and whipped cream of the news. Then they move on to whatever catches their bird-like attention.

The highest-scoring Internet news source was podcasts. I would qualify that by saying that podcasts are really radio that happens to be delivered over the Internet. Like a radio show, a podcast is normally listened to from beginning to end with little interruption.

Newspapers, whether read in print or online, generally fared better than television news. *The Daily Show* and its spin-offs were, as I've said, TV's true outlier, scoring higher than serious news shows and channels. Despite the notion that *The Daily Show* is its viewers' only source of news, it wasn't. The average *Daily Show* viewer in my sample followed 6.5 other sources of news. Most *Daily Show* viewers said they listened to NPR (fifty-nine percent). They also got news from Facebook (fifty percent), PBS (thirty-eight percent), CNN (thirty-four percent), MSNBC (thirty-one percent), the *New York Times* (twenty-eight percent), and nonfiction books (twenty-eight percent). They were less likely than other news audiences to list news aggregators as sources.

In summary, the news sources that correlate with being well informed have several features in common.

- *They are not too customized.* The highest-scoring sources present a balanced survey of the news to audiences with the attention span to consume it in full. These audiences are willing to devote drive time to listening to NPR, to page through a print newspaper or skim all the headings in a paper's app, to listen to an entire podcast or watch a full *Daily Show* episode. It is attention span that accounts for much of the variation between media. The lowest-scoring news sources are the most customized or customizable—those that cherry-pick stories to appeal to their audiences or let the audience itself be DIY news editors.

- *They are smart.* News sources such as PBS, NPR, the *New York Times*, the *Wall Street Journal*, and *The Daily Show* attract educated people engaged by the news. Other news sources, such as TV news channels, Internet news aggregators, and social networks, have broader audiences that are less educated, on average, and sometimes less focused on the news. This accounts for much of the variance within particular types of media. If you want to be well informed, favour news sources that well-informed people follow.

- *They can be supplemental.* The *Wall Street Journal* and *The Daily Show* don't pretend to be stand-alone news sources. That's okay as long as their audiences seek out other sources.

Nutrition experts say that we should divide our plates into four imaginary quarters. Fill one quarter with meat or the equivalent, another with starches, and the remaining two with vegetables and fruits. This is a desirable balance. It looks nothing like the typical fast-food meal of a hamburger, a giant Pepsi, and… does ketchup count as a vegetable?

We sometimes have a hard time striking a balance between instant gratification and long-term consequences. Fast food isn't so cheap if it means you have to have a heart bypass operation in twenty years. Our sources of information are subject to the same market forces that have shaped the Western diet (well, except for NPR, which received $200 million from Joan Kroc, widow of McDonald's founder Ray Kroc, in 2003).

The most informative news sources embody the divide-your-plate philosophy. There are slots for national news, international news, pop culture, high culture, technology, health, and sports. The size of these slots has more to do with an editor's or producer's notion of an ideal balance than with what the audience wants or thinks it wants. By the prevailing philosophy of media, news sources such as NPR, the *New York Times,* and the *Wall Street Journal* are throwbacks—"elitist" gatekeepers that make little use of customization and crowdsourcing. They are also most effective at informing their audiences.

The Popcorn Gets Eaten

It is one thing to talk of having a rational, balanced information diet. But no one I know gets news exclusively from newspapers or public radio. Only a media hermit can avoid news channels, social networks, and news aggregators. With them comes the ever-present temptation to click on news links. I work in front of a screen, as do many of us. This is like sitting in front of a bowl of popcorn. The popcorn gets eaten.

The website DigitalDetox.org, which organizes Internet-free retreats for corporations, claims that:

- The average American dedicates 30% of leisure time to perusing the Web...

- One out of ten Americans report depression; heavy Internet users are 2.5 times more likely to be depressed...
- The average employee checks 40 websites a day, switching activities 37 times an hour, changing tasks every two minutes...

Too much work time and playtime are devoted to unsatisfying searches for information. But I suspect that the "digital detox" route, like all crash diets, is of limited value. We live in a media-rich age and must find ways to work with it, not against it.

I have grappled with this problem over the past couple of years. In that time I have tried to improve my own media diet in accordance with what I've learned from surveys. The following are a few techniques that have worked for me.

No news source is good or bad in isolation. It's how it fits together with other news sources. Just as dieters find it best to cut down on snacking and plan balanced meals, anyone who cares about being informed should set aside time for one or more high-quality news source: a good newspaper, or a radio or TV news show. The most important thing you get from this daily ritual is the big picture.

Customization is a baby that shouldn't be thrown out with the bathwater. It's great when it directs you to stories of personal interest that you wouldn't find otherwise. It's bad only when it encourages you to live in a bubble of stated preferences. My strategy is to make the most of customization but avoid using customized sources as substitutes for better news sources.

The part of Facebook that's valuable to me is the news of friends and family—milestones, travels, and photos. I focus on that and ignore the news links, as I've got better sources of news.

The Google News home page is divided into newspaper-style sections—headings such as "Top Stories," "World," "Technology," and "Suggested for You." The only one I care about is "Suggested for You." It appears for anyone who has a Google account and is logged in. Click on "Suggested for You," and you'll get a page of bespoke news stories that Google's algorithms have decided you'll want to see. A widget with sliders lets you improve the selection by telling Google what sorts of topics and news sources you like or prefer to avoid. You can add specific key words, such as the name of a sports team, a celebrity, a political philosophy, or a video game. I bookmark the "Suggested for You" page so I can navigate directly to it without having to stop on the home page.

Information is being consumed on screens that are getting smaller and smaller. Were the size of a typical print newspaper measured diagonally, as screens are, it would be twenty-five inches. Much of the reading public migrated from that to fifteen-inch laptops to ten-inch tablets to five-inch phones in just a few years.

Designers are still exploring how best to fit news content to small screens. Inevitably solutions involve seeing less content at a glance as well as more scrolling and other methods of deliberate navigation. I used to dutifully flip through every page of a print newspaper, even sections that didn't interest me. In this way I glanced at every headline, or nearly so. The paper had a beginning, middle, and an end, and it was easy to gauge progress along that linear path.

Many newspaper apps abandon linearity for a labyrinth. The newsfeed keeps refreshing as you scroll and is dishearteningly endless; the reader is expected to navigate to favoured sections and subsections, then skip back. This renders the reader a wanderer in a vast forest who may encounter the same stories many times over while never being sure that he has seen everything.

Tablet apps are usually better than phone apps for reading news. The extra size helps, as does a squarer (4:3) aspect ratio than the video-friendly 16:9.

It's not hard to foresee a future in which news apps could implement a divide-your-plate strategy. A Flipboard-like app could potentially generate a balanced news magazine, with desired proportions of serious, uncustomized news alongside the fluff. It could work as a fitness app, motivating users by keeping track of their news-viewing habits and scoring them. As you flip through the app, it could supply more pages of whatever was missing in your news diet and less of what you've been bingeing on. This wouldn't be to everyone's taste, just as fitness apps aren't, but it could be valuable for the motivated.

I have found two pain-free ways to dial down my "junk" browsing. My browser's home page used to be set to a news aggregator. That meant that every time I opened a new browser window I saw a list of headlines. I had reasoned that since there is a search box at the top of every modern browser, it's redundant to make Google.com your home page. You might as well make a news site your home page so you can multitask by getting a quick look at the latest news—right? *Wrong.* An aggregator's news is engineered to make you click. Even the most worthwhile news is a demand on time and attention. Much of the time, my work-related searches were sidetracked by a tantalizing link (that didn't lead to much of a news story).

My solution was to change my browser's preferences so that new windows open to Google.com. There are no distractions (other than the Doodles); I just type what I want in the search box and go from there. Or I choose a site from my bookmarks menu. That way I choose when I'm willing to be distracted. I don't automatically hand over my time and attention to the eyeball monetizers.

If you don't like looking at the occasional Google Doodle, you can set most browsers to open to a blank page for even less distraction.

My second trick is to put away the popcorn bowl some of the time. I permit non-essential, recreational browsing only in the afternoon and early evening, between noon and 8:00P.M. This reduces my junk browsing by almost half and eliminates a prime distraction from my mornings—my most productive time of day. My schedule also frees time in the evening for more civilized things, and I'm not exposed to the baleful blue light of screens before bedtime, to disrupt my sleep.

Do I fear missing out? No. I read the *New York Times* and the *Los Angeles Times* in the morning, so I'm well informed by breakfast. I'm then on an information fast until noon. It's not hard to stick with that because I know I'll be able to check the news and social nets, and even waste some time, in just a few hours. If there is any news I must know about to enliven my dinner conversation, I've got access to it in the afternoon.

I have thought of cutting back further—maybe even to an hour a day for non-essential browsing. But I think the eight-hour window gives me the best bang for the buck. It doesn't feel like a sacrifice, and it restores several hours a week that had been lost to clickbait.

I'll close by disposing of a bad idea. A lately popular bit of advice is to seek out news sources that challenge one's ideology. The Farleigh Dickinson survey provided no evidence that that would have done any good. It found that the lowly standing of Fox News was mainly attributable to the liberals and independents who watch the channel. You may be surprised that *any* liberals watch Fox News. They do, and they're dumber than the conservatives.

That survey asked five fairly difficult questions about domestic current events. The average Fox News viewer answered 1.04 of them correctly. The liberals among the Fox audience rated only 0.82. The conservatives answered 1.28 questions right.

The opposite pattern was seen for liberal channel MSNBC. The conservatives watching MSNBC were less informed than the liberals.

The survey couldn't say whether those watching a politically antithetical news channel were looking for balance or laughs—or whether they were so clueless that they didn't understand they'd landed on the "wrong" channel.

Opposing viewpoints are hardly in short supply. Every news source presents them. I'm not aware of any solid evidence that antagonistic political slants are a bitter medicine that is good for you. If anything, the data is consistent with the idea that people absorb more from sources compatible with their own views. Maybe life is too short to dedicate time to a news source you believe to be biased, inaccurate, or just plain annoying.

Eighteen

The Ice Cap Riddle

Following current events is more demanding than ever. Consider this puzzler, devised by Dan M. Kahan, Yale professor of law and psychology.

> Climate scientists believe that if the North Pole ice cap melted as a result of human-caused global warming, global sea levels would rise—true or false?

Got your answer? Great. Now go to the refrigerator and throw a handful of ice cubes into a glass or measuring cup. Fill the glass with water, and mark the water level with masking tape (or note it on the measuring cup). Set it aside. Check the water level when all the ice has melted. You will find that the water level is exactly the same.

The North Pole ice cap is a sheet of ice floating in the Arctic Ocean. It floats for the same reason ice cubes do, because ice is less dense than liquid water. Like every other floating object, the Arctic ice pack displaces its own weight in the water. As it melts, the effect on the world's ocean levels is…zilch. The correct answer to Kahan's puzzle is "false." (Climate scientists predict sea levels will rise due to the melting of ice on land—mostly Antarctica and Greenland—and the thermal expansion of the oceans.)

Kahan has posed this question in surveys and found that only fourteen percent get it right. What's interesting is that liberals and conservatives are equally bad at answering it. There is a bipartisan, supermajority consensus—on the wrong answer. Needless to say, most of those liberals and conservatives have strong and antithetical opinions about climate change. Kahan's riddle demonstrates that most of those opinions are not accompanied by any deep understanding of the science involved.

True or False: You and Everyone You Know Are Idiots

Are conservatives more likely to disagree with scientific consensus than liberals are? It is not difficult to generate survey data consistent with that premise, but some perspective is in order. As always, survey results depend on the precise wording of the question.

For instance, Kahan posed a different version of a true-false question to each of two randomized groups:

A. Human beings, as we know them today, developed from earlier species of animals.
B. According to the theory of evolution, human beings, as we know them today, developed from earlier species of animals.

There was a big difference! Barely half of the group that saw version A marked it true. More than ninety percent of the other group said version B was true. Practically everyone has absorbed the basic concept of natural selection. It's hard to miss, given that it's an omnipresent theme of cartoons, science shows, and religious tracts. But a survey taker who asked only version A would find the public much less informed than one who asked only version B. And mainly it would be the conservative public that was less informed.

Both conservatives and liberals are happy to claim that science is on their side—when it is and, sometimes, when it's not. But that's an ex post facto justification. Rarely do scientific facts determine a choice of political philosophy. What is demonstrable is that people tend to echo the beliefs of those around them. They don't always accept a scientific consensus because many of those they trust most—neighbours, colleagues, clergymen, and political leaders—tell them, in Kahan's words: "If you are one of us, believe this; otherwise we'll know you're one of them." On politically sensitive topics, then, survey results are, at least partly, expressions of community and culture. "Obviously," as Kahan says, "no one will answer 'true' when asked, 'true or false—you and everyone you are intimately connected to are idiots?'"

The North Pole ice pack question asks what climate scientists believe, not what the survey participant believes. Had it not done so, more conservatives would have got the question right—for the wrong reason!

Curveball questions can be helpful in assessing what the public really knows. Using that and other science questions, some tricky and others more straightforward, Kahan found that there is only a modest correlation, overall, between knowledge of science on the one hand and belief in the threat of global warming on the other.

Kahan surveyed general science literacy using some of the questions asked in National Science Foundation polls (for example, "True or false: Lasers work by focusing sound waves…Antibiotics kill viruses as well as bacteria"). He charted the data by ideology. This produced not a hockey stick but a reclining V. The least scientifically literate, regardless of politics, have essentially identical views on

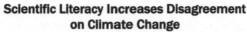

Scientific Literacy Increases Disagreement on Climate Change

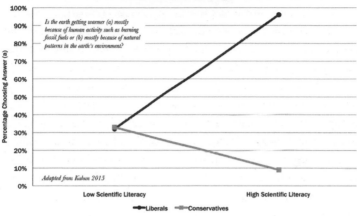

Is the earth getting warmer (a) mostly because of human activity such as burning fossil fuels or (b) mostly because of natural patterns in the earth's environment?

Adapted from Kahan 2015

Percentage Choosing Answer (a)

Low Scientific Literacy — High Scientific Literacy

Liberals — Conservatives

climate change. About thirty percent of this group say that human activity is warming the globe.

Increasing knowledge causes people to diverge in their opinions. The more that liberals know about science, the more likely they are to say that humans are causing climate change. The more that conservatives know about science, the *less* likely they are to believe in human-caused climate change.

How can this possibly be? It appears that many of the science-savvy use their knowledge to justify to themselves what they wanted to believe all along. They have often educated themselves about climate change, starting with (and sometimes ending with) popularizations congenial to their political views. They are likely to find validation in scientific uncertainties (there are many) and to characterize their opponents as knee-jerk partisans who don't know the science (most are!).

Kahan's chart is deeply disturbing. We would like to think that the ignorant may believe all sorts of crazy things but that knowledge brings us closer to consensus. If only everyone could be scientifically literate and culturally literate, the world would be a more harmonious place...Kahan's research disputes that optimism.

The issue is not just rational ignorance (remaining ignorant because the cost of acquiring knowledge outweighs the benefits) but something deeper. To form opinions on the scientific and technical issues driving public policy today—climate change, Net neutrality, stem cell research, genetically modified organisms—it is not enough to learn some facts. One must deliberate over those facts and actively seek out evidence that challenges what one wants to believe or initially suspects to be true. This is not something that many average citizens have the time or inclination to do. We fake our opinions, going along with the crowd (our crowd). Kahan warns that:

> this style of reasoning is collectively disastrous: the more proficiently it is exercised by the citizens of a culturally diverse democratic society, the less likely they are to converge on scientific evidence essential to protecting them from harm.

Deliberative Democracy

The poorly informed are not only less informed, they also deliberate less than the well informed do. Yet they believe themselves knowledgeable and come to hold firm opinions on the issues of the day. Because the ignorant and undeliberative are a plurality or even a majority, the crowd is less wise than it might be.

These aren't new worries. In 1787, the aristocratic James Madison warned that the average American was too ill informed to direct the nation's policy. It was necessary, he wrote, "to refine and enlarge the public views, by passing them through the medium of a chosen body of citizens." These chosen bodies included Congress and the Electoral College, charged with doing the learning and thinking that their constituents wouldn't undertake. These bodies would decide how best to vote on the public's behalf.

Madison's republican ideal failed to anticipate the enduring populist slant of the American electorate and the ways that future technologies would promote populism. One example is the basis of this book's research: polling, a practice that keeps getting easier and more prevalent.

In 1936 George Gallup predicted that Franklin Roosevelt would win over Alf Landon in the presidential election. Gallup was not the first pollster. He triumphed over the better-known and longer-established *Literary Digest* poll, which predicted a landslide for Landon. Gallup's poll had fifty thousand respondents, a huge number by today's standards. But *Literary Digest* had two million. The difference was that the magazine's respondents were not representative of the great mass of voters. David (George Gallup) beat Goliath by trying harder to be representative.

In the afterglow of his 1936 triumph, Gallup did what disruptive innovators generally do. He spun his brave new product as a return to an old-fashioned way of doing things, only better.

> Today the New England town meeting idea has, in a sense, been restored. The wide distribution of daily newspapers…the almost universal ownership of radios… and now the advent of the sampling referendum which produces a means of determining quickly the response of the public to debate on issues of the day, have in effect created a town meeting on a national scale.

Though we like to say that the only poll that counts is the ballot box, no politician believes it. Poll numbers become self-fulfilling prophecies. They create the sense of inevitability (or futility) that shapes who raises money, gets on the ballot, and wins the election. The omnipresent role of polling in the media, and the populist faith in direct democracy, motivated the adoption of ballot referenda. We vote for gastropubs and reality-show contestants, and now for laws, with much the same lack of attention and discernment.

Madison had a point, though. In our century, as in his, most voters are unschooled on the issues and the facts needed to put them in perspective. Political leaders have not always been much better informed. Campaigns become exercises in miseducating the public.

Cynics say that low-information voters will never be otherwise. The subtext is that such voters are lacking in mental capacity as well as knowledge. But there is evidence that the poorly informed *can* learn, given the chance and a gentle nudge. Dunning and Kruger demonstrated that. After one of their logic tests, they brought back some of the lowest scorers for a crash course in logical reasoning. It worked. Not only did their logic skills improve, they were also able to recognize their former ignorance. After the tutoring, they had much more realistic (lower) estimates of how well they had done on the original test. "One way to make people recognize their incompetence is to make them competent," Dunning and Kruger wrote. "Of course, and herein lies the paradox, once they acquired the metacognitive skills to recognize their own incompetence, they were no longer incompetent."

There is an interesting proposal for dealing with rational ignorance, the Dunning–Kruger effect, and distorted mental maps. It is known as *deliberative polling*. In 1996 several Texas electric companies contacted then University of Texas professor James S. Fishkin with a problem. A new regulation required that the utilities consult with customers when planning new power plants. They were facing two big questions. First, should they emphasize conservation, or should they move ahead with new plants? Second, should they build fossil-fuel plants or pursue solar and wind power, which are better for the environment but considerably more expensive?

In the past, the Texas electric companies had held public meetings on such matters. They knew what to expect. There would be a claque of environmentalists, another of climate-change deniers, and another of angry customers going ballistic at any talk of a rate hike. There would be radical libertarians, Nimbys, chambers of commerce, birders, and just about everyone except "real people." It's anyone's guess whether well-organized special interests speak for anyone else. They certainly speak past each other.

One alternative would be an opinion poll. The drawback is that many "opinions" are invented on the spot to satisfy a pollster. Political scientist George Bishop once demonstrated this by asking people whether they favoured repeal of the "Public Affairs Act of 1975." There was no such act. But thirty percent took the bait and offered an opinion. Bishop found that the less educated were more likely to claim an opinion.

The issues of planning energy capacity are complex, technical, and tedious. The public is rationally ignorant on how much a coal plant costs relative to a wind turbine farm and how this affects rates, the environment, and economic growth. Poll questions would have to resort to shorthand, and the result might depend on wording. All that many would hear would be political dog whistles such as "sustainable" and "free market."

A third possibility was a focus group. A small group of "real people" could be brought together at a table to express their concerns and opinions. The group setting allows for the presentation of background information, and the group can discuss the issues. But focus groups are too small to have statistical significance. The discussion tends to be dominated by one or two self-appointed leaders.

The utilities were interested in an alternative that Fishkin had described in 1988. He called it a deliberative poll: "The idea…is to find out what people would think if they really had a good chance to think about it."

A deliberative poll is an opinion poll followed by a large focus group that's closer to the size of a town meeting and that doubles as a crash course in facts. At the end of this meeting, the group answers the same questions asked in the original poll. The point is to see whether opinions have changed after exposure to facts, thought, and opposing viewpoints.

The Texas utilities agreed to Fishkin's idea. They paid to hold the initial poll and bring a subset of participants to a Dallas hotel for deliberation. The participants were given fact sheets on the issue, created with the participation of stakeholders. Each side was allowed to present all the facts and arguments relevant to its case (though it was asked not to censor the other side's facts and arguments). Much as they would at a convention, the participants met in small discussion groups with moderators and then in a full session where they could question officials and other parties.

In the original poll, fifty-two percent said they were willing to pay higher electricity bills for sustainable energy. This increased to eighty-four percent by the end of the meeting—for the group that had met and deliberated. Those willing to pay extra for conservation measures also increased, from forty-three to seventy-three percent.

Which poll number is "real"—the first one or the one after the meeting? Both are real. They measure different things. The after-deliberation opinion is the more reasoned one, however. To deny its validity, you would have to say that opinions based on knowledge and thought aren't real opinions and that the only authentic opinions are those based on ignorance and instinct.

Deliberative polls allow participants to form genuine opinions. Exposure to facts is a big part of that, but so is interacting with others of differing viewpoints. Discussion and debate hone opinions more effectively than reading the most articulate op-eds. We live in an age in which such interactions happen less often than they did in the past. We talk to neighbours who watch the same news channels we do. When we must confront different views—on a plane, in a bar, at a family reunion—we have learned the survival tactic of changing the subject. That deprives us of the town-meeting dynamic, in which views may be reconsidered and refined—and occasionally changed—by listening to others' views.

Modern democracies are modelled on those of ancient Greece. Overlooked is the most radical innovation of Athenian democracy: random sampling. In Athens, most officials and legislative bodies were chosen by lot. The goal was *not* to elect the best persons for the job(s) but rather to achieve a representative sample of the citizens.

Today we use random sampling for juries. For parliaments, it would be unthinkable. Deliberative polling is a new twist on the Athenian idea. The initial poll uses a random sample of the public. A random subset of that—about three hundred to five hundred people—is invited to meet and deliberate.

In ancient Athens, the random sample's decisions were law. In modern democracies they're not and never will be. You can say the same for opinion polls. These surveys are unofficial, private-sector efforts with no status whatsoever in law. Yet we've come to appreciate that well-designed polls are reported in the media and have become part of the political conversation. Fishkin hopes that deliberative polls could become part of that conversation, too. They send a message to voters and leaders that opinions are contingent on knowledge and deliberation and that thoughtful assessment of facts favours some policies over others. Politicians must always justify their actions to constituents, e.g. "I voted for that bill because polls say sixty percent of people in my district support it." Deliberative polls offer leaders a little more basis for favouring smart, realistic solutions over dumb ones.

The change in opinion during deliberative polls can be particularly striking with "marshmallow test" issues of long-term trade-offs. In a typical opinion poll many say they are unwilling to make *any* sacrifice now for future rewards. But rational public policy often demands just such a long-term perspective.

An interesting case in point was California's 2012 ballot initiative Proposition 31. Fishkin helped devise it, using deliberative polling. The poll and discussion presented thirty potential reforms to California law. Six received strong approval. These were packaged into Proposition 31, the Government Performance and Accountability Act.

One reform was a requirement that the state's legislature could not pass (certain types of) bills increasing spending or decreasing taxes *unless* the legislators also had a way to pay for the extra costs or loss of revenue.

This provision was neither liberal nor conservative. It was realistic. You don't decide to buy a car or a condo unless you know the price. You don't decide to quit your job without thinking about how you'll pay your bills without a salary. Why should a spending programme or a tax cut be any different? Legislators ought to vote on a law and its cost as a total package.

Little in our present system encourages this way of governing. Liberals know it's easy to get support for the government giving out free stuff. Conservatives know the public loves free tax cuts. Both know the piper must be paid (eventually), but they have different ideological ways of rationalizing the consequences away. Conservatives believe in "starving the beast." Cut taxes now, and when the government runs out of money, spending will have to be cut—somehow, and presumably without political consequences for those who cut taxes. Liberals believe that entitlements, once created, will never be rolled back, and that the government will eventually have no choice but to raise taxes. Both tactics are dishonest, as they separate the benefit from the cost. Neither engages with the real trade-offs.

The participants in the deliberative poll came to understand this. The California voters did not. Proposition 31 lost by a landslide, 39.5 percent to 60.5 percent. The post-mortems noted that the electorate never really understood what Proposition 31 was. It was a grab bag of reforms (not just the one I described), slotted under a vague name, resisting easy description. It struggled for publicity with ten other propositions on the California ballot that year.

Proposition 31 also received the kiss of death—an endorsement from the California Republican Party. Since the Republicans had little hope of ever passing anything in Sacramento, the limitation on tax cuts wasn't a concern. They saw Proposition 31 as a way to rein in the Democratic legislature's spending. The Democratic Party and unions opposed the measure. A sizeable fraction of the electorate probably encountered the proposition's name for the first time on their ballots. Skimming the endorsements, they voted along party lines.

Fishkin moved to Stanford in 2003, and the university now has a Center for Deliberative Democracy. It has organized more than seventy deliberative polls in twenty nations. They have covered such topics as snow removal in Sapporo, Japan; urban sprawl in Ghana; Korean unification; policy towards Roma peoples in Bulgaria; and the spending of natural gas revenues in Tanzania.

Deliberative polls are expensive compared to regular polls. A sponsor has to foot the bill for hundreds of participants' travel and hotel costs. But for important policy issues, this cost can be trivial. Think of all the money that has been spent trying to convince the public about climate change. A deliberative poll that supported one side could be a cheap investment—assuming it convinces.

It's possible to feel that politics has become too polarized for deliberative polling to make a difference. Fringe ideologues, who have no hope of rallying a well-informed majority, have always banked on low-information voters staying that way. No matter how carefully a deliberative poll is conducted, some will charge bias. It will be said that those who changed their minds in the deliberative poll were brainwashed and that one side of the argument was not properly presented.

Similar charges are levelled against conventional opinion polls. Anyone who is dissatisfied with a poll's result can go out and take his or her own poll. There are hundreds of opinion polls today, left-leaning ones and right-leaning ones. The news media and the public have gained considerable sophistication in reading polls. We know that the polls that count are those with a track record for accuracy and lack of bias; we also know that weighted averages of many polls are more informative than a single poll number. The mark of a losing candidate is that she says the polls are wrong and that the only polls that can be trusted are those run by her own campaign.

Deliberative polls don't have to convince everybody. They are most likely to influence those people across the political spectrum who don't know and haven't thought much about an issue. That's a large share of the public (as this book's surveys demonstrate). On one point all can agree: fact- and thought-based opinions are better than uninformed opinions.

Nineteen

The Fox and the Hedgehog

There is no first edition of the Greek poet Archilochus. His works survive only in fragments. A Greek sophist named Zenobius compiled a collection of proverbs containing this one from Archilochus: "The fox knows many things, but the hedgehog knows one big thing."

Otherwise unexplained, this vaguely ominous line has haunted the Western imagination. In 1953, Oxford philosopher Isaiah Berlin gave it the standard modern gloss: a hedgehog is an expert who relates everything to a central big idea, while a fox is an eclectic, open to many approaches and comfortable with contradiction.

So defined, *fox* and *hedgehog* have become inescapable buzzwords. Nate Silver adopted a fox as the logo of his *FiveThirtyEight* blog. The title of a 2014 *Wall Street Journal* article framed the rivalry of two fast-food chains as "A Modern-Day Fox vs Hedgehog." ("McDonald's, the fox in this scenario, has been firing multiple shots in all directions to stay on top...Wendy's...went full hedgehog—but instead of curling up into a spiky protective ball, it doubled down on its core burger line-up and introduced a very successful twist: the pretzel bun.")

Just about everyone who makes the hedgehog-fox distinction does so in order to celebrate the virtues of being a fox. A fox is a generalist—open-minded, fact-based, and entrepreneurial. A hedgehog is committed to a "big idea" regardless of its relevance—the man with a hammer who sees every problem as a nail. Philip Tetlock, a psychologist at the Wharton School, is famed for tracking the fallibility of expert predictions. For the most part, think-tank experts (hedgehogs) barely beat tabloid psychics in accuracy. Tetlock found that credentialled experts were no better at forecasting than "journalists or attentive readers of the *New York Times*."

This book's results make a case for a kind of foxiness. Knowledge that is general, contextual, and even superficial appears to be useful in unexpected ways.

Gather several of the kind of general-knowledge questions you'd find in a trivia game and pose them in a survey. You're likely to find that high scores correlate with high income, good health, and sometimes other positive attributes. It is probable that learning facts builds cognitive skills that cannot be acquired as readily in any other way (not even by learning "skills"). Breadth of knowledge can be useful in its own right. Our lives are a succession of small and medium-size decisions. A car owner weighs the need for a costly repair; a voter evaluates a campaign promise; a consumer decides whether to take a nutritional supplement advertised on TV. Most of these decisions will be made impulsively, with little or no research. There may not even be a conscious recognition that there is something to research. Those with broad knowledge are less likely to make horrifically bad decisions because they overlooked something and are more able to articulate what it is they don't know.

*Radon, Tiffany glass, urban homesteading, sous vide, annuity, checksum, bokeh, planned obsolescence, mise en scène...*A person with broad knowledge has heard of these terms or most of them.

The knowledge may be superficial—little more than the term and a vague sense of its context. But those who can put a word or phrase to a topic understand that there is a body of knowledge they lack. They can research it simply by typing the word into a browser. Those lacking the terms can't. Broad knowledge, in your head, is the key to unlocking the cloud.

The "Ground Zero mosque" is a media coinage for Park51, an Islamic community centre planned for a site two blocks from the World Trade Center site. In its original conception it was to be a thirteen-storey tower designed by Lebanese-American architect Michel Abboud, a crystalline postmodern riff on traditional Islamic patterning. Dedicated to interfaith understanding, the building was to include a prayer space, a performing arts centre, sports facilities, a food court, and a memorial to 9/11 victims. In 2010, after preliminary plans were announced, a group calling itself Stop Islamization of America dubbed the project the "Ground Zero mosque". Under that name it proved irresistible to the media, and it has been a topic of controversy ever since. The project has been downsized, assigned to a new architect, and reframed as an amenity of a luxury skyscraper. As of late 2015, only a relatively small Islamic centre has opened on the site. The centre's very existence is held by some to be insensitive to the victims of 9/11. Stop Islamization of America is held by others to be a hate group.

I ran a survey of ten assorted questions about science, business, geography, history, literature, pop culture, and sports. None of the questions had anything to do with Islam or terrorism or Manhattan real estate. The survey also included opinion questions, one being this:

Park51, a planned Islamic center two blocks from the World Trade Center site, has been called the Ground

Zero mosque. How do you feel about having an Islamic center so close to Ground Zero?

The fewer facts people knew, the more likely they were to object to the "Ground Zero mosque."

There were significant correlations even with individual questions. Those who couldn't say what nation America won its independence from were more likely to oppose the not-exactly-a-mosque. Ditto for those who didn't know what DC Comics villain is the "clown prince of crime." You might think that anyone who *can't* answer these questions must be a sleeper-cell operative who failed the How to Pass as an American training course. But no: inability to answer these questions is a good predictor of Islam agita.

My "Ground Zero mosque" question has no right or wrong answer. It asks how you feel. But emotions and facts tie together. Many of those most opposed to Park51 appear to lack context. They have heard the Ground Zero mosque is a terrible thing—which is to say, they are blindly accepting someone else's opinion. They may not know about the project's planned memorial to the victims of terrorism or, for that matter, about the food court. There are about 2,100 mosques in America, 250 in New York State, and two in Lower Manhattan (not counting Park51, since it's not a mosque). One of them (Masjid Manhattan) is six blocks from Ground Zero. It has been in operation since 1970. There had also been an Islamic prayer room on the seventeenth floor of the World Trade Center's South Tower.

You don't have to know any of the mosque statistics I just rattled off to deliberate. There are numerous mosques in New York City, and some must be fairly close to Ground Zero. Anybody want to bet there's not a Ground Zero Starbucks? (Google Maps shows seven Starbucks outlets about as close to Ground Zero as the Park51 site.) Maybe the proper conclusion is that Manhattan has lots of buildings, and everything is close to something else.

Throughout this book's research, I found correlations between knowledge and opinions on topical controversies. The well informed were more likely to have no problem with the Ground Zero mosque or genetically modified foods, to be sceptical of the need for a US–Mexico border fence and "trigger warnings." These are hot-button issues to which culture warriors offer knee-jerk responses. *Those with contextual knowledge are better able to think for themselves.*

Many individual facts seemed to be predictors of opinion. I found, for instance, that among British subjects, many types of factual ignorance correlated with the belief that Princess Diana had been murdered. (Incidentally, it was Gertrude Stein who wrote *The Autobiography of Alice B. Toklas.*)

Ignorance...	*Correlates with...*
Not knowing which famous document rebel barons had King John sign in 1215	Thinking Princess Diana was murdered
Not knowing what happened in the stock market in 1929	
Thinking Alice B. Toklas wrote *The Autobiography of Alice B. Toklas*	

I also asked questions about behaviour, ranging from the mundane to the purely hypothetical. Should people be allowed to smoke in pubs? Would you throw your pet off a cliff for £1 million?

Here, too, those scoring well in general knowledge tended to claim more sensible, pragmatic, and socially responsible behaviour. One survey that had Britons name their Member of Parliament— many couldn't, of course—also posed a contemporary ethical dilemma: "Suppose you run a small business that is getting unfairly negative reviews on social media. Is it proper for you to post favourable reviews of your own business under a false name?" The people who didn't know their MP were more likely to say it was OK to put up fake reviews.

In a US survey, those who said they'd vaccinate their children were more likely to know that humans didn't coexist with dinosaurs, to be able to identify the Manhattan Project as the nation's effort to build an atomic bomb, to know how many US senators there are, to understand that the United States is bigger though less populous than India, and to know that the War of 1812 came before the Civil War.

One hypothetical question was designed as a marshmallow test:

> Suppose there was a high-efficiency light bulb that cost $100 but would save $300 in electricity costs over its ten-year lifetime. Would you be willing to buy it?

As written, this is a no-brainer. A $100 (£66) investment would not only help the melting ice caps but also save the user $30 (£20) a year. That's the equivalent of a guaranteed tax-free thirty percent return on investment. The sensible answer is yes. The more knowledgeable people were about completely unrelated topics, the more likely they were to say they'd buy the light bulb.

Knowing which way to turn a screw to loosen it isn't rocket science. Ninety-three percent got it right. It nevertheless correlated with buying the light bulb—and with childhood vaccination and with using reusable bags in the supermarket. There is much to be said for the ultimate contextual knowledge, which we describe imperfectly as "common sense."

"Would you throw your pet off a cliff for £1 million?" Seven percent of the British public said they would. The percentage was double that for those who couldn't name their MP or the earth's largest ocean (in both cases, about fifteen percent said they'd toss their pet).

Ignorance...	Correlates with...
Thinking that early humans hunted dinosaurs	Refusal to vaccinate children for measles, mumps, and rubella
Thinking shrimp is kosher	Objecting to reusable bags in supermarkets
Not knowing which way to turn a screw to loosen it	Refusing to buy a $100 light bulb that would save $300
Not knowing one's Member of Parliament	Saying it's okay for business owners to post favourable online reviews of their own business under a fake name
Thinking the sun revolves around the earth	Wanting to ban full-face Islamic veils in public places
Not knowing which document King John signed in 1215	Believing that people should be allowed to smoke in pubs
Not knowing which ocean is the largest	Being willing to throw your pet off a cliff for £1 million

Another question asked,

> Would you push a button that made you a billionaire but killed a random stranger? No one else would know you were responsible for the death, and you could not be charged with a crime.

Nearly one in five said they'd push that button. Those who scored low on a general-knowledge quiz were more likely to push the button, and yes answers were almost twice as common (thirty-six percent) among those who couldn't name the year of the 9/11 World Trade Center attacks.

The foxlike philosophy of broad general knowledge is facing stiff headwinds. Our media zeitgeist favours a more hedgehog-like relation to facts. We are given digital tools that enable head-first dives into deep pools of interest while excluding everything else. The promise is that "everything else" will always be in the cloud, available on demand. Lost in this seductive pitch is that being well informed is about context as much as it is about factoids. It is the overview that permits the assessment of the particular, that offers all-important insight into what we *don't* know.

A broad and lifelong education is not just a means to achieving wealth and health (though it has a lot to do with that). The act of learning shapes our intuitions and imaginations. Known facts are the shared points of reference that connect individuals, cultures, and ideologies. They are the basis of small talk, opinions, and dreams; they make us wiser as citizens and supply the underrated gift of humility—for only the knowledgeable can appreciate how much they don't know.

The one thing you can't Google is what you ought to be looking up.

Acknowledgements

The writings of Robert N. Proctor were a big influence on the early conception of this book. Though my approach here is entirely tangential to Proctor's, his work on agnotology helped convince me of the importance of ignorance as a subject.

My research was aided in many ways by the SurveyMonkey team and the staff of the Charles E. Young Research Library at UCLA. Thanks also go to Tracy Behar, John Brockman, Kenneth Carlson, Brian Cathcart, Alex Christofi, David Dunning, Celia Harper, Ted Hill, Larry Hussar, Robert Luskin, Maureen Miles, Evan Miller, Drew Mohoric, Billy Neal, Laurie Ortiz, Caleb Owen, Hoda Pishvaie, Henry L. Roediger III, and Tony Scott.

Of course, this book would not have been possible without the cooperation of the thousands who found the time to take part in my surveys.

Notes

Epigraphs

p. vii *The only thing I ever learned in school*: Parker, 2009, 15n.

p. vii *Fourteen percent believe Goebbels said it*: The statistic is from my multiple-choice survey, conducted in the US. The survey offered six options (Goebbels, Oscar Wilde, Voltaire, Adolf Hitler, Winston Churchill, and Mark Twain). The quote does not appear in any of Goebbels's writings. It was attributed to Goebbels in a 1946 report of the House Un-American Activities Committee and has since been widely cited. The most popular guess in my survey was Mark Twain, chosen by thirty-eight percent.

Introduction: Facts *Are* Obsolete

p. 4 *I have to show you my first edition Torah*: Amy Miller, "New J-Lo Movie Makes 'First Edition "Iliad"' a Thing," *Legal Insurrection*, February 4, 2015: bit.ly/1aKNK0j.

p. 4 *was not something I wrote*: Hillin, 2015.

p. 4 *Sold at Sotheby's for £25,000*: Sotheby's, Auction Results, Music, Continental Books, and Manuscripts, June 5, 2013: bit.ly/1GLJ06l.

p. 5 *We were just batting around ideas*: Itzkoff, 2011.

1. "I Wore the Juice"

p. 9 *I wore the juice*: Morris, 2010.

p. 10 *WOW*: David Dunning, interview with author, June 12, 2015.

p. 11 *Gun hobbyists study*: Ehrlinger, Johnson, Banner, et al., 2003.

p. 11 *One need not look far*: Dunning and Kruger, 1999, 1132.

p. 12 *Unskilled and Unaware of It*: Dunning and Kruger, 1999.

p. 12 *is someone we've all met*: David Dunning, interview with author, June 12, 2015.

p. 12 *John Cleese's YouTube video on Dunning–Kruger*: bit.ly/1os8vxN.

p. 13 *To achieve the required standard to be licensed*: Rosen, 2014.

p. 15 *Modern research indicates*: Wagstaff, 2013.

p. 15 *Seven states have put cursive writing back in curriculum*: Wagstaff, 2013.

p. 15 *Should schoolchildren be taught*: Cathcart, 2009.

p. 16 *Now, what I want is, Facts*: Dickens, 1859. The quote is from the first paragraph of the first chapter.

p. 17 *the network of information*: Hirsch, 1987, 2.

p. 17 *How do you get to Central Square?*: Krauss and Glucksberg, 1977.

p. 17 *Yes, well you go down on the subway*: Hirsch, 1987, 4.

p. 18 *42 states and DC*: Boylan, 2014.

p. 19 *We don't ever want to educate*: Ibid.

p. 19 *Bizarre homework assignments*: For examples, see the Facebook page "Common Core Crazy Homework," on.fb.me/1EetjGk.

p. 20 *Survey on Common Core first-grade curriculum*: This was multiple choice, most questions having four options plus "don't know."

p. 21 *2010 Pew survey*: Pew Research Center, "Who Knows What About Religion," September 28, 2010, pewrsr.ch/1pD7bxq.

p. 21 *Kent State and Colorado State study*: Tauber, Dunlosky, Rawson, et al., 2013.

p. 21 *What is the last name*: Ibid.

p. 22 *ETS figures*: Educational Testing Service, 2015, 17.

p. 22 *despite having the highest levels*: Coley, Goodman, and Sands, 2015, 2.

p. 23 *Eighty-six percent of Americans under thirty*: Nielsen, 2014. Figures for China, Russia, and Brazil: Pew Research Center, 2014.

p. 23 *Most Millennials don't know*: Most are based on my own surveys with US participants. For others, see Tauber, Dunlosky, Rawson, et al., 2013.

p. 24 *Rational ignorance*: Downs, 1957, 244–46 and 266–71.

p. 25 *8 Degrees with the Worst Return on Investment*: An actual Salary.com feature: bit.ly/1e7g5cz.

p. 27 *Study of museum photos*: Henkel, 2013.

p. 28   *Research shows source memory is fallible*: Zachs, 2015.

p. 29   *Stroop experiment with hungry subjects*: Wegner and Ward, 2013, 80.

p. 29   *Trivia experiment with brand names*: Wegner and Ward, 2013.

p. 31   *Third-most-popular search containing "my penis"*: Stephens-Davidowitz, 2015.

p. 31   *Professional memorizer of Greco-Roman times*: Nestojko, Finley, and Roediger, 2013, 321.

p. 31   *As part of a plea agreement*: Quoted in Kaczynski, 2013.

p. 32   *The graduate students still see literary theft*: Fisher, 2015.

p. 32   *Study at Harvard*: Wegner and Ward, 2013, 61.

p. 33   Annie Hall *bit*: The McLuhan clip is on YouTube at bit.ly/1Dlq4dD.

p. 34   *84 percent of Americans use Internet*: Google Public Data: bit.ly/152hP8f.

p. 37   *Age differences*: The correlation between age and correct answers had a *p* value of <.001 in all three cases. (Don't know what a *p* value is? I explain it on page 108.) Sample size was 207 for senators; 445 for Brazil.

2. A Map of Ignorance

p. 38   *Susan Sherman barred from school*: Bittenbender, 2014.

p. 39   *Forty-six percent of Britons can find Austria*: Sample size of 111. The error for the Austria figure is plus or minus 9.1 percent.

p. 39   *Cartograms*: I used the proportion of incorrect responses as a density in the Gastner-Newman diffusion-based algorithm. The software was ScapeToad.

p. 43   *Only five percent*: The sample size for the US map surveys was just over one hundred. For the Republic of the Congo, the error was plus or minus 4.3 percent—nearly as big as the value itself.

p. 43   *Eighteen percent think Amazon is in Africa*: National Geographic Education Foundation, 2006.

p. 43   *Americans are far from alone in the world*: National Geographic Education Foundation, 2006, 6.

p. 44   Harvard Crimson *survey*: Lexi M. Del Toro and Bessie X. Zhang, "Roving Reporter: Canada," November 18, 2013: bit.ly/1DK92YL.

p. 44   *1.9 percent*: Tauber, Dunlosky, Rawson, et al., 2013, 1129.

p. 44   *Nine percent don't know what country New Mexico is in*: The question was multiple choice with five options (United States, Mexico, Texas, Guatemala, and South America). The United States was chosen by 91.5 percent with error of plus or minus 3.3 percent. Sample size was 282.

p. 44 *Which of the cities*: National Geographic Education Foundation, 2006, 56.

p. 46 *Impressively strong*: $p<.001$ for correlation between knowledge and border-fence support. When education and age are included in a linear regression, knowledge is still highly significant in predicting border-fence support: $p=.002$.

p. 46 *2.25 out of 10*: These figures are from a linear regression in which age and education are held constant at thirty-five years old and four years of university.

p. 46 *Those who couldn't find Ukraine wanted a border fence*: $p<.001$. Though there was a similar pattern with North Carolina, the data was not statistically significant ($p=.277$). This survey had 228 subjects.

p. 46 *Dinosaur question and border-fence support*: $p<.001$.

p. 46 *Those who said true wanted border fence*: The average border-fence rating was 7.31 out of 10 for true and 4.51 for false.

p. 47 *Survey on UK debt*: sample size of 110.

p. 50 *2006 survey on US population*: National Geographic Education Foundation, 2006.

p. 51 *net worth...defined as the total value*: Norton and Ariely, 2011, 9.

p. 53 *Seniors have eighteen times the wealth of young adults*: Schrager, 2014.

p. 54 *top twenty percent of earners makes just over half of total income*: Statista, "Shares of Household Income of Quintiles in the United States from 1970 to 2014": bit.ly/1PkkUng.

p. 55 *Survey of CEO and worker income*: Kiatpongsan and Norton, 2014.

p. 55 *Given the consensus among disparate groups*: Norton and Ariely, 2011, 12.

p. 56 *Just over half support gun rights*: Kohut, 2015.

p. 56 *Decline in crime rate; Pew poll*: Cohn, Taylor, Lopez, et al., 2013.

p. 59 *Desvousges and his colleagues*: Desvousges, Johnson, Dunford, et al., 1992.

p. 62 *Fifteen percent*: Ipsos MORI, 2014.

p. 63 *Fifty-six percent*: Ibid.

p. 63 *Fifteen percent unemployed*: Ibid.

p. 63 *People come into the country illegally*: Ibid.

p. 64 *[P]oll after poll shows that voters*: Romano, 2011.

p. 65 *Those who knew federal budget earned more*: $p=.005$ with a sample size of 462.

3. Dumb History

p. 67 *"Life in the UK" survey:* Sample size of 162.

p. 68 Newsweek *poll: Newsweek,* 2011.

p. 68 *Arizona law requiring students to pass citizenship test:* Wilson, 2014.

p. 75 *Contacted by Ford library:* Henry Roediger III, interview with author, March 16, 2015.

p. 75 *have never seen an airline "ticket":* Beloit College, Mindset List, 2016 list: bit.ly/1CpeE3G.

p. 76 *Memories of world events influenced by age at the time:* Koppel and Berntsen, 2014.

p. 77 *rank historical figures just as Google ranks web pages:* Skiena and Ward, *Time,* 2013.

p. 79 *Error bars:* Sample sizes were around 160. Error bars for figures recognized by about half the sample were plus or minus eight percent.

p. 81 *Thirty percent knew who proposed theory of relativity:* Tauber, Dunlosky, Rawson, et al., 2013, 1123.

p. 81 *a disease of white people:* Gewertz, 2007.

p. 81 *Memory experiment on three wars:* Zaromb, Butler, Agarwal, and Roediger, 2013.

p. 82 *"Einstein" insanity quote in The Basic Text of Narcotics Anonymous:* See bit.ly/1e0891p; Matt Novak, "9 Albert Einstein Quotes That Are Totally Fake," *Paleofuture,* March 14, 2014: bit.ly/17hHKK7; Brown, 1983, 68.

p. 82 *Churchillian drift:* The term was coined by British writer and broadcaster Nigel Rees. See Peters, 2009.

p. 84 *radically revisionist view of American history:* Deam, 2014.

p. 84 *I've had kids tell me:* Ibid.

p. 85 *Colorado school board policy:* Townes, 2014.

p. 85 *early American history to be less about the Pilgrims:* Kurtz, 2014.

p. 85 *Oklahoma committee banned AP history course:* Legum, 2015.

p. 85 *Entitled to land of "less advanced" people:* Cave, 1996, 35–36.

p. 86 *Roediger "cringed" at American estimates:* Henry Roediger III, interview with author, March 16, 2015.

p. 87 *Positive and factual textbook about Hitler:* See Philipp Bouhler's *Kampf um Deutschland: Ein Lesebuch für die Deutsche Jugend* [The Battle for Germany: A Textbook for the German Youth] (Munich: Zentralverlag der NSDAP, Franz Eher Nachfolger, 1938). A partial translation is online at bit.ly/1fG9qfC.

4. The One-in-Five Rule

p. 89 Huffington Post *article*: Luippold, 2010.

p. 89 *2014 survey*: Anti-Defamation League, 2014.

p. 91 *Results by nation*: I have presented the ADL data a little differently from the way it's presented on the organization's website. The site reports that ninety-three percent of Germans had heard of the Holocaust and that, of that group, eleven percent thought it had been exaggerated. I think it's more useful to be able to compare those who've never heard of the Holocaust to those who deny it or think it's exaggerated. Thus the given values for multiple-choice questions have been multiplied by the number who had heard of the Holocaust. Percentages don't always add up to 100 percent because of rounding.

p. 93 *Debunkings of the "ten-percent myth"*: See, for instance, Boyd, 2008.

p. 94 *Princess Diana study*: Wood, Douglas, and Sutton, 2012.

p. 94 *The Apollo moon landings never happened*: Lewandowsky, Gignac, and Oberauer, 2014, 2–3.

5. The Low-Information Electorate

p. 96 *It's hard to think of a major policy dispute*: Krugman, 2015.

p. 96 *The Democratic party's electoral majority*: Carl, 2013.

p. 96 *a big chunk of America's body politic*: Krugman, 2015.

p. 96 *Many liberals have a deeply ideological view*: Carl, 2013.

p. 97 *Judge Janavs lost to bagel store owner*: Garvey and Garrison, 2006.

p. 97 *You know the most frightening thing*: Garrison, 2006.

p. 98 *Vice president result better than some surveys*: Pew Research Center, "Who Knows What About Religion," September 28, 2010, pewrsr.ch/1pD7bxq.

p. 99 *No meaningful difference between politics and knowing elected officials*: $p=.742$. My sample was small, however, at 110.

p. 99 *2014 survey*: Annenberg Public Policy Center, 2014.

p. 99 *Our Constitution declares that "all men"*: Dooley, 2014.

p. 99 *Thomas Paine wrote that "the duty of a patriot"*: Gorman, 2015.

p. 99 *You're the state*: Ramer, 2011.

p. 99 *The last time I checked*: For an audio recording, go to bit.ly/1GpEhZu.

p. 100 *Twelve percent, four percent chance*: Vavreck, 2014.

p. 100 *It is tempting to think that something*: Ibid.

p. 101 *Twenty-three percent of Los Angeles voters*: Meyerson, 2014.

p. 101 Eight percent turnout for school board election: Lopez, 2014.

p. 101 Survey on voting: Ipsos MORI, 2014.

p. 102 Opinium/Observer survey: Coman and Helm, 2014.

6. Putting a Price Tag on Facts

p. 105 Post and his lottery winnings: Sullivan, 2006.

p. 106 Visitors to his crumbling mansion: Ibid.

p. 109 Spurious correlations website: tylervigen.com.

p. 110 As has been endlessly chronicled: See, for instance, the college salary report on Payscale.com.

p. 112 Score remained significant when education added to model: $p=.002$ for quiz score.

p. 112 Knowledge still a highly significant predictor: $p=.004$.

p. 116 $75,000 income: Kahneman and Deaton, 2010; Luscombe, 2010.

p. 117 No significant correlation between knowledge and happiness: $p=.371$.

p. 118 Questions from quiz: The full quiz also asked for the capital of Brazil, where a shortstop plays, the name of the Speaker of the House, the third digit of pi, and about how long it takes to double an investment at a seven percent annual return.

7. Elevator-Pitch Science

p. 119 It almost kind of looks like what the earth looks like: youtu.be/s_5j1mVE8Sk

p. 120 Science surveys: National Science Foundation, 2006.

p. 121 God created human beings pretty much: Newport, 2014.

p. 124 Disgraceful photo of recreational hunter: Luke Lewis, "A Whole Bunch of People on Facebook Thought Steven Spielberg Killed a Real Dinosaur," BuzzFeed, July 11, 2014: bzfd.it/1dzn4k0.

p. 124 15 percent believed that humans and dinosaurs coexisted: The margin of error was plus or minus 4.9 percent. Sample size was 204.

p. 125 Planets survey: Sample size was 121.

p. 126 We are made of star-stuff: Sagan wrote or mentioned this a number of times, the first apparently being in Sagan, 1973, 189–90.

p. 127 In many districts, they may have a different perspective: Candisky and Siegel, 2014.

p. 127 focus on academic and scientific knowledge: Timmer, 2014.

p. 132 Correlation to gender: p<.001; sample size, 204.

p. 132 Experiment by Ehrlinger and Dunning: Ehrlinger and Dunning, 2003.

p. 132 No significant correlation between science knowledge and income: p=.129 with sample size of 204.

p. 132 4.8 percent of workforce: John F. Sargent Jr, *The U.S. Science and Engineering Workforce: Recent, Current, and Projected Employment, Wages, and Unemployment*, Congressional Research Service, February 19, 2014: bit.ly/1amEn69.

p. 134 Pi question had correlation to income: p=.016, with sample size of 124.

p. 134 Turing-test question: Sample size was 204.

8. Grammar Police, Grammar Hippies

p. 136 47,000 Wikipedia edits correcting "comprised of": McMillen, 2015.

p. 136 Restaurant people are not writers: Black, 2008.

p. 136 I don't expect chefs to be writers: Ibid.

p. 136 GrubHub study: GrubHub, 2013; Satran, 2013.

p. 137 Misspellings of "pizza Margherita," other Italian foods: Paolo Rigiroli, "Top Misspelled," *Quattro Formaggi*, n.d.: bit.ly/1ThRAOP.

p. 137 mescaline on menu: Jane Black spotted this at the Yorktown Bistro, Arlington, Virginia.

p. 137 Fieri mispronunciation of mascarpone: Madison, 2010.

p. 139 Responses to correct and incorrect the same: The sample size was 222 for the correct menu and 215 for the incorrect one.

p. 139 Trust is something I know: Memoli, 2013.

p. 143 No correlations: Grammar quizzes had p=.605 for income and p=.086 for educational level with a sample size of 117; for age, p=.125 with a sample size of 226. The spelling quiz had p=.677 for age with a sample size of 103.

p. 143 Income failed to correlate: For spelling, p=.079 with a sample size of 103. For grammar, p=.246 with a sample size of 226.

p. 143 Earned $23,000 more a year: p=.023 with a sample size of 226. Note that the *p* value is the probability that the income is larger in the population, not that the $23,000-a-year figure is exactly right.

p. 144 FBI list of Twitter slang: Kleinman, 2014.

p. 145 Strong and negative correlation with age: It was p<.001 for both a set of eight slang questions and a set of eight acronyms and abbreviations.

p. 145 Slang and acronyms didn't correlate with income: p=.878 for acronym questions and p=.579 for slang questions. Both surveys had sample sizes of 107; for *mansplain,* it was 207.

p. 146 *The* Oxford English Dictionary *accepts both pronunciations*: O'Leary, 2013.

p. 147 *Pronunciations correlate with income*: p=.022 with a sample size of 183.

9. Nanofame

p. 148 *One way to describe Mr Jarre's life*: Bilton, 2015.

p. 149 *Turned down $1 million contract to promote "unhealthy food"*: Ibid.

p. 149 *PewDiePie makes $4 million in ad sales*: Grundberg and Hansegard, 2014.

p. 149 Californication *has been on*: January 7, 2014, post on @AnthonyDeVito Twitter feed.

p. 149 *Vine has two hundred stars with a million followers*: Williams, 2015.

p. 149 *Hi, Kanye!*: New York Post, 2013.

p. 150 *Hip-hop survey*: The sample was 261 Americans. The difference in recognition between Kanye West and Pitbull was not statistically significant. The margin of error was plus or minus 5.9 percent for West and plus or minus 5.8 percent for Pitbull.

p. 150 *Hip-hop knowledge correlated inversely with age*: p<.001. The average quiz score was about seventy percent for Millennials versus thirty percent for those over sixty.

p. 150 *Correlation to income*: p=.033. In a linear regression with age, hip-hop knowledge was no longer significant as a predictor of income; p=.371.

p. 150 *Spotify data analysis*: Kalia, 2015.

p. 151 *taste freeze; music relevance*: Ibid.

p. 152 *Celebrity endorsements*: Said, 2013.

10. Is Shrimp Kosher?

p. 155 *Jews and Mormons outscored Christians*: Pew Research Center, 2010.

p. 156 *Which of the following best describes Catholic teaching*: Ibid., 70.

p. 157 *4.6 of the Ten Commandments*: Stephen Prothero, "Religious Literacy Quiz," Pew Research Center, 2007: pewrsr.ch/1aLl9bd.

p. 157 *Americans are both deeply religious*: Prothero, 2007.

p. 157 *Bush didn't mean, and was not understood*: Sontag, 2007.

p. 158 *Believers an overwhelming majority*: Pew Research Center, 2010, 2015.

p. 159 *No matter what the results*: Pew Research Center, 2010, 4.

p. 159 *Religious knowledge had no correlations*: p=.680 for income, p=.580 for happiness, and p=.839 for being married. The sample size was 118.

p. 160 *Religious knowledge is not necessary*: Oppenheimer, 2007.

p. 160 *Last Supper and Gautama Buddha questions*: The sample size was 118.

11. Philosophers and Reality Stars

p. 161 *All art is quite useless*: In Wilde's preface to *The Picture of Dorian Gray* (1890). See e-book at bit.ly/1KfBR0J.

p. 166 *Contemporary art survey*: The sample size was 164. The margin of error for the lowest-scoring artists was about four percent.

p. 167 *Auctioned for $26 million*: Christie's, Post-War and Contemporary Art sale results, November 12, 2013: bit.ly/1Ic0g77.

p. 167 *Shibboleth names...by which the privileged*: The Tumblr blog *454 W 23rd St New York, NY 10011-2157* coined that term and supplies a list of correct pronunciations. See bit.ly/1yTivoP.

p. 168 *Correlated with income*: p=.026 with a sample size of 183.

p. 169 *Estimate of percentages who saw movies*: See box-office figures at The-Numbers.com. I'm guesstimating an average $10 ticket price.

p. 170 *Every few weeks, my wife mentions*: Greenfeld, 2014.

p. 171 *Recognizing Nabokov correlated with education*: p<.001 for education, p=.082 for income. The sample size was 119.

12. Sex and Absurdity

p. 172 *a girl is no longer clean*: Semuels, 2014.

p. 172 *Almost $1 billion on abstinence-only programs*: Audrey Tang with Matt Itelson, "Center Tests Americans' Sexual Literacy," *SF State News,* July 11, 2005: bit.ly/1OaylEz.

p. 173 *If you have sex, you will get AIDS*: Semuels, 2014.

p. 173 *Two of the curricula*: Vine, 2008.

p. 173 *The whole lesson here*: Post on @AliceDreger Twitter feed, April 15, 2015. See also Nelson, 2015.

p. 174 *Circumcision study*: Lilienfeld and Graham, 1958.

p. 174 *Seventy-nine percent of American men circumcised*: Xu, Markowitz, Sternberg, and Aral, 2006.

p. 174 *the vast majority of my female students*: Proctor and Schiebinger, 2008, 112.

p. 175 *San Francisco started programme for teens' sex questions in 2006*: Allday, 2006.

p. 176 *socioeconomic status, paranoia*: Oliver and Weed, 2014.

p. 177 *Gluten-free diet survey*: Consumer Reports, 2015, 37.

p. 177 *Jimmy Kimmel bit*: The clip is on YouTube at bit.ly/1hxnfrr.

p. 177 *Perception is reality*: Consumer Reports, 2015, 40.

p. 178 *Gluten survey*: The sample size was 151.

p. 179 *Reality is that which*: This quote comes from Dick's 1978 speech, "How to Build a Universe That Doesn't Fall Apart Two Days Later." See bit. ly/1koJyFx.

p. 180 *the knowledgeable more likely to be married*: p=.014 for the fifteen-question quiz that also asked about health.

p. 180 *Positive correlation between quiz scores and health*: p=.029.

p. 180 *Correlations to health*: These questions were on the fifteen-item quiz I discussed, and they were individually predictors of health as well. For Kant: p=.027. Sun: p=.008. The sample size was 445.

13. Moving the Goalposts

p. 182 *One in five Britons don't know number of players*: The UK sports survey had a sample size of 152. US sports survey: sample size of 154.

p. 183 *Sports knowledge correlated with income*: For UK survey, p=.039; for US, p=.009.

p. 183 *Women make eighty percent as much*: CONSAD Research Corporation, 2009.

p. 183 *Linear regression predicted incomes of £25,122 and £50,920*: This survey did not have education data, so figures represent the household incomes of a 35-year-old (of unspecified educational level).

p. 184 *Gender not significant in model*: p=.742. For sports knowledge in the model, p=.014. Both figures are from a US survey with sample size of 154.

p. 185 *Difficult quiz had no correlation to income*: p=.359 with a sample size of 104.

p. 185 *Reran the "easy" sports quiz*: In the second survey, p=.044, and the sample size was 110. The income gap was somewhat bigger: $29,511 per year (household) for those scoring zero percent versus $87,092 for those scoring 100 percent.

p. 185 *Happiness correlation to "easy" sports questions*: $p=.009$ with a sample size of 110. The regression projected an average score of 3.89 out of 10 for someone who scored zero percent versus 6.45 for someone who scored 100 percent.

p. 186 *Wimbledon question*: The sample size was 162.

p. 186 *Ted Williams question*: $p=.024$ for correlation to income. The sample size was 117.

14. Marshmallow Test

p. 187 *Eighty-four-year-old woman won $590 million*: New York *Daily News*, June 3, 2013.

p. 187 *What made me play... You pay $1*: Piore, 2013.

p. 188 *Fifty-nine percent of British adults bought lottery ticket*: British Gambling Prevalence Survey, 2010.

p. 189 *Those who answered correctly had higher incomes*: $p=.035$ with a sample size of 322.

p. 189 *Twenty-four percent happier*: The correlation between quiz score and self-reported happiness had $p<.001$.

p. 190 *2010 study of Federal Reserve Bank of Atlanta*: Gerardi, Goette, and Meier, 2010.

p. 191 *In a sale, a shop is selling*: Ibid., 11.

p. 191 *financial knowledge gap*: Maranjian, 2015.

p. 192 *rule of 72*: This financial rule of thumb says you divide 72 by the annual rate of return, in percentage points, to get the number of years it will take to double an investment. In this case you'd divide 72 by 7 to get 10.29 years. The answer is not mathematically exact, but it's close enough for investors who are usually guesstimating the rate of return anyway.

p. 193 *Reported $32,000 more income*: The correlation between the correct answer and income had $p<.001$. The sample size was 427. For savings, the correlation had $p=.012$ with a sample size of 322. Happiness ratings, on a scale of 0 to 3, were 2.091 for those who answered the compounding question correctly and 1.815 for those who didn't ($p=.004$).

p. 194 *Obesity, crack cocaine, divorce*: Casey, Somerville, Gotlib, et al., 2011; Schlam, Wilson, Shoda, 2013.

p. 195 *An uneducated individual armed with a credit card*: Pelletier, 2013, 2.

p. 195 *2013 report found that only seven states*: Pelletier, 2013.

p. 196 *Financial literacy in college*: Matthew Reed and Debbie Cochrane, "Student Debt and the Class of 2011," Project on Student Debt of the Institute for College Access and Success, October 2012: bit.ly/21wksZ2.

p. 196 *Several recent studies have poured cold water*: See S. H., 2014.

p. 196 *Follow-up study on Midwestern high school students*: Mandell and Klein, 2009.

p. 197 *No correlation between financial instruction and investment income*: Cole and Shastry, 2008.

p. 198 *Those who answered retirement-account question correctly earned more*: $p=.004$. Were happier: $p=.012$. The sample size was 322.

15. The Value of Superficial Learning

p. 201 *We are what we do*: Quoted in Sweet, 2010, 51.

p. 201 *Knowing how to spell* prerogative *correlates with* consensus: $p=.019$. With *supersede*: $p=.002$. The p values are impressive despite the modest sample size of 103.

p. 202 *Asian map test a strong predictor*: $p=.014$ with a sample size of 100.

p. 203 *Survey shown by hollow dot not statistically significant*: $p=.132$ with a sample size of 207.

p. 203 *Both "easy" surveys highly significant*: $p<.001$ with sample sizes of 228 and 207. Other "hard" survey: $p=.003$ with a sample size of 228.

p. 204 *Chess is an analogy*: LoBrutto, 1997, 19.

p. 205 *Simon and chunks of knowledge*: Chase and Simon, 1973.

p. 207 *Graham's invention of Liquid Paper*: See the entries for Bette Nesmith Graham at *Famous Women Inventors* (bit.ly/1Fn7Chu) and Wikipedia.

p. 207 *Imagination is more important than knowledge*: Einstein, 1931, 97.

p. 207 *Other examples*: For Einstein and Darwin-Wallace, see Asimov, 2014.

p. 208 *Posterior hippocampus is larger*: Rosen, 2014.

p. 208 *Money can buy better education*: Mohan, 2015.

16. When Dumbing Down Is Smart

p. 213 *mystery meat*: Mobley, 2014.

p. 216 *Young people recognize icons*: Correlation with age was steeply negative and had $p<.001$ with a sample size of 106.

p. 217 2006 study in Annals of Internal Medicine: Davis, Wolf, Bass, et al., 2006.

p. 219 Inserts are legal, not medical documents: Brown, 2014.

p. 219 145,000 measles deaths a year: This is the World Health Organization figure for 2013. See bit.ly/1myPji2.

p. 219 If it takes 5 machines 5 minutes: Frederick, 2005.

p. 220 MIT requires two semesters of calculus: See the "Admissions" page at the MIT website: bit.ly/1Qfyhfo.

p. 220 Britain replaced "avoid alcohol" warning: Paddock, 2011.

p. 220 Seventy-eight percent comprehension for deductible: Loewenstein, Friedman, McGill, et al., 2013.

p. 220 Consumer mistake of overpaying for low deductibles: Ibid., 860.

p. 221 Hard-boiled egg, steak survey: The sample size was 268.

p. 222 Ingredients in bread: The sample size was 121.

p. 222 $24,000 income difference for oysters question: p=.048 with a sample size of 267.

p. 222 Half gave the correct answer, three: The sample size was 268.

p. 223 Tool questions: The sample size was 268.

p. 223 Thirty-eight percent chose 3,000 miles: The sample size was 268.

p. 224 7,500 or ten thousand miles, Mobil guarantee: Reed and Montoya, 2014.

p. 225 Psst…this is your engine speaking: Prange, n.d.

p. 225 a marketing tactic that dealers use: Reed and Montoya, 2013.

17. Curating Knowledge

p. 227 Actor Adam Sandler is reported: See the "Celebrity Fake News Hoax Generator" story on FakeAWish.com at bit.ly/1n0YtS7.

p. 228 seems to make it harder: Miller, 2014.

p. 229 It might not be all that different: Henry Roediger III, interview with author, March 16, 2015.

p. 229 cognitive load comment: Ibid.

p. 229 I was in Paris: Brian Cathcart, interview with author, June 5, 2015.

p. 230 Quiz of twelve questions: The sample size was 458, and the Fox News score was 56.6 percent plus or minus 4.4 percent at the 95 percent confidence level.

p. 233 Tabloids are factually accurate: Should you doubt this claim, see Poundstone, 1990, 311–15. I tried to verify all the stories appearing in six weekly US tabloids. I was able to confirm all 196 *National Enquirer* stories as substantially factual. Even the *Weekly World News*, famed for made-up stories (LOVE-STARVED ORANGUTAN GOES APE FOR DWARF), was ninety-six percent factual.

p. 236 Don't watch the news: Marshall, 2013.

p. 238 Differing habits of rolling and prime-time news viewers: Vavreck, 2015.

p. 240 twenty-five pages viewed versus five pages: Ibid.

p. 242 The average American: "The Facts: Why Digital Detox?" at bit. ly/1aLo1F9. No sources are given for the statistics.

p. 246 Fox News viewers answered 1.04 questions: Farleigh Dickinson, 2012, 3.

18. The Ice Cap Riddle

p. 248 Climate scientists believe: Kahan, 2014, 22.

p. 249 14 percent got North Pole question right: Ibid., 42.

p. 250 If you are one of us: Kahan, 2012.

p. 250 Obviously, no one will answer: Kahan, 2014, 29.

p. 251 Thirty percent say it's a real threat: Ibid., 12.

p. 252 this style of reasoning: Ibid., 14.

p. 252 to refine and enlarge the public views: Quoted in Fishkin, 2006.

p. 253 Today the New England town meeting: Quoted in Fishkin and Luskin, 2005, 286.

p. 254 One way to make people recognize their incompetence: Dunning and Kruger, 1999, 1131.

p. 255 The idea…is to find out what people would think: Aizenman, 2015.

p. 256 52 to 84 percent shift, 43 to 73 percent: Fishkin, 2006.

p. 259 More than seventy polls in twenty nations: See website of the Center for Deliberative Democracy, cdd.stanford.edu.

19. The Fox and the Hedgehog

p. 261 The fox knows many things: Berlin, 1978, 22.

p. 261 Berlin's interpretation: Ibid., 23.

p. 261 McDonald's, the fox in this scenario: Gara, 2014.

p. 262 journalists or attentive readers: Tetlock, 2005.

p. 263 hate group: The Southern Poverty Law Center so terms it. See Wikipedia entry for Stop Islamization of America, bit.ly/1Q91MGd.

p. 264 *Strong correlation between knowledge and "Ground Zero mosque" attitudes*: p=.02.

p. 264 *Correlation with US independence*: p=.004. DC Comics villain: p=.004. The correct answers are Great Britain and the Joker.

p. 264 *About 2,100 mosques in the United States*: See Wikipedia entry "List of Mosques in the United States," bit.ly/1GBdPeT.

p. 264 *Masjid Manhattan is four blocks from Ground Zero*: Barnard, 2010.

p. 264 *Prayer room in World Trade Center*: Freedman, 2010.

p. 265 *Individual facts predicted opinions*: I should warn readers about *multiplicity*, a statistical hazard too little appreciated by journalists and decision makers. The convention is that a result is deemed significant when the probability of its occurring purely by random-sampling error is five percent or less. This comes from a traditional conception of science in which collecting data (and forming hypotheses) is labour-intensive. Today it is easy and cheap to collect data online and let software search for any correlations that may exist. This may be tantamount to testing thousands of potential hypotheses. In such contexts p values are less able to separate wheat from chaff. The researcher must expect to find about one "significant" but bogus correlation for every twenty hypotheses checked.

p. 265 Multiplicity is a potential concern here, as I have selected correlations that are more or less amusing and illustrative of general connections between knowledge and opinions or self-reported behaviours. I have therefore been cautious in favouring single-fact correlations with highly significant p values, representative of correlations between performance on general-knowledge quizzes and beliefs.

p. 265 *Not knowing which famous document*: p=.009, sample of 206.

p. 265 *Not knowing what happened in the stock market*: p=.038 with sample of 206.

p. 265 *Thinking Alice B. Toklas wrote*: p=.03 with sample of 206.

p. 265 *People who didn't know their MP were more likely to post fake reviews*: p=.016

p. 266 *Those who said they'd vaccinate*: p<.001 for all other cited opinions; the sample size was 207.

p. 266 *More knowledgeable, more likely to buy the light bulb*: p=.020.

p. 267 *Screw question correlated strongly*: p<.001 (would vaccinate child); p=.002 (approve reusable bags); p=.009 (would buy $100 light bulb). The sample size was 207.

p. 267 *Seven percent of the British public would throw pet*: Sample size of 206. Error was plus or minus 3.6 percent. Correlation with not knowing largest ocean and MPs had p values of .015 and .006 respectively.

p. 267 Shrimp; reusable bags: $p=.005$ with a sample size of 207 Americans.

p. 267 One in five would push the button: The exact result was 18.9 percent plus or minus 4.8 percent. Correlation to knowing or not knowing year of the 9/11 attacks has $p=.001$. The sample was 254 Americans.

Sources

Aizenman, Nurith. "It's Not a Come-On from a Cult. It's a New Kind of Poll!" NPR *Morning Edition* story, aired May 18, 2015. n.pr/1Afszii.

Allday, Erin. "Safer Sex Info Goes High-Tech." *SFGate*, April 26, 2006.

Annenberg Public Policy Center. "Americans Know Surprisingly Little About Their Government, Survey Finds." September 17, 2014. bit.ly/1IsSaqy.

Anti-Defamation League. "ADL Global 100," 2014. Global100.adl.org.

Asimov, Isaac. "Isaac Asimov Asks, 'How Do People Get New Ideas?'" *MIT Technology Review*, October 20, 2014.

Barnard, Anne. "In Lower Manhattan, 2 Mosques Have Firm Roots." *New York Times*, August 13, 2010. nyti.ms/1FNjkWV.

Berlin, Isaiah. *Russian Thinkers.* Edited by Henry Hardy and Aileen Kelly. Vol. 1 of *Selected Writings.* London: Hogarth, 1978.

Bilton, Nick. "Jérôme Jarre: The Making of a Vine Celebrity." *New York Times*, January 28, 2015.

Bishop, George F., Robert W. Oldendick, Alfred Tuchfarber, and Stephen E. Bennett. "Pseudo-Opinions on Public Affairs." *Public Opinion Quarterly* 44, no. 2 (1980): 198–209.

Bittenbender, Steve. "Kentucky Teacher Resigns Amid Parents' Ebola Fears: Report." Reuters, November 3, 2014.

Black, Jane. "Typos à la Carte, Ever a Specialty of the House." *Washington Post*, June 18, 2008.

Boyd, Robynne. "Do People Only Use 10 Percent of Their Brains?" *Scientific American*, February 7, 2008. bit.ly/1lYfJv9.

Boylan, Jennifer Finney. "A Common Core for All of Us." *New York Times*, March 22, 2014.

British Gambling Prevalence Survey, 2010. See bit.ly/1OWAuGs

Brown, Eryn. "Doctors Learn to Push Back, Gently, Against Anti-Vaccination Movement." *Los Angeles Times*, October 21, 2014.

Brown, Rita Mae. *Sudden Death*. New York: Bantam, 1983.

Campbell, Colin. "Obama Can't Stop Using Sports Metaphors to Explain Foreign Policy." *Business Insider*, May 29, 2014.

Candisky, Catherine, and Jim Siegel. "Intelligent Design Could Be Taught with Common Core's Repeal." *Columbus Dispatch*, August 20, 2014.

Carl, Jeremy. "Liberal Denial on Climate Change and Energy." *National Review*, October 23, 2013.

Casey, B. J., Leah H. Somerville, Ian H. Gotlib, Ozlem Ayduk, et al. "Behavioral and Neural Correlates of Delay of Gratification 40 Years Later." *Proceedings of the National Academy of Sciences* 108, no. 36 (September 6, 2011): 14998–15003. bit.ly/1Cg7lw6.

Cathcart, Brian. "Is Google Killing General Knowledge?" *Intelligent Life*, Summer 2009.

Cave, Alfred. *The Pequot War*. Amherst: University of Massachusetts Press, 1996.

Chase, W. G., and H. A. Simon. "Perception in Chess." *Cognitive Psychology* 4 (1973): 55–81.

Cohn, D'Vera, Paul Taylor, Mark Hugo Lopez, et al. "Gun Homicide Rate Down 49% Since 1993 Peak; Public Unaware." Pew Research Center, May 7, 2013.

Cole, Shawn, and Gauri Kartini Shastry. "If You Are So Smart, Why Aren't You Rich? The Effects of Education, Financial Literacy and Cognitive Ability on Financial Market Participation." Harvard Business School Working Paper 09-071, November 2008.

Coley, Richard J., Madeline J. Goodman, and Anita M. Sands. "America's Skills Challenge: Millennials and the Future." Princeton, NJ: Educational Testing Service, January 2015.

Coman, Julian, and Toby Helm. "Voters can't name their MEPs as poll highlights disengagement with EU." *The Observer*, May 10, 2014.

CONSAD Research Corporation. "An Analysis of Reasons for the Disparity in Wages Between Men and Women." Prepared for the US Department of Labor, January 12, 2009. bit.ly/1ie1UWk.

Consumer Reports. "The Truth About Gluten." January 2015: 37–40.

Davis, Terry C., Michael S. Wolf, Pat F. Bass III, et al. "Literacy and Misunderstanding Prescription Drug Labels." *Annals of Internal Medicine* 145, no. 12 (December 19, 2006): 887–94.

Deam, Jenny. "New US History Curriculum Sparks Education Battle of 2014." *Los Angeles Times*, October 1, 2014.

De Groot, Adriaan. *Thought and Choice in Chess*. The Hague: Mouton, 1965. Reprint of the 1946 Dutch edition.

Desvousges, William H., F. Reed Johnson, Richard W. Dunford, Kevin J. Boyle, Sara P. Hudson, and K. Nicole Wilson. ("Measuring Nonuse Damages Using Contingent Valuation: An Experimental Evaluation of Accuracy." Research Triangle Institute Monograph 92-1, 1992.

Dickens, Charles. *Hard Times—For These Times*. Originally published in 1854. A Project Gutenberg eText is available at bit.ly/1pH9ASu.

Dooley, Erin. "Oops! Va. Judge Confuses Constitution, Declaration of Independence in Gay Marriage Ruling." ABC News, February 14, 2014.

Downs, Anthony. *An Economic Theory of Democracy*. New York: Harper & Brothers, 1957.

Dropp, Kyle, Joshua D. Kertzer, and Thomas Zeitzoff. "The Less Americans Know About Ukraine's Location, the More They Want US to Intervene." *Washington Post*, April 7, 2014.

Ehrlinger, Joyce, Kerri Johnson, Matthew Banner, David Dunning, and Justin Kruger. "Why the Unskilled Are Unaware: Further Explorations of (Absent) Self-Insight Among the Incompetent." *Organizational Behavior and Human Decision Processes* 105, no. 1 (January 2008): 98–121.

Einstein, Albert. *Cosmic Religion: With Other Opinions and Aphorisms*. New York: Covici-Friede, 1931.

Fairleigh Dickinson University PublicMind Poll. "What You Know Depends on What You Watch: Current Events Knowledge Across Popular News Sources." May 3, 2012.

Fisher, Marc. "Steal This Idea." *Columbia Journalism Review*, March/April 2015.

Fishkin, James S. "The Nation in a Room." *Boston Review*, March 1, 2006.

Fishkin, James S., and Robert C. Luskin. "Experimenting with a Democratic Ideal: Deliberative Polling and Public Opinion." *Acta Politica* 40 (2005): 284–98.

Foster, James. "Do Users Understand Mobile Menu Icons?" Exis, n.d. bit.ly/1DRUqpK.

———. "Don't Be Afraid of the Hamburger: A/B Test." Exis, n.d. bit.ly/1Cxj6NB.

Frederick, Shane. "Cognitive Reflection and Decision Making." *Journal of Economic Perspectives* 19: 25–42.

Freedman, Samuel G. "Muslims and Islam Were Part of Twin Towers' Life." *New York Times*, September 10, 2010.

Gallup, George. "Public Opinion in a Democracy." The Stafford Little Lectures, Princeton University Extension Fund, 1939.

Gallup News Service. "Lotteries Most Popular Form of Gambling for Americans." June 17, 1999.

Gara, Tom. "McDonald's and Wendy's: A Modern-Day Fox vs Hedgehog." *Wall Street Journal*, January 24, 2014.

Garrison, Jessica. "Guesswork Is the Norm When Voting for Judges." *Los Angeles Times*, May 28, 2006.

Garvey, Megan, and Jessica Garrison. "Judge's Loss Stuns Experts." *Los Angeles Times*, June 8, 2006.

Gerardi, Kristopher, Lorenz Goette, and Stephan Meier. "Financial Literacy and Subprime Mortgage Delinquency: Evidence from a Survey Matched to Administrative Data." Federal Reserve Bank of Atlanta Working Paper 2010-10, April 2010.

Gewertz, Ken. "Albert Einstein, Civil Rights Activist." *Harvard Gazette*, April 12, 2007.

Gorman, Sean. "Rick Perry Errs in Tying Patriotism Quote to Thomas Paine." *Richmond Times-Dispatch*, March 9, 2015.

Greenfeld, Karl Taro. "Faking Cultural Literacy." *New York Times*, May 24, 2014.

GrubHub. "Family Favorites Top the List of Most Misspelled Food Names." Press release, May 28, 2013. bit.ly/1HGxs7V.

Grundberg, Sven, and Jens Hansegard. "YouTube's Biggest Draw Plays Games, Earns $4 Million a Year." *Wall Street Journal*, June 16, 2014.

Henkel, Linda. "Point-and-Shoot Memories: The Influence of Taking Photos on Memory for a Museum Tour." *Psychological Science* 25, no. 2 (February 2014): 396–402. doi:10.1177/0956797613504438.

Hickey, Walter. "A New Poll Shows Americans Don't Actually Understand Anything About the Deficit." *Business Insider*, October 9, 2013. read.bi/1Cg9Iid.

Hillin, Taryn. "*Boy Next Door* Screenwriter: That Cringe-y 'First Edition *Iliad*' Scene Was Not in My Script." *Fusion*, February 6, 2015. fus.in/1ukOyBl.

Hirsch, E. D., Jr. *Cultural Literacy: What Every American Needs to Know.* New York: Houghton Mifflin, 1987.

Huber, Jeanne. "The Dirt on Furnace Filters." *Washington Post*, January 19, 2006.

Ipsos MORI. "Perceptions Are Not Reality: Things the World Gets Wrong." Perils of Perception Study, October 29, 2014. bit.ly/1ydnOFb.

Itzkoff, Dave. "Where the Deer and Chameleon Play." *New York Times*, February 25, 2011.

Kaczynski, Andrew. "Section of Rand Paul's Book Plagiarized Forbes Article." BuzzFeed, November 5, 2013. bzfd.it/1GLxbwP.

Kahan, Dan M. "Why We Are Poles Apart on Climate Change." *Nature* 488, no. 7411 (August 15, 2012): 255.

———. "Climate-Science Communication and the Measurement Problem." *Advances in Political Psychology* 36 (2015): 1–43.

Kahneman, Daniel, and Angus Deaton. "High Income Improves Evaluation of Life but Not Emotional Well-Being." *Proceedings of the National Academy of Sciences* 107, no. 38 (September 21, 2010): 16489–93. bit.ly/1yW8S9h.

Kahneman, Daniel, Ilana Ritov, and David A. Schkade. "Economic Preferences or Attitude Expressions? An Analysis of Dollar Responses to Public Issues." *Journal of Risk and Uncertainty* 19 (1999): 203–35.

Kalia, Ajay. "'Music Was Better Back Then': When Do We Stop Keeping Up with Popular Music?" *Skynet & Ebert*, April 22, 2015. bit.ly/1HvgYMA.

Kiatpongsan, Sorapop, and Michael I. Norton. "How Much (More) Should CEOs Make? A Universal Desire for More Equal Pay." *Perspectives on Psychological Science* 9, no. 6 (November 2014): 587–93.

Kleinman, Alexis. "FBI Crafts 83-Page Report on What Things Like 'LOL' and 'BRB' Mean." *Huffington Post*, June 18, 2014.

Kohut, Andrew. "Despite Lower Crime Rates, Support for Gun Rights Increases." Pew Research Center, April 17, 2015.

Kopan, Tal. "Rand Paul on Plagiarism Charges: If Dueling Were Legal in Kentucky…" *Politico*, November 3, 2013. politi.co/1N9Vlqm.

Koppel, Jonathan, and Dorthe Berntsen. "Does Everything Happen When You Are Young? Introducing the Youth Bias." *Quarterly Journal of Experimental Psychology* 67 (2014): 417–23.

Kruger, Justin, and David Dunning. "Unskilled and Unaware of It: How Difficulties in Recognizing One's Own Incompetence Lead to Inflated Self-Assessments." *Journal of Personality and Social Psychology* 77 (1999): 1121–34.

Krugman, Paul. "Hating Good Government." *New York Times*, January 18, 2015.

Kurtz, Stanley. "How the College Board Politicized U.S. History." *National Review*, August 25, 2014.

Legum, Judd. "Oklahoma Lawmakers Vote Overwhelmingly to Ban Advanced Placement U.S. History." *ThinkProgress*, February 17, 2015.

Lewandowsky, Stephan, Gilles E. Gignac, and Klaus Oberauer. "The Role of Conspiracist Ideation and Worldviews in Predicting Rejection of Science." *PLoS ONE* 8, no. 10 (2013). doi:10.1371/journal.pone.0075637.

Lilienfeld, A. M., and S. Graham. "Validity in Determining Circumcision Status by Questionnaire as Related to Epidemiological Studies of Cancer of the Cervix." *Journal of the National Cancer Institute* 21, no. 4 (October 1958): 713–20.

Liu, James H. "Narratives and Social Memory from the Perspective of Social Representations of History." In *Narratives and Social Memory: Theoretical and Methodological Approaches*, edited by Rosa Cabecinhas and Lilia Abadia, 11–24. Braga, Portugal: University of Minho, 2013.

LoBrutto, Vincent. *Stanley Kubrick: A Biography*. New York: D. I. Fine, 1997.

Loewenstein, George, Joelle Y. Friedman, Barbara McGill, et al. "Consumers' Misunderstanding of Health Insurance." *Journal of Health Economics* 23 (2013): 850–62.

Lopez, Steve. "Idea of an LA Voteria is Gaining Currency." *Los Angeles Times*, August 19, 2014.

Los Angeles Times. "A Textbook Case of Meddling in California." June 15, 2014.

Luippold, Ross. "The Craziest Beliefs Shared by 'One-in-Five' Americans." *Huffington Post*, August 24, 2010. huff.to/1O9CzMP.

Luscombe, Belinda. "Do We Need $75,000 a Year to Be Happy?" *Time*, September 6, 2010.

Madison, Jillian. "The Food Network Loves Mascarpone." *Food Network Humor*, April 15, 2010. bit.ly/1ydqmTQ.

Mandell, Lewis, and Linda Schmid Klein. "The Impact of Financial Literacy Education on Subsequent Financial Behavior." *Journal of Financial Counseling and Planning* 20, no. 1 (2009): 15–24.

Maranjian, Selena. "The Simple 3-Question Financial Quiz Most Americans Fail: Can You Pass It?" *The Motley Fool*, March 10, 2015.

Marshall, Perry. "Why I Don't Watch the News & Why You Shouldn't Either." July 15, 2013. bit.ly/1GLARii.

McMillen, Andrew. "One Man's Quest to Rid Wikipedia of Exactly One Grammatical Mistake." *Medium*, February 3, 2015.

Memoli, Michael A. "Louisiana Congressman 'Very Sorry' After Video Shows Romantic Encounter." *Los Angeles Times*, April 8, 2014.

Meyerson, Harold. "How to Boost Voter Turnout in LA—and It Isn't Offering Prizes." *Los Angeles Times*, August 19, 2014.

Miller, Dean. "News Literacy Is Not Optional If You Need to Be Well-Informed." *New York Times*, February 28, 2014.

Mobley, Eric W. "The Ambiguous Hamburger Icon: Is the Icon Mystery Meat to Users?" February 12, 2014. bit.ly/1HR6Xb1.

Mohan, Geoffrey. "Can Money Buy Your Kids a Bigger Brain?" *Los Angeles Times*, March 30, 2015.

Mooney, Chris. *The Republican War on Science*. New York: Basic Books, 2006.

Morris, Errol. "The Anosognosic's Dilemma: Something's Wrong but You'll Never Know What It Is." *New York Times*, June 20, 2010.

National Geographic Education Foundation. "National Geographic–Roper Public Affairs 2006 Geographic Literacy Study." May 2006. on.natgeo. com/QrP3aj.

National Science Board. "Science and Engineering Indicators 2006." Arlington, Va.: National Science Foundation (vol. 1, NSB 06-01; vol. 2, NSB 06-01A). 1.usa.gov/1c9bk7i.

Nelson, Libby. "Read a Professor of Medicine's Outraged Tweets from Her Son's Abstinence-Only Sex Ed Class." *Vox*, April 15, 2015.

Nestojko, John F., Jason R. Finley, and Henry L. Roediger III. "Extending Cognition to External Agents." *Psychological Inquiry* 24, no. 4 (2013): 321–25.

Newell, Allen, and Herbert A. Simon. *Human Problem Solving*. Englewood Cliffs, N.J.: Prentice-Hall, 1972.

Newport, Frank. "In US, 42% Believe Creationist View of Human Origins." Gallup Politics, June 2, 2014.

Newsweek. "Take the Quiz: What We Don't Know." March 20, 2011. bit. ly/1y56VvY.

New York Post. "Diddy Mistaken for Kanye West at Art Basel." December 6, 2013.

Nielsen. "Mobile Millennials: Over 85% of Generation Y Owns Smartphones." September 5, 2014. bit.ly/1pyhyfG.

Noble, Kimberly G., Suzanne M. Houston, Natalie H. Brito, et al. "Family Income, Parental Education and Brain Structure in Children and Adolescents." *Nature Neuroscience* 18, no. 5 (May 2015): 773–78. doi:10.1038/nn.3983.

Norton, Michael I., and Dan Ariely. "Building a Better America—One Wealth Quintile at a Time." *Perspectives on Psychological Science* 6, no. 1 (January 2011): 9–12.

O'Leary, Amy. "An Honor for the Creator of the GIF." *New York Times*, May 21, 2013.

Oliver, J. Eric, and Thomas Wood. "Medical Conspiracy Theories and Health Behaviors in the United States." *JAMA Internal Medicine* 174, no. 5 (May 2014): 817–18. doi:10.1001/jamainternmed.2014.190.

Oppenheimer, Mark. "Knowing Not." *New York Times*, June 10, 2007.

Paddock, Catharine. "Medicine Labels to Carry Clearer Instructions, UK." *Medical News Today*, March 4, 2011.

Parker, Dorothy. *Not Much Fun: The Lost Poems of Dorothy Parker*. Edited by Stuart Y. Silverstein. 1996. Reprint, New York: Scribner, 2009.

Pelletier, John. "National Report Card on State Efforts to Improve Financial Literacy in High Schools." Burlington, Vt.: Champlain College Center for Financial Literacy, 2013.

Peters, Mark. "If 'Mark Twain Said It,' He Probably Didn't." *Good*, September 27, 2009.

Pew Research Center. "America's Changing Religious Landscape." May 12, 2015. pewrsr.ch/1FhDslC.

———. "Emerging Nations Embrace Internet, Mobile Technology." February 13, 2014. pewrsr.ch/1mg8Nvc.

———. "Public's Knowledge of Science and Technology." April 22, 2013. pewrsr.ch/1Cp50xP.

———. "US Religious Knowledge Survey." September 28, 2010. pewrsr. ch/1Cxom3u.

Piore, Adam. "Why We Keep Playing the Lottery." *Nautilus*, August 1, 2013.

Poundstone, William. *The Ultimate*. New York: Doubleday, 1990.

Prange, David. "A Sign of the Times." *National Oil and Lube News*, n.d. bit. ly/1c9d7JK.

Proctor, Robert, and Londa Schiebinger, eds. *Agnotology: The Making and Unmaking of Ignorance*. Palo Alto, CA: Stanford University Press, 2008.

Prothero, Stephen. *Religious Literacy: What Every American Needs to Know— And Doesn't*. San Francisco: HarperOne, 2007.

Ramer, Holly. "Bachmann Flubs Revolutionary War Geography in NH." Boston.com, March 13, 2011.

Reed, Philip, and Ronald Montoya. "Stop Changing Your Oil." Edmunds. com, April 23, 2013.

Roediger, Henry L., III, and Robert G. Crowder. "A Serial Position Effect in Recall of United States Presidents." *Bulletin of the Psychometric Society* 8, no. 4 (October 1976): 275–78.

Roediger, Henry L., III, and K. A. DeSoto. "Forgetting the Presidents." *Science* 346, no. 6213 (November 2014): 1106–9.

Romano, Andrew. "How Ignorant Are Americans?" *Newsweek*, March 20, 2011.

Rosen, Jody. "The Knowledge, London's Legendary Taxi-Driver Test, Puts Up a Fight in the Age of GPS." *New York Times*, November 10, 2014.

Sagan, Carl. *The Cosmic Connection*. Garden City, NY: Doubleday, 1973.

Said, Sammy. "The Most Expensive Celebrity Endorsements." *The Richest*, October 5, 2013. bit.ly/1Cp80dK.

Satran, Joe. "Misspelled Food Names: The 11 Dishes GrubHub Users Get Wrong the Most." *Huffington Post*, May 30, 2013. huff.to/1O9JlSN.

Schlam, Tanya R., Nicole L. Wilson, Yuichi Shoda, et al. "Preschoolers' delay of gratification predicts their body mass 30 years later." *Journal of Pediatrics* 162, no. 1 (January 2013): 90–93.

Schrager, Allison. "Are Americans Saving Too Much and Spending Too Little?" *Bloomberg Business*, October 27, 2014.

Seaman, Andrew M. "You're Not Alone: Medical Conspiracies Believed by Many." Reuters, March 19, 2014.

Semuels, Alana. "Sex Education Stumbles in Mississippi." *Los Angeles Times*, April 2, 2014.

S. H. "Financial Literacy: Back to Basics." *The Economist*, July 11, 2014.

Skiena, Steven, and Charles B. Ward. *Who's Bigger? Where Historical Figures Really Rank*. Cambridge, UK: Cambridge University Press, 2013.

———. "Who's Biggest? The 100 Most Significant Figures in History." *Time*, December 10, 2013.

Sontag, Susan. *At the Same Time: Essays and Speeches*. New York: Farrar, Straus and Giroux, 2007.

Sparrow, Betsy, Jenny Liu, and Daniel M. Wegner. "Google Effects on Memory: Cognitive Consequences of Having Information at Our Fingertips." *Science* 333, no. 6043 (August 2011): 776–78.

Stephens-Davidowitz, Seth. "Searching for Sex." *New York Times*, January 24, 2015.

Sullivan, Patricia. "William 'Bud' Post III; Unhappy Lottery Winner." *Washington Post*, January 20, 2006.

Sweet, Leonard. *Nudge: Awakening Each Other to the God Who's Already There*. Colorado Springs: David C. Cook, 2010.

Tauber, Sarah K., John Dunlosky, Katherine A. Rawson, et al. "General Knowledge Norms: Updated and Expanded from the Nelson and Narens (1980) Norms." *Behavioral Research Methods* 45, no. 4 (December 2013): 1115–43.

Terkel, Amanda. "Texas Board of Education: Jefferson Davis and Obama's Middle Name Are Essential for Students to Learn." *ThinkProgress*, May 21, 2010.

Tetlock, Philip. *Expert Political Judgment: How Good Is It? How Can We Know?* Princeton, NJ: Princeton University Press, 2005.

Timmer, John. "Ohio Lawmakers Want to Limit the Teaching of the Scientific Process." *Ars Technica*, August 26, 2014.

Vavreck, Lynn. "The Power of Political Ignorance." *New York Times*, May 23, 2014.

———. "Why Network News Still Matters." *New York Times*, February 18, 2015.

Vine, Katy. "Faith, Hope, and Chastity." *Texas Monthly*, May 2008.

Wagstaff, Keith. "Forget Cursive: Teach Kids How to Code." *The Week*, November 14, 2013.

Way, Wendy L., and Karen Holden. "Teachers' Background and Capacity to Teach Personal Finance: Results of a National Study." National Endowment for Financial Education, March 2009. bit.ly/1Y4HW4Z.

Wegner, Daniel M., and Adrian F. Ward. "How Google Is Changing Your Brain." *Scientific American*, December 2013: 58–61.

Weinberger, Hannah. "Changing Gears: Is Knowing How to Drive Stick in America Still Essential?" CNN, July 19, 2012. cnn.it/1JoPpUJ.

Williams, Alex. "15 Minutes of Fame? More Like 15 Seconds of Nanofame." *New York Times*, February 6, 2015.

Wilson, Reid. "Arizona Will Require High School Students to Pass Citizenship Test to Graduate. Can You Pass?" *Washington Post*, January 16, 2015.

Wood, Michael J., Karen M. Douglas, and Robbie M. Sutton. "Dead and Alive: Beliefs in Contradictory Conspiracy Theories." *Social Psychological and Personality Science* 3, no. 6 (November 2012): 767–73.

Wu, Suzanne. "USC Survey Reveals Low Health Care Literacy." *USC News*, March 24, 2014. bit.ly/1GLGHjy.

Xu, Fujie, Lauri E. Markowitz, Maya R. Sternberg, and Sevgi O. Aral. "Prevalence of Circumcision in Men in the United States: Data from the National Health and Nutrition Examination Survey (NHANES), 1999–2002." XVI International AIDS Conference, 2006.

Zachs, Jeffrey M. "Why Movie 'Facts' Prevail." *New York Times*, February 13, 2015.

Zamon, Rebecca. "Dr. Oz Says Gluten-Free Diets Are a Scam." *Huffington Post Canada*, May 26, 2014.

Zaromb, Franklin, Andrew C. Butler, Pooja K. Agarwal, and Henry L. Roediger III. "Collective Memories of Three Wars in United States History in Younger and Older Adults." *Memory & Cognition* 42: 383–99.

About the Author

William Poundstone is the author of fourteen previous books, including *How to Predict the Unpredictable*, *Are You Smart Enough to Work at Google?*, and *Fortune's Formula*. He has written for the *New York Times*, *Harper's*, *Harvard Business Review*, and the *Village Voice*, among other publications, and is a frequent guest on TV and radio. He lives in Los Angeles. Follow Poundstone on Twitter (@WPoundstone) and learn more at his website, william-poundstone.com.

Index